Changing Status of Women in Central Asia

A Comparative Study of Kazakhstan and Uzbekistan

Changing Status of Women in Central Asia

A Comparative Study of Kazakhstan and Uzbekistan

Mukta Tanwar

GYAN

The Publication of this thesis was financially upheld by ICSSR and the responsibility of the facts stated, opinions expressed or conclusions reached are entirely that of the author and ICSSR accepts no responsibility for them.

ICSSR Consultant

Professor Chandrakala Padia, IIAS Shimla and Vice-Chancellor MGS University, Bikaner.

ISBN : 978-81-212-1344-8

Price : ₹

First Published, 2017

Published by

Gyan Publishing House
5, Ansari Road
Daryaganj, New Delhi-110002
Phone: 9811692060
E-mail: books@gyanbooks.com

Printed at: G. Print Process, Delhi.

Cataloging in Publication Data—DK
Courtesy: D.K. Agencies (P) Ltd. <docinfo@dkagencies.com>

Tanwar, Mukta, author.
Changing status of women in Central Asia : a comparative study of Kazakhstan and Uzbekistan / Mukta Tanwar.
pages cm
Includes bibliographical references.
ISBN 9788121213448

1. Women—Kazakhstan—Social conditions. 2. Women—Uzbekistan—Social conditions. 3. Women—Kazakhstan—Economic conditions. 4. Women—Uzbekistan—Economic conditions. 5. Women in development—Government policy—Kazakhstan. 6. Women in development—Government policy—Uzbekistan. I. Title.

HQ1742.T36 2016 DDC 305.420954 23

To my godly parents

Contents

Foreword

Central Asian Women gained a lot from USSR's women emancipation policies but after gaining independence women's status has been declining slowly in Turkmenistan and Kazakhstan while a rapid down fall has been recorded in Uzbekistan and Tajikistan. Free market economy, democratic political system and new socio-economic challenges (Human and drug trafficking, unemployment and welfare policies withdrawn by state etc.) have made a negative impact on the status of women in Central Asia. The participation of women in the sphere of education, employment, politics and decision making is decreasing day by day. In fact, Central Asian women are facing 'multiple burdens' in the present scenario. Kazakhstan and Uzbekistan have similar legacies and religion tradition but the condition of women is different in each. Women in these states are facing some similar problems in the new context. But there are many differences as well.

Socialist views about women were introduced in Soviet Union and since Central Asian Region was also part of the Soviet Union, it was also influenced by Soviet policy on women. In order to explain the source of women's problematic position in Central Asia, we need to turn to history. Scholars and politicians of both the left and right agreed that women in late nineteen century and early twentieth century in Central Asia lived in the most oppressive, conservative and unfriendly environment to be found in the territory controlled by the Russian Empire. Very often, relatives, parents or husbands viewed women as their property. They were given a sub-human status in the ruthless and exploitative system of patriarchal society; their lives were a tale of suffering and degraded existence. It did not mean that women had no right in Central Asia. They always had legal rights both under

Adat and *Shariah* but those law and rights were granted in the local context where local policies, courts, governments and economy were exclusively dominated by men.

The situation in the area populated by nomads was significantly different but not much better. Women there enjoyed more freedom in their personal lives, as a large part of everyday economy very much depended on their contributions. Central Asia was the only place in the nineteen century Muslim world where queens could rule their communities as did Kurmanjan – Datha of Kyrgyz tribes and Guljamal Khanum of the Turkmen tribes. Yet, even nomad women were after forced to marry leaders or representative of other tribes in order to seal a peace or a political and military union.

After the disintegration of the Soviet Union and the subsequent emergence of independent Central Asian States, these societies did undergo substantial changes in all aspect. However, different republics in the Central Asian Region have been moving in different directions. Kazakhstan and Kyrgyzstan have established more liberal form of polity. Yet, all states encouraged Islamic observance as a means of promoting an independent national identity. Revival of religion has adversely affected women's status in Central Asia. Professional women, especially from the middle class, struggle to maintain decent living standards. In contradiction, the market pressure has energized many women as many of their men could not adapt to the transition or were consumed by alcoholism or depression or the stress of new ways of life. The weakening of state institutions has been hard for the working class, especially women, although many privileges and guarantee of women's rights and freedom are written clearly into the new constitution and law.

State institutions are increasingly unable to enforce those laws and rules. Drug mafias tied to fundamentalist groups meanwhile have involved and exploited women in drug trade and human trafficking. The number of women in Central Asian prisons is increasing. These women are victims of economic and social policies that result in reduced jobs and educational opportunities. They are also vulnerable to extremist groups that threaten and exploit them and to law enforcement and judges who send them to jail while men who reap the profit from drug trade remain free. Due to globalization and new business owners did enormous profit on women by expanding already existing segregation in the labour market vertical as well as horizontal.

Professor Ajay Patnaik

Centre for Russian and Central Asian Studies

School of International Studies

JNU, New Delhi

Acknowledgements

In the process of completing my book I have received encouragement from many quarters. I would like to acknowledge all those people who gave me generous support to do my study. First of all, I would like to express my deep appreciation and sincere thanks to my supervisor Professor Ajay Patnaik, Professor, Centre for Russian & Central Asian States, SIS, JNU, New Delhi who encouraged me towards pursuing this topic and gave me enough space, support and importance to my independent ideas. He was always ready to help me accomplish a clear vision during this study.

I would also like to express my sincere thanks to Professor Anuradha M. Chenoy, late Professor Tulsi Ram, Dr Arun Mohanty, Dr Phool Badan, Dr Preeti Das, Dr Rajan Kumar, and all other distinguished faculty members and staff of CR & CAS for their kind help and valuable suggestions. I am grateful to all those learned academicians and scholars; their books, articles and research works I valued while developing my own point of view.

This book would not have been possible without the precious support of the libraries of JNU, JMI, DU, IDSA, Teen Murti and special thanks to Computer Maintenance Cell and Subscribed Online Database services of Jawaharlal Nehru University that made it possible to access all the leading journals and research articles around the world from the campus itself. My special thanks also go to the organizations like ADB, UNDP, UNICEF, UNIFEM, ICG, CEDAW, ILO and OSCE etc. for their reliable reports and data. All such material indeed strengthened my argument during this study.

I owe my special thanks to another of my respected teacher Professor R.S. Yadav, Chairperson, Department of Political Science, Kurukshetra University, Kurukshetra, who encouraged me to pursue my Doctorate studies in JNU, New Delhi. I also express my heartfelt thanks to very renowned Prof. Chanderkala Padia, Chairperson IIAS, Shimla & Vice-Chancellor of MGS University, Bikaner for evaluating my thesis as a subject expert of ICSSR for publication and Sh. Ajay Kumar Gupta, Deputy Director, Publication and Research Division of ICSSR, New Delhi for timely processing my case in his office. I am also grateful to the Gyan Books for taking my study for publication under their rich gamut of publications.

Finally, I am also thankful to my godly parents, it is only due to their support that I was able to continue my studies again after a long break. This work could never be accomplished without their support and constant encouragement. Thank you for teaching me to believe in myself, in my dreams and above all in GOD. I am also grateful to all other family members for their consistent support and help all the time. I extend my special thanks to my husband, Rajesh Chauhan and my daughters, Kulvibha and Sakranti for their love and support; perhaps this book would not have been possible without their steady help.

Mukta Tanwar

Preface

In the last two decades, uneasy global changes have been observed. Particularly, related to this study were disintegration of the Union of Soviet Socialist Republics (USSR) and the birth of unstable Commonwealth of Independent States (CIS). A number of textbooks have analysed the changes in this region, at the same time gender issues have also received sufficient attention, though female scholars are still filling the gaps left in the conventional monographs. All the former republics are in periods of state building, but despite these changes in economic and political direction, institutions of the past have not been completely shattered.

After the USSR, all Post-Soviet republics witnessed deterioration in women's condition and women were pushed out of power structures. All these states largely outdated the Soviet traditions in actual practice. During this transition period, the difficulties of transition from Socialism to Market Economy and Democracy had to be faced by women population in a different manner. A woman in this chaotic transition, from socialism to new market mechanism, was really the most unsafe. Thus, the transition to democracy forced women to uncertainty in the environment of proclaimed democratic values. In fact, while building a new type of democratic society, it is required to follow the best experiences of other countries that gender perspectives may be applied in modern conditions. The creation of different attitudes and decisions demands critical thinking and practice.

In this background lively debates have taken place about the transformations in the lives of women in this region. The inevitable issues that came up during this time were unemployment and poverty. Women were perhaps largely worst affected by these issues. The reduction in women's employment was a primarily female problem in government, to achieve economic independence and to be protected from gender violence and discrimination will be the day when the promise of gender equality is realized and fulfilled in real sense. Lastly, needless to mention that if there is some fault or omission in this work is solely my responsibility and I'll try to surmount those gaps with readers' critical inputs and valuable suggestions in the next edition.

Mukta Tanwar

List of Abbreviations and Acronyms

ADB	–	Asian Development Bank
AIDS	–	Acquired Immune Deficiency Syndrome
CAW	–	Central Asian Women
CAS	–	Central Asian States
CAR	–	Central Asian Republics
CEDAW	–	Committee on the Elimination of Discrimination against Women
CIS	–	Commonwealth of Independent States
DHS	–	Demographic and Health Survey
EU	–	European Union
GAP	–	Gender Action Plan
FDI	–	Foreign Direct Investment
GBV	–	Gender Based Violence
GDI	–	Gender Development Index
GDP	–	Gross Domestic Product
GNP	–	Gross National Product
HIV	–	Human Immunodeficiency Virus
HDI	–	Human Development Index
HDR	–	Human Development Report
IDUs	–	Injecting Drug Users
ILO	–	International Labour Organisation
IMF	–	International Monetary Fund
IOM	–	International Organisation for Migration
KCLF	–	Kazakhstan Community Loan Fund
KZT	–	Tenge (Kazakhstan national currency)
LDC	–	Least Developed Country

Chapter - 1

Introduction

The women question is one of the issues in the history which has had its own specific and complicated fate. There are biological as well as social differences between the sexes, but in this context gender refers to the latter. Biological differences between the sexes sometimes favour women other times men. Gender differences, instead, generally favour men because they are the result of women's disadvantaged position in the society (Mayra Buvinic, 1999: 568). Gender is seen as a social construction, which determines what it means to be male or female in any particular place or time. In an early feminist intervention in this discipline Cynthia Enloe asked the question: where are women? And she found the answer that they were often there but all the time in a sub-human status. The realisation of this unequal status of women and efforts to change it is generally associated with the term 'Feminism'. The goal of feminism can be seen as an attempt to improve the quality of women's lives by promoting a world in which they can thrive equally with men. Feminists have divided this movement's history into three waves (The Oxford Companion to Politics of the World, 1993: 298-300).

The first wave of feminism was mainly concerned with woman's legal and civil rights. This movement focused primarily on education, individual political rights and legal rights (including voting and property rights in the West and participation in the independence struggles in the East) or on women's special needs as mothers and keepers of society's virtue. The second wave of feminism began its theoretical revival with the publication of '*The Second Sex*' (1949) by Simone De Beauvoir. She challenged the secondary status of the women in society that assumed men as the subject and maleness as the norm. Beauvoir asserted that women are made subordinate by patriarchy; she is not born but rather made by the society. The third wave feminism, also known as Post-modern feminism, came during the 1980s.

A defining feature of third wave feminism is its focus on multiplicities or the belief that there exists multiple gender, race and sexualities. With this idea in mind and echoing earlier criticisms, many third wave feminists expressed dissatisfaction with the insufficient treatment of race, class, sexuality and other locations of inequality in mainstream feminist scholarship. As a result, it is during contemporary third wave feminism that inter-sectionality first appeared (Price and Sokoloff, 2004). In other words post-modern feminism departs from the other feminist perspectives by questioning the existence of any one pattern of truth including women's oppression. Post-modern feminism rejects fixed categories and universal concepts in favour of multiple truths and as such examines the effects of discourse and symbolic representation on claims about knowledge (Amanda Burgess, 2006: 26).

In the context of information society and neo-liberal, global politics, the third feminist wave from the mid-1990s onward sprang from the emergence of a new post-colonial and post-socialist world order. Third wave feminism manifests in itself 'girl'. It seeks to overcome the theoretical question of equity or difference and the political question of evolution or revolution while it changes the notion of "universal womanhood" and embraces ambiguity, diversity and multiplicity in transversal theory and politics (Three Wave of Feminism, 2). Actually, the third wave feminists have no intentions of thinking, speaking or writing themselves and other women out of existence. They aim to answer the 'woman question' in a way that has never been answered before that who is she and what does she want? (Rosemarie Tong, 2009: 9).

In the 1970s and 1980s these differences were often summed up under labels liberal, radical and socialist feminism. Liberal feminism is one of the earliest forms of feminism stating that women's secondary status in society is based on unequal opportunities and discrimination from men. This stream of feminism focuses on eliminating gender inequality through legal support because it enables and facilitate them in achieving the same rights and opportunities as men. Further, liberal feminists believe that by removing legal obstacles can overcome women's subordination. The basic belief is grounded in liberal philosophical traditions, as well as French and British feminist theories. Society consists of individuals who are equals and therefore all people must have equal rights.

There is clear division between the role of state (Public) and individual freedom (Private). Liberal feminism wants to transform and revise by working within the existing social structures and changing people's attitudes (Kristina Wolff, 2007: 14). The important issues of liberal feminist movement include reproductive right and abortion access, sexual harassment, voting, education, fair compensation for work, affordable childcare, affordable healthcare and freedom from sexual and domestic violence against women and equal employment opportunity.

Mary Wollstonecraft (1759-1799) was one of the key thinkers of the liberal feminist movement. She wrote '*A Vindication of the Rights of Woman*' in which she makes the case that women need to be educated just as well as men so that they can grow up to be honourable and autonomous human beings. Then in nineteenth century John Stuart and Harriet Taylor Mill wrote about women needing to be more involved in society. They consider that the overall goal of liberal feminism is the worthy one of creating "a just and compassionate society in which freedom flourishes." Women and men can prosper equally in such social order (Rosemarie Tong, 2009: 13). While Harriet Taylor called for women to work outside the household as well as raise children, John Stuart Mill believed that women should "Be recognised as fully rational and worthy of the same civil liberties and economic opportunities as men" (Bryson, 1992: 55-63).

Liberal feminists believe that the principle of liberty and justice should be applied to women and the society must work to remove laws and reform institutions that impinge upon equal rights. Therefore, liberal feminism focuses on systematic changes. The epistemological view of liberal feminists is indicated by the following statement:

> "The liberal feminist agenda is political and moral.... It takes no epistemological revolution to see what a liberal feminist.... sees

> in the plight of women. It takes no uncovering of "new ways of knowing" to understand that women are politically and socially disadvantaged....what the gender feminist is hailing is not a newfound ability to see that women are unfairly treated, but a perspectival, scientific revolution that identifies the underlying causes of injustice by exposing the pervasive sex/gender system that subordinates women and holds them in thrall" (C. Sommers, 1994: 153-54).

But it does not mean that the liberal theory is perfect for feminism. There are several critiques of liberal feminism. One is that liberal feminism focuses too much on women becoming like men and it unnecessarily denigrates the importance of traditional female role. Other thinkers attack liberal feminism because it emphasises the rational above the emotional while individual need both. It also questioned liberal feminism's focus on the individual and not the community. A historical critique of liberal feminism focuses on its racist, classist and heterosexist past (Wallin, Dawn C., 1999: 5-7).

Radical feminism seeks to redress the power balance between women and men in society. Rather than equalising women and men through legal processes, radical feminism focuses on patriarchy as a system of power that organises society with men dominance what radical feminists claim is "male supremacy" that oppresses women. Radical feminism aims to challenge and to overthrow patriarchy by opposing standard gender roles and what they see as male oppression of women, and call for a radical reordering society (Gerald Atkinson, 1-2). Therefore, Radical feminists professed themselves as revolutionaries rather than mere reformers.

Early radical feminism, arising within second-wave feminism in the 1960s, typically viewed patriarchy as a "trans-historical phenomenon" prior to or deeper than other sources of oppression, "not only the oldest and most universal form of domination but the primary form" and the model for all others. The term radical in radical feminism (from Latin, meaning root) is used as an adjective meaning of pertaining to the root or going to the root. Radical feminists locate the root cause of women's oppression in patriarchal gender relation, as opposed to legal system (Liberal feminism) or class conflict (Socialist feminism and Marxist feminism) (Shahrzad Mojab, 2001: 2-6).

According to this approach the distinguishing character of women's oppression is their oppression as women, not as members of other group such as their social class. Hence, the explanation of women's oppression is seen as lying in sexual oppression. Women are oppressed because of their own sex. The notion of shared oppression is intimately connected with a strong emphasis on the sisterhood of women and encourages some degree of separatism from men. Furthermore this identification with women and rejection of male dominance involves both a critique of the existing organisation of heterosexuality as prioritising men and recognition of lesbianism as a challenge to that priority. Only the elimination of patriarchy and the destruction of male control will liberate women.

Radical feminists suggest and begin by eliminating gender, specifically sexual status, role, temperament and social construction as they have been constructed under patriarchy. As patriarchy is organised through men's relationship with other men, unity among women is only effective means for liberating women. Separatist women lobby calls for their seclusion from men and from institutions, relationships, roles and activities that are male-defined and male-operated, benefits males and maintain male privilege. Female separation often fills into the trap of essentialism, the belief in natural or innate differences between men and women (Bryson, 1992: 201-204).

Radical-libertarian feminists rejected patriarchal society's assumption there is a basic connection between one's sex (male or female) and one's gender (masculine or feminine). In its place, they claimed that gender is divisible from sex and that patriarchal society uses rigid gender roles to keep women passive ("affectionate, obedient, responsive to sympathy and approval, cheerful, kind and friendly") and men active ("tenacious, aggressive, curious, ambitious, planful, responsible, original and competitive") (Hester Eisenstein, 1983: 8).

With emergence of so called essentialism in feminist thought, radical feminists were divided into two camps: radical libertarian feminists and radical cultural feminists. Radical libertarian feminists generally espouse the idea of 1960s and 1970s radical feminists who drew attention to the ways in which women's reproductive and sexual role and responsibilities often limit women's development as full human beings. These radical feminists longed for androgyny. Although this concept of androgyny is flawed due to its male bias, it captured radical feminists desire to transcend the limits of the sex/gender system by daring to be masculine as well as feminine. Radical libertarian feminists desire to free women from the constraints of female biology. So that they can choose their gender role and identities, mixing and matching them at their own will (Rosemarie Tong, 2009: 50).

Alternatively, cultural-radical feminists rejected androgyny as a desirable goal, replacing it with a proposal to embrace women's essential "femaleness". Instead of believing liberated women must exhibit both masculine and feminine traits and behaviour, these cultural-radical feminists expressed the view that it is better to be female than it is to be male. Thus, women should not try to be like men; they should try to be more like women emphasising values and virtues culturally associated with women ("interdependence, community, connection, sharing, emotion, body, trust, absence of hierarchy, nature, immanence, process, joy, peace and life") and deemphasising values and virtues culturally associated with men ("independence, autonomy, intellect, will, wariness, hierarchy, domination, culture, transcendence, product, asceticism, war and death"). Moreover, women should recognise that despite of cultural disparities among themselves, all women share one and the same female nature (Bryson, 1992: 204).

This theory of feminism is also not beyond criticism. Radical feminism falls into the trap of essentialism, the conviction that men are men and women are women and there is no way to change either's nature. Such a trap represents an analytic dead end as well as political danger. Agreeing, for example, that woman is by nature compassionate and nurturing and that man is aggressive and competitive suggests that radical feminists accept and promulgate the very stereotypes they are trying to avoid. How does one alter or change that from which one cannot escape? Women are trapped inside their bodies and biology becomes their destiny.

Marxist feminist theory is the gist of Marx and Engels' view about feminine ferment. Marx wrote that great social revolutions are impossible without the feminine ferment. Social progress may be measured precisely by the social position of women. In 1884, Engels, working from Marx's notes wrote 'The Origins of Family, Private Property and the State' which opened way to the understanding of the root of women's oppression.

Engels showed how changes in the material conditions of people affect the organisation of their family relations. He argued that before the family, or structured conjugal relations; there existed a primitive state of "promiscuous intercourse." In this early state, every woman was fair game for every man, and vice versa. All were essentially married to all. In the process of natural selection, suggested Engels, various kinds of blood relatives were gradually excluded from consideration as eligible marriage partners. As fewer and fewer women in the tribal group became available to any given man, individual men began to put forcible claims on individual women as their possessions. As a result, the pairing family, in which one man is married to one woman, came into existence.

Noting that when a man took a woman, he came to live in her household, Engels interpreted this state of affairs as a sign of women's economic power. Because women's work was vital for the tribe's survival and because women produced most of the material goods (e.g., bedding, clothing, cookware, tools) that could be passed on to future generations, Engels concluded that early pairing societies were probably matrilineal, with inheritance and lines of descent traced through the mother. Later, Engels speculated that pairing societies may have been not merely matrilineal societies but also matriarchal societies in which women ruled at the political, social, and economic levels. But his main and less debatable point remained that whatever power women had in past times, it was rooted in their position in the household, at that time the centre of production. Only if the site of production changed would women lose their advantaged position. As it turned out, said Engels, a site change did occur. The "domestication of animals and the breeding of herds" outside the household led to an entirely new source of wealth for the human community. Somehow, men gained control of the tribe's animals (Engels did not tell us why or how), and the male-female power balance shifted in favour of men, as men learned to produce more than enough animals to meet the tribe's needs for milk and meat.

Marxism sees class division rather than gender as the root of women's oppression. Because a great deal of time and efforts was needed to reproduce the workforce comes from the private family, Marxism sees this as the key to women's oppression: despite education and healthcare in advanced capitalist countries, the system largely depends on women's unpaid labour for the creation of a healthy workforce (Frederic Engels, 1884: 8-12).

Women's generally lower economic and social status grows out of this. In this classic Marxist statement of this position, Friedrich Engels's above mentioned work argues that the bourgeois family rests on a material foundation of inequality between husband and wife, where the latter is kind of unpaid prostitute, producing heirs for transmission of property in exchange for board and lodging.

In Marxist feminism, the work of Karl Marx '*The Communist Manifesto*' (1848), hierarchical class relations (built on unequally distributed or owned sources of wealth, including monetary and other resources) are seen as the sources of coercive power and oppression, of all inequalities ultimately. Sexual oppression is seen as a dimension of class power. In this model the earliest form of class division historically gave rise to male dominance; class oppression predates sex oppression (Marx and Engels, 1848).

The emerging organisation of the first forms of private wealth, and therefore a class hierarchy, led to the treatment of women as property. In other words Marxist feminism offers a version of history and society which is in some ways the opposite of that proposed by radical feminism. In radical feminism the earliest forms of male domination over women produce a framework of hierarchical social relations in which class divisions arise; sexual oppression predated class power.

Engels argued that the rise of class society brought with it rising inequality between the rulers and the ruled, and between men and women (Sharon Smith, 1997: 8). His theory of women's oppression rests on the relationship between the sexual division of labour and the mode of production, which underwent a fundamental transformation with the onset of class society. In hunter-gatherer and horticultural societies, there was a sexual division of labour and rigidly defined set of responsibilities for women and men. But both sexes were allowed a high degree of autonomy in performing these tasks. Moreover and this is an element, which has been learned since Engels' time, women not only provided much of the food for the band in hunter-gatherer societies, but also in many cases they provided most of the food (Karan Sacks, 1975: 211-212).

So women in pre-class societies were able to combine motherhood and productive labour, in fact there was no strict demarcation between the reproductive and productive spheres. All of that changed with the development of private property. According to the sexual division of labour, men tended to take charges of heavier agricultural jobs like ploughing, since it was more difficult for pregnant and nursing women and might endanger small children to be carried along. Moreover, since men traditionally took care of big game hunting, again it made sense for them to oversee the domestication of cattle. Engels argued that the domestication of cattle preceded the use of the plough in agriculture, although it is now accepted that these processes developed at the same time (Frederic Engels, 1884: 13).

As production shifted away from the household, the role of reproduction changed substantially. Thus, unlike hunter-gatherer societies which sought to limit the number of offspring, agricultural societies sought to maximise women's reproductive potential, so the family would have more children to help in the fields. Therefore at the same time that men were playing an increasingly exclusive role in production, women were required to play a much more central role in reproduction. Women became trapped within their individual families as the reproducers of society cut off from production (Jonah Horowitz, 2005: 3-4).

According to some Marxist feminists' conclusion that private property was almost exclusively the cause of women's oppression was overly simplistic, but not surprising given the fact that they were approaching the problem from only an economic standpoint. Other forms of feminism more accurately hold men and more specifically patriarchy as the primary causes of women's oppression. Friedrich Engels came up with a theory as to the origins of patriarchy titled '*The Origins of Family, Private Property and the State*'. In this work, he describes hunter-gatherer society as a matriarchy. Only once civilisation developed into an agrarian society did patriarchy become into existence. This idea was interesting, even if he had no evidence to back it up, according to Peter Custers, Engels completely misses the complexities of human interaction in reducing marriage to a relationship of only sex for money he adds (Peter Custers, 1997: 88-89).

Private property, according to Marxists, transformed the relations between men and women within the household only because it also

"unpaid service" within the home. The main reason for women's lower status in relation to men is the fact that they are generally economically dependent upon this male partner. Male power over women is consolidated by ideological myths about women (that they are naturally passive, that they have maternal instincts and so forth). These myths are part of a powerful socialising influence upon women that leads them to define their major role as that of mother, housekeeper and child rearer.

In other words all socialist feminists assert along with radical feminists that women's subordination predated the development of class based societies and hence that women's oppression could not be caused by class division. Socialist feminism connects the oppression of women to Marxist idea about exploitation, oppression and labour. Socialist feminists see women as being held down as a result of their unequal standing in both the workplace and the domestic sphere (Faith Wilding, 2007).

Prostitution, domestic work, childcare and marriage are all seen by Socialist feminists as ways in which women are exploited by a patriarchal system which devalues women and the substantial work that they do. Socialist feminists focus their energies on broad change that affects society as a whole, rather than on an individual basis. Socialist feminism centred on the question of gender constitution and oppression sees history in the materialist tradition. Socialist feminist analysis thus focuses on the institution and social practices of capitalism, promote to collective confrontation with these institutions and practices in such a way as to challenge the capitalist system as a whole and set in motion a transition toward a non-sexist socialism.

Socialist feminists therefore ask: How do gender relations articulate class relations? How does the constitution of gender articulate class formation and change? The most socialist feminists have discussed such questions using a framework which argue that gender constitution is a process implicated within a complex of 'productive' and 'reproductive' and that women's position can be located in terms of the relations of production and reproduction at various moments in history. The analysis is focused around understanding why these relations constitute gender and way in which this process articulates class formation and class action (Michele Barrett, 1980: 22).

Clara Zetkin, a German socialist who was a founder member of the German Communist Party, argued that class must take primacy over gender interests. She refused to cooperate with other women in campaigns for improved education, employment prospects and legal status, on the grounds that 'proletarian' and 'bourgeois' women had nothing in common. She argued, "This structure is built upon sand and has no basis in reality, the emancipation of women will take place only with the emancipation of labour from capital" (Susan Groag Bell and Karan M. Offen, 1981: 87-91).

However, socialist feminists could be criticised for not accepting that some women might go into and make a success of business. Their dynamism and entrepreneurial flair should be both rewarded and acknowledged, and to regard feminism as a class question might be unhelpful and narrowing. All women could benefit from a free system of production, based on the market and capitalism. Secondly, women are individuals who should be entitled to exercise choice, and the tendency by socialist feminists to seek work outside the home as crucial for emancipation is not borne out by the fact that many women who choose to stay at home and live fulfilled and happy lives.

Radicals are sceptical that the problems facing women are simply to do with capitalism. It is true that some socialist feminists have argued that there is a dual system which oppresses women – capitalism and patriarchy. Capitalism may reward men as 'breadwinners', thereby creating a division of labour that disadvantages women. Writers such as Ann Ferguson see patriarchy as semi-autonomous sexual oppression that exists alongside class oppression and is not reducible to it. But radicals feel that this argument merely serves to deepen the theoretical crisis faced by socialist feminist, since there is no reason to believe that pornography, prostitution and male chauvinist attitudes are specifically linked to a particular mode of production (Bryson, 1992: 243-45).

Some of the other types of feminism were also being observed in the end of twentieth and the beginning of twenty-first century e.g. Cultural Feminism, Black Feminism, Colonial Feminism and Islamic Feminism. An in-depth study of the Islamic feminism and the socialist feminism is required in the present research work because the study is based on the changing status of CAW (Central Asian Women). Both these two types of feminism have changed the status of CAW and between these both the more important is Islamic feminism in the context of CAW. In pre-USSR, USSR and post-USSR period, there were great changes in the system and standards but the impact of Islam was all the time present over CAW. A stream of Islamic feminists has worked for the development of women in Central Asian States.

The concept of 'Islamic feminism' is of recent origins, the term was used for the first time in 1990s in the growing Western literature on 'Women and Islam'. Response was diverse ranging from advocacy of women's emancipation to its outright rejection.[1] Islam was clearly present in much of the early confrontation between feminism and the religious and secular forces that reacted to the challenge. In this conflict, the Quran, the *Shariah* (Islamic law) and health were all used by contending forces, ranging from secular modernists to the religious guardians of patriarchy.

From the very beginning, the debate was centred on the compatibility of the idea of women's emancipation with the principle of Islam. One category of writers emphasised that Islam was compatible with demands for equality between men and women. For instance, reinterpreting the Quran, some early reformist women in Egypt claimed that the seclusion, segregation and veiling imposed on urban women were not sanctioned by Islam (Badran and Cooke, 1990: xxiv). Similar positions were formulated in many Islamic countries, whereas the other group argued that the demand for gender equality was Western and anti-Islamic.

The first woman to offer a detailed reinterpretation of the texts in favour of the women's rights was probably Nazira Zain al-Din. She was born in Lebanon in 1905 and her father was a scholar of Islamic jurisprudence. Her first book '*Unveiling and Veiling: Lectures and Views on the Liberation of the Women and Social Renewal in the Arab World*' was an indictment of patriarchal oppression, which she declared to be against the principles of Islam. She said that the veil was an insult to men and women. When the book was published in 1928, men of religion announced their stand against Zain al-Din and started distributing pamphlets against her. Nazira's second book '*The Young Women and the Shaikhs*' (Al-Fatahwa al-Shuyukh) was a response to the conservatives especially to Shaikh Mustafa al-Ghalaini's

'*Islam, the Spirit of Civilisation*' (Al-Islam Ruh al-Madanniyya) published in 1929. The Shaikh had accused her of sectarian and colonial persuasions, and alleged that her book had been written by Christian missionaries (Zain al-Din in Badran and Cooke, 1990: 275).

Some of the newly established States, such as Turkey and Iran appropriated the feminist movement by dissolving independent organisations and their press, and granting women certain rights. The term Islamic feminism is used more specifically to refer to activism of a relatively small number of Iranian women who seek the amelioration of the Islamized gender relations, mainly though lobbing for legal reform within the framework of the Islamic republic. However, it is difficult to define Islamic feminism. Margot Badran defines that:

> "It is a feminists discourse and practice articulated within an Islamic paradigm. Islamic feminism, which derives its understanding and mandate from the Quran, seeks rights and justice for women, and for men, in the totality of their existence. Islamic feminism is both highly contested and firmly embraced."

On the other hand, Shahidian has argued that 'Islamic feminism' is an oxymoron, a contradiction in term:

> "If by feminism is meant easing patriarchal pressures on women, making patriarchy less appalling, 'Islamic feminism' is certainly a feminist trend. But if feminism is a movement to abolish patriarchy, to protect human being from being prisoners to fixed identities, to contribute towards a society in which individuals can fashion their lives free from economic, political, social and cultural constraints, then Islamic feminism proves considerably inadequate. I define feminism in these latter terms and for that reason, I consider 'Islamic feminism' an oxymoron" (Hammed Shahidian, 1998: 51).

In reality, in most of the advanced Islamic States such as Iran, Turkey or South Arabia Islamic feminism advocates that women should be given legitimate rights to protect themselves but not to the extent that they can raise their voice against male domain. However, to understand Islamic feminism properly one has to analyse some of the Islamic religious books in which these women rights are discussed in detail, without which all the explanations of this stream of feminism would be incomplete in itself.

Islamic feminists are reinterpreting Islamic sources in order to achieve equal rights for women within an Islamic framework. They have challenged traditional interpretation of scripture and received notions of interpretive authority, both in Muslim majority societies as well as in the diasporic Islamic world. With their new interpretation they have contributed to the transformation of the legal, political and social rights of Muslim women. There are however also limitations to the feminist interpretation of scripture and their potential to deliver gender equality.

First of all, the status of Muslim women is to be viewed in reference to *the Quran*. With the advent of Islam, the position of women was radically redefined. Firstly, it prohibited the practice of 'female infanticide' and restored the birth of women. The Prophet asserted the right of a female child to be treated on an equal footing with her brother. There are few Hadiths in which he encouraged Muslims to be gentle and caring to their daughters: "if a daughter is born to a man and brings up her affectionately, shows her respect and treats her in same manner as treats his son, the Lord will reward him with paradise." (Haifaa A. Jawad, 1998: 12) Hence, Islam elevated the status of women being as worthy of human dignity as were men. The Quran refers, "Allah created you from a single soul, and from the same soul created his mate" (S.A.A. Mawdudi, 1976: 154).

It also says O mankind; we created you all from a male and female, and made you into nations and tribes, that ye may know each other not that ye may despise each other (The Quran, Surah 49: Verse 13). They are wives, your garments and you (husbands) are their (The Quran, Surah 2: Verse 187). Women have rights to what is responsible, over their husbands' rights over them (The Quran, Surah 2: Verse 228). In terms of moral responsibility, both men and women are equally accountable for their actions e.g. the Quran decrees that the same punishment has to be applied on the thieving men as well as the thieving women (The Quran, Surah 4: Verse 15).

If any of your women are guilty of fornication, take the evidence of four witnesses from amongst you against them, and if they testify, then confine them to houses until death comes to them or Allah ordains a way of release for them. On other hand, Surah 4, Verse 16 tells, "If two males among you commit lewdness, punish them both and then if they repent and amend, leave them aside; for Allah is acceptor of repentance most merciful."

All it means, if man does something unethical he can be forgiven or can be given religious asylum. But woman is quite far from such favour for herself. If she is accused for some wrong doing then her own statement or the statement of her favoured fellows is no more acceptable but to prove her innocence before four persons who are an opposite party to her, have to favour her argument otherwise she would lose chance to save her. According to the Quran man is allowed to have many wives at the same time, means his salacious behaviour is acceptable and woman's sexual behaviour is completely restrained. Even if her character is slightly suspicious then again she has to face extreme consequences.

Men are protectors and maintainers over women. By reason of superiority over one another Allah has given this privilege (The Quran, Surah 4: Verse 34). However, a Muslim woman is at liberty to buy, sell, mortgage, lease, borrow or lend, signs a contracts and legal documents. And do not desire by which Allah has made some of you excel others; men shall have the benefit of what women earn; and women shall have the benefit of what they earn themselves (4: 32).

Marriage in Islam is a union between two consenting adults. Its aim is to perpetuate human life and achieve spiritual and emotional harmony (Jamal Badawi, 1980: 137-38). The Quran refers, "And of his signs is that he created you from dust and beholds: you became men and multiplied throughout the earth. And of his signs is that He gave you wives from among yourselves that you might live in tranquillity with them, and put love and kindness in your hearts (The Quran, Surah 30: Verse 20). According to the prophet, "A widow or divorcee is not to be married before her consent is sought" and no virgin girl is to marry without first consulting her and her approval is her keeping silent (M. Siddiqui, 1988: 49).

Related to the right to education, both the Quran and Shariah advocate the rights of women and men equally to seek knowledge. The Quran encourages Muslims (irrespective of their sex) to read, think, contemplate and learn from the signs of Allah in nature: Are the wise and the ignorant equal? Truly, none will take heed but men of understanding (The Quran, Surah 39: Verse 9). Allah will raise to high ranks those that have faith and knowledge among you (The Quran, Surah 58: Verse 9).

The Quran has allotted a sphere for the women in the inheritance of her parents' property. Her share is guaranteed by law and it is completely hers. The Quran asserts, "Men shall have a share in what their parents and kinsmen leave; and women shall have a share in what their parents and kinsmen leave; whether it be little or more, it is legally theirs." (The Quran, Surah 4: Verse 7). However, it has been stated that Islam has firmly established and secured forever the legal right of inheritance. The woman's share is by no means fair and equal to that of her brother, who is allowed to take twice as much as the share of his sister (The Quran, Surah 4: Verse 10).

The Quran states that Allah direct you as regard you and as regard your children's (inheritance): to the male, a portion equal to that of two-females; if there are only daughters more than two, they will get two third in the heritance; and if only daughter is a heir she should be given a half share (The Quran, Surah 4: Verse 11). And in that inheritance which your wives leave, your share would be half if they leave a child, you get one-fourth share out of that which remains after the fulfilment of legacies and the payment of debts they may leave incurred. And your wives shall get one-fourth share out of what you leave; provided you have no child; but if you leave a child, your wives shall get an eighth share in distribution out of what remains after the fulfilment of legacies you had made and payment of debt you had to pay (The Quran, Surah 4: Verse 12).

Polygamy is also permitted in Islam. The verse read as follow, "If you fear that you cannot treat orphan with fairness, then you may marry such women as seen good to you; two, three or four of them. But if you fear that you cannot do justice, one only of those you possess, this will make it easier for you to avoid injustice" (The Quran, Surah 4: Verse 2). The Quran gives men and women equal rights to solve their marital problem. The Quran refers: "And if you fear that because of strained relations between husband and wife opposition or rift is widening, then set up an arbitrator from her family; if these two wish settlement, Allah shall bring harmony between those two because Allah only has full knowledge and acquainted with all thing" (The Quran, Surah 4: Verse 35).

The Quran also gives them (husband and wife) equal right to be separated from each other or dissolve their marriage. It further refers that "and then if (reconciliation has failed) they got separated, then Allah will provide in abundance to everyone and shield against dependency to one another; and Allah is all sufficient, all wise" (The Quran, Surah 4: Verse 130). The Quran exhorts the man to be considerate and kind to his former wife (The Quran, Surah 2: Verse 231) and (The Quran, Surah 65: Verse 2). Here the Quran says, "Do not expel them (wives) from their houses or let them go away unless they commit a proven immortality. Such are the bound set by Allah; he that transgresses Allah's bounds wrongs his own soul" (The Quran, Surah 65: Verse 1).

With the establishment of Islamic states the role of women in the political affairs of the new society gained momentum. Right from the beginning, women like men, gave support and loyalty to the political system which was set up under the leadership of Prophet Muhammad. This was done through the so called 'baya'. The 'baya' is an important political institution by which the nation or the Umma grants or ensures legitimacy for the political system. In addition to 'baya' women also participated in 'Shura' (mutual conservation) which is one of the foundations of the Islamic political system.

However the Quran, Surah 4, Verse 34 reads thus; "Men have authority over women because Allah has made the one superior to the other and because they spend their wealth to maintain them." This has virtually closed the door to women's advancement to higher positions. Two Hadith are of particular importance in this issue. The prophet is reported to have said 'O Women! Give alms, as I have seen that the majority of dwellers of hell fire were you (women). They asked why it is so, O Allah's messenger. He replied, you curse frequently and are ungrateful to your husbands. I have not seen anyone more deficient in intelligence and religion than you. A cautious, sensible man could be led astray by some of you. The women asked, O Allah's messenger! What is deficient in our intelligence and religion? He said, is not the evidence of two women equal to the witness of one man? They replied in the affirmative. He said, this is the deficiency in her intelligence. Is it not true that a woman can neither pray nor have fast during her menses? The women replied in affirmative. He said, this is the deficiency in her religion (Haifaa A. Jawad, 1998: 90).

The second Hadith which is reported in Bukhari and reads as thus: "Abu Bakr said when Allah's messenger was informed that the Persians had crowned the daughter of Kisra (Khosrau) as ruled by lady will never be successful" (Haifaa A. Jawad, 1998: 92). These Hadiths are used by opponents of women's rights in politics, to prove their point in saying that women cannot be trusted with handling public matters.

After making the review of religious literature of Islam, it is quite sure that it favours male dominance and patriarchal system. But simultaneously it also gives reflection that this religion is not favouring women's exploitation. It has presumed somewhere the male domain in society and at the same time, instructed male to provide some equal rights to women. But at so many spheres (e.g. property inheritance, two witnesses for man and four for woman) woman is really subordinate to man, which strengthens the view that woman is treated secondary in Islamic world. If someone analyses feminism as an ideology that interrogates patriarchal format and talks about women empowerment then it is quite confirmed that there is no existing Islamic feminism. But when someone talks about some of fundamental rights and some ease from exploitation then this phrase 'feminism' is having some existence in Islamic world.

To understand Islamic feminism properly it is essential to compare and contrast its features with Western feminism. Islamic feminism is very difficult explain in terms of Western feminism because a mutual incompatibility exists between the two. No Islamic feminist movement can relate to Western feminism because of the way feminists formed their groups. Western feminism is grounded in Western values and their ideology and values entirely differ from those of Islam and Arab tradition. Many problems exist because of resistance of cultural conversion.

Historically feminism started in the West particularly in France. Though the term originated in the West, Egypt was the primary pioneer of feminism. Contrary to popular belief Egypt was the one of the first countries to demonstrate feminist thinking. There is a lot of literature that can document the varied and diverse movement among feminists, but the West believes they own the concept of feminism. Although, it is true that Islamic feminism is a recent concept and as for modern day Islamic feminism, women have had a strong active presence only since the 1990s Islamic reawakening in the Arab and Islamic countries (Badran, 1990: 196).

Feminism is a concept that is unique to each culture or geographic location. In order to get a clear picture of the various attitudes of Muslim communities one has to look at predominantly Muslim countries like Saudi Arabia, Iran and Turkey. In each of these countries primary religion is Islam, but each country has its different national language and different attitudes toward the status of women. Saudi Arabia and Iran actually established the Quran as their constitution, while Turkey does not and tends to be the most liberal towards women. Saudi Arabia has the tightest restrictions on women. For instance, women cannot drive nor can they be educated in fields such as engineering and law. They are only allowed to teach and provide medical care to other women. In a report from Amnesty International, it is stated that despite an encouraging emerging debate on women's rights in Saudi Arabia, women still face extreme form of discrimination (Robert Spencer and Phyllis Chesler, 2007: 6-7).

Iran has also adopted the Quran as the basis of its constitution. Iranians, however believe existence is a "unified and interrelated divine system". Men and women complement each other and should have equal status. The differences defined in the laws of Islam for men and women are based on the roles they play and the responsibilities each assume. They believe that the law of Islam gives special privilege to women because of their physical characteristics and their role in creation. If they were to see women as equal in all aspects of life, it would violate some of their natural rights. So it is best for a woman to participate in development with consideration of their physical and spiritual needs. They believe the Islamic dress (Hijab) actually protects women from abuse and cruelty. Iran emphasises the positive interpretation of the Quran and should not be regarded as negatively as Westerners try to portray many Muslim communities (Hammed Shahidian, 1998: 11-12).

Muslim women in Turkey are most liberated because they enjoy a professional life that is not only impressive compared to other Islamic countries, but even for the European nations. In November 2002, the Turkish parliament reformed family law, by abolishing the law of men being head of the household and allows women to make decision concerning children. The law established community property in marriages and raised the legal age of marriage for girls from fifteen to eighteen. The Turks abolished the law of polygamy in 1925 and laws were amended to give women equal rights of divorce and inheritance. Under Islamic law, women were not granted these rights. Turkey is a positive example of an Islamic community that treats women well (Women in Contemporary Turkey, *http://www.tawsf.org/Women.htm*).

Although religion was an enemy for the Western feminist movement, Muslim women tend to embrace Islam and believe religion is a guiding source for their movement. The legal rights of Western women sought in the eighteenth century were incompatible with the Islamic religion because Muslim women were granted those same rights in the seventh century. Women are portrayed as negative beings in Christianity whereas there is not a negative depiction of women in Quran. But the interpretations of the Quran are different in some societies and there are at least two school of feminist thought throughout the Arab world (Hammed Shahidian, 1998: 14).

First, the apologetic view claims that Islam has liberated women and that Muslim women have more rights than Western women. Another branch of this school contends that the harsh conditions of Muslim women are the responsibility of male jurists who interpreted the Quran in a conservative and misogynist way. Then there is the feminist movement that tries to reinterpret Islamic texts from a female point of view. Western feminists believe that discrimination against women imbedded in the religion of Islam. The prophet Muhammad determined the inequality of women and passed it as god's commandments and recorded them in Quran. In the Quran it is written that men are 'one degree' above women in rank, and that men are guardian to women. At the same time, in the Quran, women's religious status is as high as that of men. It states:

> Lo! Men who surrender unto Allah and women who surrender, men who believe and women who believe, and men who obey and women who obey, and men who speak the truth and women who speak the truth, and men who preserve and patient men patient women and the humble men and humble women, and the charitable men and the charitable women, and the fasting men and the fasting women, and men who guard their chastity and women who guard

their chastity and men who remember Allah has prepared for them forgiveness and a mighty reward (The Quran).

This verse explains that women can attain every good quality to which men can have access and posits that in the Quran women have the same spiritual level as that of men. But in another verse of the Quran, it is stated, "men are maintainers of women as Allah has made to excel others and as they spend out of their wealth on women". On that verse Islamic feminists say that Quran gives man a slight edge over woman. It is not due to any inherent weakness of the female sex, but because of the social context (The Quran, Surah 4: Verse 34).

Besides, Muslim feminists criticise Western feminists for their view that Muslim women are oppressed because they are veiled and less career oriented as compared to Western women. Muslim feminists treat this veil as a guard and feel that a mother (housewife) is no less than a career woman. One American Muslim woman states, "When non-Muslim Americans meet Muslim women, they tend to feel sorry for them. 'Your husband makes you wear that?' They don't understand its personal choice". A Muslim woman in return says, "Oppression is not the scarf; oppression is wearing the Western fashion, which turns women into objects to be coveted by men" (Fernea, Elizabeth, 1998: 32-36).

It is true that in some countries Muslim women are weak, passive and oppressed but this is also true that women have many political and social rights in various Muslim countries. A few examples are Bangladesh, Pakistan and Turkey. In reality, the important fact about this conflict is women's issues are important for all cultures because they address the needs of the family and have an impact on society in general. Western feminists need to recognise other form of feminism and not try to impose their beliefs on other cultures. The goals of Western feminists are not compatible with Islamic feminists and should not be forced upon Muslim women.

The structure of family is also one of the reasons behind the differing social status of Islamic and Western women. Muslim women have a negative view as regards to Western family structure. They believe that Western societies have moved away from bonding and instead have smaller alternative family style. Those styles are opposite to the traditions and customs found among Islamic societies.

Islamic societies normally have an 'extended family' rather than a nuclear family. They also believe that the family as a whole should participate in preserving and contracting marriages. Another tradition that is arranged marriage has a negative impact on female liberation and is against individual freedom. Muslim women on the other hand believe that arranged marriages have distinct advantages for the individual and the society as a whole (Hammed Shahidian, 1998: 15).

Western society belittles traditional female roles such as child-rearing and reverence to those positions identified with males such as providing financial support. This concept is a major hurdle for Muslim women because they believe that both types of roles are necessary when coupled with religion and the division of labour is a great benefit for all members of society. Islamic tradition maintains that women's rights are equal to man but they are different rights. In Islamic societies, it is necessary to maintain the individual rights and complement one another rather than competing for same positions in society.

Western society also tends to criticise the concept of polygamy found in Islam and believes that Islam uses polygamy to subjugate women of Islam. Although it is true that Islam allows men to have more than one wife as written in the Quran, polygamy is not a common practice for all Muslims. Muslims resort to polygamy only in exceptional circumstances. For instance, it was earlier started and promoted to support war widows and their daughters so that they could be treated equally. Polygamy is not widespread phenomenon among Muslims. Therefore, the women of Islam would not support Western feminists' ideas of eliminating this practice.

Islamic feminists think that when the US promoted Taliban there was no anxiety for Muslim women then. But after 9/11 Muslim women are seen as victims everywhere. The US did not try to intervene with human rights of Muslim women until it was attacked. Besides, the Taliban's war on women was a key example of how the Quran was misinterpreted to oppress women, e.g. the Quran states, "men are the protectors and maintainers of women, because Allah has given the one more than the other, and because they support them from their means. Therefore, the righteous women are devotedly obedient" (The Quran, Surah 4: Verse 34).

This verse is the basis of Western feminists' argument against Islam. One Islamic feminist (Rifat Hassan) believes that the interpretation of the verse is wrong because of the way differences in understanding the context. She cites the errors in the verse by stating, "Where the Quran says that 'men are protectors and maintainers of women', it means that men are supposed to take care of the women when women are preoccupied with duties where they cannot take care of themselves, such as child rearing and child birth" (Jennifer S. King, 2003: 56).

Islamic feminists have been trying to engage with Islamic values and teachings rather than trying to reject the religion as such as Western feminist have done. One of the reasons is that when feminists groups attempt to ignore religion and pursue a Western based view of feminism, they have failed because Islam does not provide secular positions when discussing feminism. If Western feminists continue to deny or try eradicate Islam than any attempt at an Islamic feminist movement will fail. They need to understand that the women of Islam are not oppressed in all Muslim societies. All religions have positive aspects as well as negative ones. But to relate any one type of feminism is not possible on Central Asian women. It can be easily seen that all these feminist theories (especially Socialist/Marxist and Islamic Feminism) have influenced and changed the status of Central Asian women at large.

Chapter - 2

Women in Central Asia: A Historical Background

The social status of women in Central Asian society is shaped by myriad of invisible social and cultural customs, religion, tradition, family experiences, educational achievements and the history of local development. In order to explain the sources of women's changing problematic position in Central Asia one needs to turn to history. Because the Central Asian women's rights, liberties and her identities were shaped and reshaped in each period in which they lived. Women's position was greatly influenced by the social, economic, political and religious conditions during all these particular periods. However it is essential to analyse all these factors need a detailed study to know the contemporary status of Central Asian women in each times.

Central Asian Women in Pre-Soviet Period

Pre-Soviet period is considered here from Tsarist colonisation in 1865 to 1920 A.D. The scholars and politicians of both the left and the right agree that women in late nineteenth and early twentieth century Central Asia lived in most oppressive, conservative and unfriendly environment to be found in the territory controlled by the Russian empire. In Pre- Soviet period the social structure of the society was patriarchal and of big families which is an indication of traditional agricultural society. Within these big families the eldest male and female used to be in authority. While the brides that became the part of the family lived under the control of both men and elderly women, especially of their mother-in-law or their husband's elderly wives.

Therefore, it is not only men who reproduced this family structure but women too contributed to the reproduction of this structure of this relationship, which exploited and suppressed women. The social and agrarian economic structure was inclined towards the male in the society (Suna Gulfer Ihlamur, 2003: 175-221).

Patriarchal relations that are very much related with the economic structure have therefore not changed. But rather continue with redefinitions and negotiation within the context of society, identity and culture, which are themselves in constant flux and transformation (Isenbike Togan, 1999: 122). Patriarchal ideologies give less value to feminine roles and identity in comparisons to masculine ones (Anuradha M. Chenoy, 2005: 169). It is the winner of all the time, which is successful in the representing itself with a different face by establishing multi-dimensional relations with those in power and different periods. Women's destiny has been shaped in Central Asia by patriarchy having different faces at different periods. Thus, CAS is having a history of male dominance and simultaneously it is also true that male dominance and feminism cannot pace together.

Besides, in the history of Central Asia, Islamic religion has been in dominance for a very long time, though it had different roles in pre-Soviet, Soviet and post-Soviet period. It is a truism that women living under Islamic law are visibly the most suppressed. Islam provides women many rights which we have discussed earlier and all these rights aim at to save women from exploitation. But at the same time it is also true that the same religion compels women to obey numerous traditions and customs in a rigid manner which is liable for women's oppression.

For instance, the pre-USSR period Central Asia is associated with the practice bride-purchasing and bride-price (*kalym*), bride-kidnapping, child marriage, female isolation at the back of the house (*ichkari*), isolation through the veil (*paranja*), polygamy, violence, complete domination over the lives of women (Anuradha M. Chenoy, 1996: 516-518). *'Kalym'* is bride price which is paid by the bridegroom family. Since the family of bridegroom pays *'kalym'* (price) for the bride while the marriage is arranged, it increases domestic violence.

The fact that the groom's family pays bride price helps to build special relationship with the bride and her family and turns her to a free (unpaid) house servant. Besides the family of a bridegroom covers all expenses related with wedding ceremony and party; buys house and furniture for the new couple. These also make women vulnerable and in case of her disobedience she is fully blamed by *mahalla* (community people). People consider that if price is paid for the bride then she should obey her husband and his relatives (Rafis Abazov, 2007: 212).

Another discriminatory custom was bride-kidnapping, which was an ancient tradition in nomadic societies in Central Asian States. Often, it took place in the circumstances of mutual agreement, but only few people were aware that the kidnapping of bride without her wish is a crime (Alena Aminova, 2005: 3). Women wore conservative dress according to strict Islamic norms. They were like human puppets that were visible in the street of Central Asia as moving bundles whose feet were only visible to the passerby. The *paranja* or the veil symbolises the enslavement of women, her ignorance and her subjection to men. Behind the veil the human being that existed was regarded only as an object of lust, meant for pleasure and production (Ajay Patnaik, 1989: 10).

Mostly marriages were arranged and women had no choice about her partner, early marriages were common in practice and marriages between a minor girl and an old man were widespread. In many cases of that time women could not bear the pain of child birth at such an early age and died as a result. Life expectancy of women was very low and woman was not mere a slave to one man who happened to marry her rather of the whole family of her husband. Girls as young as 10 or 11 years old were pushed to become wives or concubines in the *harems* of wealthy man who might be of the age of their grandfathers (Rafis Abazov, 2007: 216).

In many parts of the Central Asian region a widow was obliged to marry her husband's younger brother or a relative, even if he was just a boy or an invalid (Frederick Burnaby, 2002: 357-358). In some places, women were married out by their families to the highest bidder – the person who would pay the highest *kalym* (bride price) or were not allowed to marry the man they loved just because the fiance was unable to afford the appropriate dowry (Ajay Patnaik, 1989: 12). The Turkmen society in Central Asia used to have a rare custom that only married people had rights over the natural resources like water and land. In such a situation rich people promoted the evil of *kalym* and minor marriages to occupy these natural sources, on the other hand poor people saved money all their lives to acquire a wife or were quite deprived to marry (Fannina W. Halle, 1938: 83-85). In this way, such orthodoxy had enhanced the number of minor marriages and *kalym* cases in the region and the fundamental element of human need like water and land had played a significant role in shaping society.

Virginity and modesty were considered issues of reputation for women in Central Asian societies; and a woman could be stoned to death just for talking or having a secret meeting with men other than her husband, father and her male blood relatives. Divorce was not allowed to women even if her husband was abusive or a paranoid. Dating was absolutely unacceptable, and almost all marriages were arranged by parents or elderly persons of the family (Frederick Burnaby, 2002: 179-180). Most of the women were secluded and isolated behind the high walls of *Ichkari* (individual houses for women) or harems and never had an opportunity to get a proper education and job. The local population gained their formal education from religious institutions which neither taught modern curriculum nor encouraged girls to study. This system prevented the growth of an educated and skilled labour force among the native population and the literary rate was extremely low in Central Asia and was decimal as far as women were concerned (Ajay Patnaik, 1989: 9).

In Tzarist regime girls in Central Asia could only attend religious school which were hypothetical. The girls had to go to the mullah's house where his wife used to teach the lessons. These lessons were given in the kitchen or in the cowshed. The classroom and equipment of learning were not in existence, the girls had to remain on their feet in the preaching family during their learning and this process of learning was also very short. After attaining a certain age they were bound to remain at home and got married. Such education was meant for some fundamental training for women in religion (Lyudmila Dubrovina, 1957: 256).

Table 2.1: Literacy Level, 1897

(In per cent)

	Men	*Women*
RSFSR	44.4	15.4
Uzbekistan	5.6	1.2
Kirghizia	5.0	0.8
Tajikistan	3.9	0.3
Turkmenia	11.5	2.7

Source: Ajay Patnaik (1989), *Perestroika and Women Labour Force in Soviet Central Asia,* New Literature, New Delhi, p. 9.

The above figures included all nationalities in Central Asia and the rate of literacy among Central Asian women was very low as compared to men in these states and it was approximately 2 per cent of the total strength of women collectively.

Women were completely segregated from the main stream of life and even could not dream of equality. They had a very inferior status in their social lives, they were considered *"impure"* as a wife and an *"alien burden"* as a daughter. They were not allowed to share their meals with male members in the family but had to wait in a corner for the order of males even to fulfil their hunger. The families were mostly in extended form and in these families a childless woman was considered the greatest shame and a pregnant woman was regarded as most impure. Husband could take another wife if the existing wife had no children, all the blaming of having no children always lay with the woman.

Many rural Uzbek women knew little about the world and were not allowed to set outside of their homes without the permission of their husbands or relatives. Such was an extended form of degradation for women in Turkmen society. The term used to define their spouse or wives as *"slave"* or *"concubine"*. The Turkmen women could rock the cradle by a cord tied its feet while she worked, if it was a girl, but in the case of a boy she never used to do so (Fannina W. Halle, 1938: 79-82). All this shows that women were the victim of society from their childhood and all her upbringing were meant to mould her personality from the very beginning.

In traditional Central Asian families children, male and female, understood their gender identity at a very early age. The birth of boy was joyfully celebrated by everyone and girls were rarely given such attention. The parents, especially fathers openly expressed emotional attachment to their young sons, even through games emphasising the boy's gender significantly and were less attentive towards female child. The mothers prepared girls to take care of themselves and to take on their allocated obligations. At the age of five or six girls took care of younger siblings. From earliest childhood girls were taught to tolerate deprived and limitations in food, sleep and comfort. A capricious girl was not tolerated, while the family accepted capricious and demanding boys. Mothers and grandmothers promoted such attitudes based on their own experiences as they prepared their daughters for their subsequent difficult life as a wife in the husband's home, where she would be subservient to the husband and his relatives (Sofia Kasymova, Gender Socialisation: Central Asia: 159).

Observing father's power in the family's daily life, the boys came to recognise their superiority over girls; they knew that they had the rights to punish them if they deviated from the norms of their gender status. The boys were encouraged to act, to self-defence, and to aggressiveness (Sofia Kasymova, Gender Socialisation: Central Asia: 159). They spent a great deal of time outside the home in company of men. Both family and community exercised strict control over girls who knew that they must serve other members, especially the males in the family. They must be modest, obedient, and fear all men; male could punish them for disobedient and relation with some strangers on the basis of their reputation and good name in the society. A girl's good name included not only preserving virginity until her marriage but modesty in clothing and speech, and not showing herself in social spaces with unrelated men. Control over girls' and women's sexual behaviour was a fundamental element in Central Asian gender socialisation (Sofia Kasymova, Gender Socialisation: Central Asia: 159).

Women had no right to divorce and had to accept the condition of her existence without any way to escape from it. Men could buy them as wives and discard them as per their own will. The husband, who bought her could sell her like any other object and could even kill her

Yet even nomad women were often forced to marry leaders or representatives of tribes in order to strike a peace or a political and military union; sometimes they were taken as kind of a trophy in the horse racing competitions or were simply stolen by bachelors who for some reasons could not get married through legitimate means. This tradition was called bride kidnapping or *kyzula kachu* in Kyrgyz. Such tradition also exists in some parts of Kazakhstan, Karakalpakistan and Turkmenistan (Rafis Abazov, 2007: 217).

It does not mean that no steps were taken to improve the condition of Central Asian women from her deplorable social setting. Some Russian elites and reformists within Muslim religion tried to enhance women's position in this region and undertook a number of positive measures. For example, in the beginning the Russian empire used Central Asia merely for their political and economic interests. They did not worry about the social and cultural structure of the region. They thought that if they would intervene in private matters like religion and conventional customs then it could bring great troubles in their ruling system because most of the region was dominated by Muslim community and their great inclination towards the neighbouring Pan-Islamic states. But during the reign of Peter the great, the Russian policy towards Muslim society began to change, since Westernisation and modernisation paved the way for the emergence of processes such as systemisation and homogenisation of Russia's complex socio-cultural structure. The Russian elites ran a civilising mission in order to convince the backward people of Central Asia to adopt Russian culture and if necessary to implement it even by force (Suna Gulfer Ihlamur, 2003: 175).

"The status of Central Asian Muslim women had been a target of Russian missioners and Orientalists. Orientalism which means the knowledge of the West on the East goes beyond an endeavour to give meaning or to explain. The knowledge of the West goes beyond constructing the East; it constructs the facts about the East, and by this way enables the West to take the East under control." (Suna Gulfer Ihlamur, 2003: 184) The same goal to take Central Asia under control was hidden within the facts constructed by the Russian Orientalists with regard to Central Asia. From the nineteenth century to the twentieth century there emerged reformists within Islamic world who were (under the influence of the Orientalist discourse) trying to find means to overcome the low profile of the Islamic communities and transform them.

In order to achieve this goal they aimed at improving the position of women in the society. The freedom of women became the core claim of intellectuals that held progress and modernisation as the most important goals for their societies. According to both Jadidism (reformism), which could be defined as the modern struggle of the Islamic civilisation in Russia and Ismail Bey Gasprinsky, who has been the leading figure of this movement, modernisation was deemed necessary in order to overcome the "backwardness" of the Russian Muslims. According to Gasprinsky, who deemed the position of women in the society as important for his modernisation project, the status of women within the society should be improved and women should have the right to education. The restrictions upon dressing up of women, unequal treatment of women in regards to marriage, divorce and practices such as polygamy should be done away with. The conservatives, who were against the modernisation goal of the Jadidists, rejected these claims regarding the rights of women (Suna Gulfer Ihlamur, 2003: 186).

The Russian Muslims' alliance in January 1906, after long discussions about the political rights of women and despite the efforts of the Jadidists gave women only the right to vote (Suna Gulfer Ihlamur, 2003: 186). At the third meeting of the alliance in August 1906, it was accepted that both men and women were equal before the law arguing that religion was not a restricting factor for Central Asian women status. Tzarist Russia considered keeping the structure and not interfering with the traditions of the region as the best way to preserve Russian rule over the region. This attitude of Tsarist Russia had limited the influence of enlightened Russia to eliminate the patriarchal structure or to transform the society in the Central Asian region (Suna Gulfer Ihlamur, 2003: 189).

The Religion as a unifying factor for Russia's Muslim and increasing influence of Pan-Islamic movement made Russian Muslims open to the influence of other Muslim societies, which preoccupied Tzarist Russia. This led Russia to consider keeping the existing structure and not interfering with the traditions of the region as the best way to preserve Russian rule over the region, while playing the trump card of ethnic identity against Pan-Islamism and religious conservatism against Jadidism.

The differences between traditionally settled and nomadic people of Central Asia have remained considerable throughout the history of their co-existence. In settled regions Islam had intense history of more than one thousand years. Establishment of Islam protracted upto the seventeenth and eighteenth centuries among the nomadic people of Central Asia and Sufi saints and orders (Tarikats) played an important role in converting the nomads into Islam. An important feature of the Sufi saints' activity was a tolerance to some animistic nomadic traditions and a flexible approach to dealing with the nomads in their everyday life. Sufi teaching was closely inter-twined with local tribal habits and rituals and even with the pre-Islamic beliefs (Rafis Abazov, 1998: 12).

Islam is not only faith but also a socio-cultural system for the people of Central Asian region. Islam came to Central Asia is 642 A.D. when Arabs defeated the Persian Sassanid Empire. By the eighth century Islam became a dominant religion in Central Asia. The complete Islamisation of nomadic people took several more centuries (Muriel Atkin, 1992: 60). The system, regardless of religion, featured kin-based extended families, male domination, early marriage and consequent high fertility, restrictive code of female behaviour, the linkage of family honour with female virtue and occasionally polygamous family structure. In Muslim areas, veiling and sex segregation formed part of the gender system. Muslim women in Central Asia lived under the family or personal status of law, which is mainly built upon Shariah, Islamic religious-based law. However, Islamic family law as variously manifested in Muslim nations posed obstacles to women's equality.

Central Asian Women in the Economic Structure of Pre-USSR Period

Under the Tzarist's rule the economy of Central Asia depended mainly on agriculture and like other colonisers the industrial revolution of Russia was accomplished on the basis of the feudal agrarian policy of Central Asian states. Central Asia had become a major source of raw silk and cotton for Russian industrialists and the manufacturing of textiles was prohibited in this region due to the exploitative relation between the European industrial region and Central Asia.

During this time whatsoever steps were taken to enhance the economy of Central Asia came only under a policy to maintain a good colony or under a colonial strategy, it was not meant for the real economic development of this region. In those times feudal relations of production remained predominant. The feudal and clan nobility, which owned the land, the irrigation systems, the cattle and so forth, oppressed the mass of peasantry with shackling labour rents. Mediaeval form of rent paid in labour and in kind, still existed on the eve of the October Revolution, though money rent had also come into use with commercialisation of agriculture under colonial rule (Ajay Patnaik, 1996: 10-11).

Central Asian agriculture was characterised by the small size of holding and ancient techniques of cultivation which kept productivity of labour extremely well. There were an excess number of landless peasants in Central Asia that enhanced the *Chairikers* (share-croppers) system in the region, under which the share-croppers received as little as one-fourth or even one-fifth of the total production (R.R. Sharma, 1979: 12-13). The enormous masses of peasantry lived a wretched life, more so under the colonial system which exposed the peasantry to the twofold exploitation of feudal land tenure system as well as the capitalist cash nexus. Central Asian farmers under the Russian rule were incurably suppressed by host landlords, merchants, usurers and tax collectors, and continued to pay the feudal dues and additionally they also toiled for building, dredging and repair work on canals, roads and bridges (Ajay Patnaik, 1996: 10).

All this made the life extremely harsh in rural areas. Landlords and capitalists hired peasants on very cheap wages from the villages and women and children were widely involved in this process. Wages were so low that after working for a whole year many labourers did not earn enough to pay even for the food (A Leap Through Socialism, 1968: 200). Besides, Central Asian societies were divided mostly into two classes. In one class there were extremely poorest peasants, the landless and the tenant farmers and in other class there were extremely rich landlords, usurers and the *kulak* (the capitalist farmers) class (Ajay Patnaik, 1996: 10).

The urban centres of Central Asia during Tzarist period were basically centres of commerce and handicrafts. The town were situated in the midst of rich valleys, especially cotton valleys. This was so because the town mainly functioned as assemblage points where agricultural produce from the surrounding countryside was gathered to be transhipped to Russia. Central Asian working class was not skilled but the Russian migrants were generally skilled because of their urban background and almost all the skilled jobs in Central Asia were monopolised by Russians. Central Asians remained mainly unskilled workers or labour class even after the industrialisation of their area. Russian were 76 per cent of persons operating and maintaining machine and engines and 70.3 per cent of those engaged in equipment repair in the railways. The proportion of unskilled workers in the industry of Turkistan in 1914 was 13.2 per cent Russian, 50.4 per cent Uzbek and 36.4 per cent from other nationalities (R.T. Kamilov, 1964: 32).

In Central Asian working class there was the lack of participation of women in the work force. There were only 65 Uzbek women employed in industry in Turkistan. In Tzarist period there was no Uzbek woman engineer or technician in Central Asia. The subsistence of a feudal-patriarchal system and low level of urbanisation barred the involvement of women in industrial labour force (Ajay Patnaik, 1996: 13). In this period women were busy in her domestic work, field work, handicraft work and other domestic industry in which their wages were grabbed by their husband or other family members. Hence, in these work places there were no financial outcomes for them.

The economic structure of Central Asia in Tzarist period was agrarian and feudal. They were living in miserable conditions even after industrialisation. Russian empire used this region as supplier of raw material and unskilled labour. This economic structure had affected women adversely. First of all their status was lower than men because they were not considered breadwinner in that patriarchal society. Secondly, if their family were living in poor conditions then also they were lower in status though working to support the family. Because in poor families their health, food culture, working conditions were more affected they suffered more, rather they were bearing large family burden also. In absence of education and technical knowledge they remained unskilled and low wages labourers. Generally, they earned less than men because they were given low wages than men.

In such economic setting, there was no working culture for women in Central Asian society and if something like that existed there then it was simply unskilled labour or domestic working traditions during the Tzarist period. There was no trade training for women in Central Asia. The few private vocational schools that existed taught housekeeping, needle work and dress making; none of them instructed women in skilled industrial occupation (Nina Popova, 1957: 96). The Tzarist civil service regulation categorically prohibited the employment of women in any administrative capacity. It is a well known fact that unless and until the economic situation are not developed suitably the women in the family even cannot dream a quality life in such social order. Because a low profile economic setting affects women more than men in a society.

Central Asian Women in the Political Structure of Pre-USSR Period

During the Tzarist period the Central Asian region was treated as a colony. The political structure of Russian regime was based on monarchy in which there was no participation of common man. On regional level there was feudal system that was only based on economic exploitation. The Central Asian region was actually ruled under the Russian regime and it was not a part of it. In this way all major developments were made in Russia and this region was merely manipulated for Russian benefits.

All the welfare schemes which were meant for masses reached to neither Central Asian people nor Russian rulers were liable for all such lapses in administration in anyway. In such a situation the participation of women in politics was a distant dream, and not any steps were taken to reduce their exploitation in this region. Central Asian women were under a great burden due to the bindings made by religion. According to Islamic Holy Scripture Quran, women should dress modestly rather than attempt to confront the forceful external gaze of patriarchal society. Thus, the existing system had pushed women of Central Asia into a dark cell.

Besides all this, the traditions like *ichkari* (women section in a house), polygamy, bride price, early marriages and the secondary status of women were a pest for women in this region. Despite such pathetic conditions of women, the Russian rulers didn't give any attention to improve their position at political level. The one major cause for all this was that the Russian rulers never took any risk by interfering in religious matters because the religion is commonly considered the most sensitive aspect of human beings in general and also as this region was surrounded by Pan-Islamic countries. Secondly, the Russian rulers had always used this region mere as a colony and did nothing for its development. The rulers desired that there should not be any social, political and economic awakening in the masses particularly in this region because such stirring might have become a hindrance in their smooth ruling.

Tzarist Russia, where both social and nationwide subjugation were at its most horrible, was inevitably also a state of crying disparity for women. Old Russian legislation downgraded women, in both society and the family, to a status that was not only unequal but downright embarrassing. Women had no political rights, and were deprived even of the insufficient electoral civil rights, which the Tzarist regime had been obligated to grant the male population after the revolution of 1905. Women could neither take part in election nor be elected to any agency or organisation of local self-government, they had no right to raise their voice in Duma (national parliament of Russia), which was a very poor impression of parliament in reference to women. The civil service code then in force in the Russian Empire explicitly prohibited the appointment of women to clerical and other offices in any government departments where posts were assigned by the decision of a superior or as a result of election (Anna Pankatova, 1957: 16).

The law and the entire Tzarist system cynically approved the oppressed the working women who were deprived of all rights and had to bear all kinds of degradation. Women especially from the working strata of population were deprived of any participation in the social and political life of the country. Their position in the family was that of a subsidiary, a fact which found striking reflection in old proverbs and folk sayings. In accordance with the code of laws of the Russian Emperor (Volume X, Part 1, Article 107 and 109) the husband was considered the head of the family and the wife was obliged to obey him implicitly (K. Gorsghenin, 1957: 51).

The law gifted the husband with limitless power over his wife. For instance, if he changed residence the wife was forced to follow him unconditionally. She had no right to take on a job or enter an educational institution without the husband's consent. She had to take her husband's family name and nobody even asked whether she approved it. Women in the faraway regions of the country were exploited with extreme cruelty which was characteristic of the entire landlord – bourgeois system of the Tzarist Russia. In those regions the Tzarist tyranny and the ruling group of feudal lords and gender biased attitude twisted the women into practical slaves. Kalym, bride-kidnapping, early marriage and minor and unmatched marriage, polygamy and bigamy were the sanctioned customs in the tribal areas of Central Asia (K. Gorsghenin, 1957: 52).

Thus, the Tzarist period worked as preserver of traditional system and worsened the political, social and economic conditions in the region. It never worked for the progress and improvement of Central Asian region. In such a situation there was no space and scope left for analysing anything good about women. On the basis of all this one can infer that during this phase the entire setting was almost having an anti-woman force and to talk about women empowerment was a far-off vision. The whole political environment was having an anarchist character and so far as the matter of women empowerment was concerned, it was not even contemplated in that time.

During that time the socio-economic conditions was predominantly based on agrarian sector and that merely approved women to stay only within the four boundaries of the house. Though at the same time it was also a reality that women's labour was very imperative in domestic industry, but whatever in her hand were only manual labour and not its outcome. She was all the time under the shadow of male members and not given any financial independence. The social structure was totally based on patriarchy and favouring male in society. Women were not given equal social rights and her actual position was inferior to men in society, a variety of social customs were against women's right and liberty.

So far as the matter of cultural structure of society is concerned women were designed for subjugation and the cultural life of Central Asian region had sanctioned the veiling and polygamy to crush women in society. The cultural life was greatly influenced by Islam and religion had shaped and reshaped women's position in society. As it was mentioned in first chapter that religion was largely a prerequisite for male domination and women were nowhere considered and placed identical to men in reality and later on the followers of this religion explained and used it for their own interests.

All these reveal that women's state was really pathetic and sub-human in society in those times and there was hardly any meaningful step taken to improve women's position in society. Thus, it can be observed that issues, for instance, feminism, equal status for women and women empowerment did not figure at all at that time. All such notions came as ideas at some stage in the period of the USSR. The Soviet Union was the first state that well thought-out steps to make women equal to men and took some constructive measures to enhance women's position in society.

Central Asian Women in the USSR

The Russian revolution of 1917 had vibrated almost every part of Russian empire. The chief goal of this revolution was to establish equality in society in terms of rich and poor; men and women; and the Russian region and Central Asian region. At that time Central Asia became the part of USSR on an equal political basis. As a part of political modernisation of the early 1920s, Stalin by his directive significantly redrew the map of Central Asia during 1924-26 and the region was subdivided into union republics. The territorial borders were slightly altered in 1936 and the areas occupied by each of the five Central Asian republics (Kazakhstan, Uzbekistan, Kyrgyzstan, Tajikistan, and Turkmenistan) remained unchanged until the disintegration of USSR.

After the socialist revolution in USSR great concern was shown for women's emancipation especially for Central Asian women. Marx wrote that great social revolutions are impossible without the feminine ferment and social progress measured precisely by the social position of women. From the very beginning, the Bolsheviks were determined to abolish primitive practices and customs that degraded and oppressed women believing that this would help to clear the way for the construction of socialism (Adrienne Edgar, 2006: 252). The "women question" was a matter of concern throughout the Muslim world of Central Asian States in the early part of twentieth century, with intellectual and reformers questioning practices such as veiling and polygamy and demanding education and a greater public role for women (Leila Ahmad, 1992: 15).

Status of Central Asian Women in the Constitutional Structure of USSR

The state wanted to remove all hindrances to women's full participation in labour force and politics. Lenin believed socialism was not possible without the full emancipation of women and also that full equality was not possible without socialism. He further says, "Unless women are brought to take an independent part not only in the political life generally, but also daily and universal public, it is no use talking about stable democracy, let alone socialism" (V.I. Lenin, Vol. 24, 1965: 70) and "To effect complete emancipation and make her equal to men it is necessary for the national economy to be socialised and for women to participate in common productive work." (V.I. Lenin, Vol. 30, 1965: 43)

All Russian Congress of Soviet, held in July 1918, legalised women's new political and civil rights through Article 22, which guaranteed the equality of all citizens of the Soviet republics regardless of sex, race or nationalities, Article 64 guaranteed right to Soviet women on an equal footing with man, irrespective of nationality, creed etc. (K. B. Usha, 2005: 146) In the 1920s the Soviet state initiated a very determined assault on certain Islamic customs relating to women. Laws were passed outlawing the payment of bride price, child marriage and polygamy. Women were also given the right to divorce, the right to equal inheritance of property, the right to education without discrimination, the right to vote, the right to be witness in courts on the same basis as men, and the right to hold public offices (Greagory J. Massal, 1974: 152). According to Article 122, in the USSR, women enjoyed equal rights with men in all spheres of economic, state, culture, social and political life. This right was guaranteed by granting women equal right with men to work, remuneration of labour, leisure and rest, social insurance and education (K. B. Usha, 2005: 146).

Religion was regarded as 'vestige of the past' in Soviet period, which would be fought against by scientific persuasion or, if necessary, by force. From the mid-1920 onwards, anti-religious machinery was set in motion and the Muslim regions were flooded with anti-Islamic posters and publications. The enforced collectivisation of farm lands in the late 1920s and early 1930s was accompanied by a direct assault on the traditional practices of Muslim communities: almost all mosques were closed down and thousands Muslim scholars, Imams and Sufi saints were imprisoned, exiled or excluded from public life. Muslim newspapers and Islamic literature were banned, and Muslim libraries were destroyed. The communist youth activists took the lead in bulldozing Muslim shrines (Studying Islam in the Soviet Union, 2008: 5-6).

A major goal of the early Soviet policy in Muslim regions was banning of traditional female clothing; the unveiling of Muslim women, by persuasion of by force, was regarded as women's liberation, with no regard for the women's preferences and for the vulnerable situation of the unveiling women in the their traditional societies (Studying Islam in the Soviet Union, 2008: 7). Since the 1930s, the Soviet Union was completely secular but the Soviet totalitarian state was not able to eradicate the influence of religion. It was in private, mainly in the family or at unofficial communities meeting that Muslims continued to perform Islamic rituals.

The Bolsheviks changed the social and political setting in which Islam existed in Central Asia and cut short its modernising tendencies (this modernising movement was known as Jadidism, which was particular focused on education including women and was at least sceptical of tradition and custom) curtailed. The closed border also isolated Soviet Muslims from the broader Muslim world. Central Asia remained beyond the reach of much mid and late century Islamist phenomenon of "political Islam" (Central Asia: Islam and the State, 2003: 2).

Soviet rule had recognised that a complex and significant relation was subsisted between gender and religion in Central Asian region. Because the religion was functioning as a negative key stakeholder for Central Asian women, it was observed that if the religion itself is completely uprooted then women's condition can be improved to a great extent. Marx and Engels had earlier repeated this argument again and again that women are having the half sky and they should be given their due. To establish a secular society by eliminating religion was an imperative step in this direction.

Status of Central Asian Women in the Social Structure of USSR

The state promoted the interest of mothers and children; they gave proper assistance to unmarried mothers and mothers of extended families. The USSR government made provision of paid maternity leave, childcare leave, and provided safe and sound environment and good facilities in maternity hospitals. They provided such conveniences as collective kitchen, nurseries, and kindergartens for working women. Actually, the USSR government desired and to some extent created all the facilities for women so that they could symbolise a spirit of equality and common welfare in society and all the barriers which were coming in between were sought to be removed by making some significant laws and regulation in support of women.

To minimise the burden on the working women regarding the responsibility of upbringing their children and domestic works in general and to make a shift from household work to professional work in particular, the communist government started a number of kindergartens and nursery schools.

Table 2.2: Kindergartens and Nursery Schools in the USSR

(*in thousands*)

Year	*Number of kindergartens and nursery schools*	*Number of children*	*Directors and Teachers*
1927	2.1	107.5	6.1
1940	24	1171.5	75.2
1950	25.6	3115.1	243.4
1970	83.1	8099.7	576.3
1971	86.6	8463.4	602.9
1972	89.4	8870.5	636.4
1973	93	9361	669.8

Source: V.S.Yazykova (1975), "The Socialist Mode of Life and Women's Free Time" in *Soviet Women: Some Aspects of the Status of Women in the USSR,* Progress Publishers, Moscow, p. 120.

By relieving women of a certain portion of burden of caring for children, society enabled them to devote more attention to their own development on educational and professional skills level.

The household duties have an equally damaging impact on women's social role because they swallowed up a large portion of their free time. Therefore, the equal distribution of housework was regarded as very important. The communist mode of life presupposes not an equal sharing of family responsibility, but the abolition of the domestic bondage as social institutions, not equal division of housework between wife and husband, but the transference of the most unproductive, most monotonous odd jobs in the household to community services (V.S. Yazykova, 1975: 121-122).

Any survival of the feudal-bias treatment of women was considered in the Soviet Union as grave crimes punishable by law. Marriages and divorces were legalised and prohibited any religion or customary restrictions on them. Women were given the right to divorce; according to law they cancel decide the question of divorce themselves, as citizens and members of the family in full standing (K. Gorshenin, 1958: 53). The first code on civil right which was published in 1918 stipulated, that persons entering into marriage have the right to decide whether they will take the husband's family name, or the wife's, or a combined family name. It also provided that a change of domicile by one of the spouses involved no obligation on the other to follow. Parental rights were exercised by father and mother jointly and all measures in respect of the children were taken by the parents through mutual consent; in case of disagreement the question in dispute was settled through court procedure with the participation of the parents (K. Gorshenin, 1958: 53).

According to the law of the Russian Federation marriage age was 18 and the difference between bride and groom should not be more than one or two years. Soviet law provided for the mutual consent of both the parties, entering into marriage; the law prohibited any type of forced or arranged marriage or the marriage without consent of women. In Soviet Union there was no racial or national discrimination in the sphere of marriage as well. Moreover, Soviet Union even gave the right of citizenship to women who were Soviet citizens but married foreigners (K. Gorshenin, 1958: 56).

The Soviet law have given the equal right of property to both husband and wife. The property of the couple before marriage was separate property of each. Property acquired by husband and wife in the married state was common property, even if the wife was engaged exclusively in housekeeping and bringing up children. The *Zhenotdel* (women's department) of the communist party of the USSR was setup to guarantee that the new rights granted to Soviet women were actually made available (D.M. Heer and Nadia Youssef, 1977: 157). In order to draw women into public life, the Zhenotdel devised a system of 'delegate meetings' which operated in both towns and villages throughout the 1920s. In the meetings women learned to sew, trade, read and write without encountering men (Susan Bridger, 1970: 10-15). Besides, during these meetings all the problems related to women were raised and efforts were made to make efficient solutions. Zhenotdel benefited the Central Asian women in two ways, first, it encouraged women to participate in public life without obliging them to join political parties and secondly, Zhenotdel provided a platform to women to discuss their problems openly and it enhanced the mental awakening in them about their social status and rights in society.

Zhenotdel served as a link between the party and the female masses. It was true that the Zhenotdel delegates' assemblies were not tainted by feminism and did not articulate the radical demand of equal of rights for women. But it was perhaps the emergence of the gender notion of women as social activist (Melanie Ilic, 2001: 4). During the 1920s certain amount of success was achieved in the area of women's rights and in drawing them to productive and social activities. Poor people greatly appreciated the fact that women's work contributed to the family budget. Peasants were satisfied that their wives earned in the cartel without violating social norms since they were among women only (Dilarom A. Alimova, 1998: 148-149). Zhenotdel (Department of women) was the very first effective, practical and successful step taken by the USSR. It made women financially independent and broke the four boundaries around and gave a little breathing space to them.

In the beginning no one raised the issue of casting off *Paranjas* or unveiling. However, the majority of women were left in *Ichkari* behind the high walls. Moreover, the slow pace of this development did not affect the oppressive organisation already in place. The government initiated an interventionist and aggressive campaign called *Hujum.* Shedding of veil or unveiling was the main part of this movement. Neither the party members and Soviet workers, regardless of the position they occupied, nor the simple people were prepared to understand or accept the fact that women could go out without *paranjas* (Dilarom A. Alimova, 1998: 148-149). There were a number of cases reported where the workers of the Communist party and even the government employees used to have a different point of view on the issue of *paranjas*. For instance, a member of Central Executive committee, Karimov, arrested a worker of Tashkent Tram Park because his wife took off her *paranjas*.

In the village named Yallama in the Tashkent region officials prohibited farm labours from opening their wives faces and letting them go out into the street (Dilarom A. Alimova, 1998: 148-149). One cruelly painful story from the early period of this movement was of a young girl who after she discarded her veil, had her hands, her ears and her tongue cut off by her family and was then thrown into a pit. She was subsequently rescued by red army soldiers (Caroline Kennedy-Pipe, 2004: 97). At the time (1927) the Communist parties of Central Asian Republics appointed 40,000 members and delegates, 25,000 of whom were the representative of local nationalities. It was assumed that these communists should act as an example of progressive ideology. But in fact they took their wives to the squares where *paranjas* were publically brunt into the fire, and on the next day they made them wear them again.

According to Uzbek archival data, in just over two years between 1926 and 1928, more than 2500 women who were activists, members of rural regional committees dealing with women's clubs and libraries, died and this was a conservative estimate (Rafis Abajov, 2007: 148-149). Veil has had such a symbolic customary importance that many women, once they were unveiled, suffered at the hands of their fathers, brothers and husbands. Even men who supported his sisters, daughters and wives in their unveiling process were discarded from their religious group. There were evidences that a number of Muslim men left the Communist party because they did not support this Soviet policy of *Hujum* (John Anderson, 1993: 206-228).

The movement proceeded amid bloody reprisals from the reactionary and conservative camp. There were further numerous cases in Turkmenia, where hundreds of women were estimated to have been murdered for their disregard for the veil. In 1926, about thirty were murdered in three districts of this republic alone ((Fannina W. Halle,

1938: 196)). In 1928, as many as 235 Uzbek women, who had discarded the veil, were murdered. Such happenings had made Central Asian women frightened and worried one side, while on the other hand it also made a positive impact by making them determined not to subjugate themselves.

Even after such a grand upheaval the Soviet rule continued this movement and encouraged individual women who recorded their participation in such activities. According to an Ikramov's data in Uzbekistan, in mid 1927 about 100,000 women took off their *paranjas*, 5000 women enrolled in literacy classes and 5202 women were selected as people's life of the republic (Dilarom A. Alimova, 1998: 150). This movement achieved success to a great extent. Central Asian women's extensive involvement in public life was confirmed and the pressure of religion, traditions and the fear of patriarchal system was also curtailed largely. During such movement, women even staked their life to confront the family, religion and dogmatic customs of Central Asian society. This way, for first time women were projected as social and political activists in their community. As a result of all this, for the first time women were recruited on a large scale in factories and this campaign served the goal of involving Central Asian women in production (Dilarom A. Alimova, 1998: 150).

The new social mode of Central Asia was a result of radical social transformation which came in the course of socialist construction. This programme was meant to release women from her traditional role and to remove all those barriers that caused her to be submissive and interrupted her position in social, economic and political spheres. The Soviet state launched its mother and child care system after the October Revolution in a decree passed by the Soviet Government on January 31st, 1918. All expected mothers were placed under thorough medical supervision from the very first months of pregnancy. Women's Consultation Centres performed all the necessary medical analysis. Systematic attention for women's health made it possible to prevent diseases and establishing the necessary condition for normal child birth. As a rule all women gave birth in maternity homes under expert medical supervision. Children were regularly examined by doctors at children's polyclinics and consultation centres (Maria Kovrigina, 1957: 186-220). A large number of research institutes related mothers and childcare were established at government level.

Table 2.3: Data of Child and Women care Centres and Other Facilities in USSR

(In thousands)

Years	*1940*	*1950*	*1965*	*1970*	*1972*	*1973*
Obstetricians-gynaecologist	10.6	16.6	35.4	41.4	45.9	48.1
Paediatricians	19.4	32.1	71.7	80.8	88.8	94
Surgeon's assistants and midwives	12.8	42	79.3	81.3	79.8	78.6
Midwives	68.1	66.5	171.4	216	231.7	243
Women's consultation centres, children's consultation centres and polyclinics	8.6	12	19.3	21	21.3	21.8
Number of beds for expectant mothers and women recently confined	147	143	227	223.8	223.6	224
Number of beds for sick children, having tuberculosis	5.3	10.2	29.2	26.7	24.8	23.9
Contagious diseases	31.9	43.8	75.8	92.6	99.6	101.9
Non-contagious diseases	52.5	79.1	247.8	324.8	344.6	352.9

Source: Z.A.Yankova (1975), "The Women and the Family" in *Soviet Women: Some Aspects of the Status of Women in the USSR,* Progress Publishers, Moscow, p. 118.

In this way, for the first time the safety measures for women's motherly obligation were considered as a state responsibility during the Soviet period and mother and child were given good medical facilities. All this had a very positive impact on the life expectancy of mother and child and women were liberated from the health compromises due to the financial constraints.

The better health services helped in the decrease in the death rate during the duration of the Soviet regime. The following figures show the birth rate, death rate and net increase in the population of the Soviet Union.

Table 2.4: Figures Showing Death Rate and Increase in Population from 1913 to 1955

Year	*Deaths per 1000 inhabitants*	*Net increase in population per 1000 inhabitants*
1913	30.2	16.8
1926	20.3	23.7
1940	18.3	13.4

(Contd...)

1950	9.6	16.9
1951	9.6	17.2
1952	9.3	17.1
1953	9.0	15.9
1954	8.9	17.6
1955	8.4	17.2

Source: Maria Kovrigina (1957), "Public Health and Mothers and Child Welfare in the USSR", *Equality of Women in the USSR,* Foreign Language Publishing House, Moscow, p. 199.

As a result of the advance of public health and medical services in the Soviet period, the death rate dropped 2.2 times by 1940 and 3.6 times by 1955 as compared to 1913. The post natal cases of sepsis almost disappeared.

Status of Central Asian Women in the Educational Structure of USSR

Education was taken as the most important agenda of the Soviet government. The communist policy had felt that only education could save the Central Asian masses from the bondage of religion, poverty and feudal system. They had started a battle against illiteracy and Soviet regime realised that only education was a necessary condition for raising the socio-cultural activities of Central Asian women. The abolition of illiteracy, including female illiteracy, became a genuinely national task. The slogan advanced was, "every literate fellow must teach an illiterate". A big role in helping the women to overcome illiteracy was played by the so called "women's delegate conference" formed immediately after the revolution, and by other organisations set up to help women workers and peasants. Schools and classes were arranged for people who could neither read nor write and in many cases they were given individual tuitions (Lyudmila Dubrovina, 1957: 241).

However, Central Asian women were unable immediately to take advantage of the right to education given by the Soviet rule. Enormous difficulties were encountered in getting girls and older women to attend classes in the prevailing patriarchal feudal form of society. Some of the leading women were murdered. The life of the Kyrgyz woman Tursun Usmanova, a former illiterate who became People's Commissar for Social Security of the Kyrgyz Republic in 1930, can be cited as an example of the path taken by women in their fight for freedom and knowledge. At the age of 13 she had been sold in marriage; when she began to study she was beaten up, and on one occasion the Kulaks poured oil on her and tried to burn her alive (Fannina W. Halle, 1938: 183-190).

There is another famous story of Gul Bibi, who defied the orders of her parents and mullah and married a school teacher whom she loved. This incident took place on International Women's Day and gave inspiration to Central Asian women to throw off their traditional standards and ignored the consequences (Fannina W. Halle, 1938: 183-190). Such happenings gave a momentum to women liberation movement in Central Asia. But with the support of government machinery and their self-conscious urge for emancipation they had to overcome all these bondages. They began to take a more active part in economic, political and social way of life in their own region and even of their countries.

In the beginning millions of working women grappled with alphabet. The children of workers burdened with large families were looked after in special cares while women attended classes. The Soviet government was well aware of the problem like veiling and other domestic orthodoxy related to Central Asian women. Although such customs were made illegal by making some laws, but Central Asian women required more and more female teachers to obtain education and the Soviet government took a number of measures in this direction. Girl schools were opened on large scale and female teachers were appointed in these schools. Mobile schools were organised for nomad areas, with boarding facility, free supply of clothes and food being given in these schools (Z.A.Yankova, 1975: 257).

Female teachers even came to Central Asian women's houses and they were given time off work to learn their letters. In addition these women were also taught professional and industrial trade skills. The acquisition of knowledge enabled women to get more skilled jobs in industry, to occupy leading posts and brought them more and more into social and political spheres.

Table 2.5: The Girl Students during the Period of 1927-28 and 1935-36

(in percentage)

Years	*1927-28*	*1935-36*
USSR (as a whole)	39.6	46.9
RSFSR (Union Republics)	40.2	47.7
Ukraine (Union Republics)	39.8	47.0
Byelorussia (Union Republics)	37.6	46.9
Uzbekistan (Union Republics)	4.0	40.2
Turkmenistan (Union Republics)	29.8	42.5

Source: Z.A.Yankova (1975), "The Women and the Family" in *Soviet Women: Some Aspects of the Status of Women in the USSR,* Progress Publishers, Moscow, p. 257.

The above data gives an idea of the growth in number of girl students during the first years of compulsory education in the Soviet Union as a whole and in various republics and one can observe the constant increase in the number of girl students in less than a decade.

Table 2.6: The Structure of Public Education in the USSR

Higher education—universities and institutes(daytime, evening and by correspondence)
1. Secondary Vocational Technical Schools
2. Complete Secondary General Education School (10-year curriculum)
3. Technical Schools
4. Evening (Shift) Complete Secondary General Education School
(a) Vocational Technical Schools
5. Secondary Specialised and Technical Schools (Daytime, Evening and by Correspondence)
(a) Incomplete Secondary General Education School (8-year curriculum)
(b) Primary General Education School (4-year curriculum)
(c) Children's Pre-School Institutions

Source: G.P.Sergeyeva (1975), "Women's Education and Scientific and Technological Progress" in *Soviet Women: Some Aspects of the Status of Women in the USSR,* Progress Publishers, Moscow, p. 77.

The above chart illustrates the Soviet education system which was organised in such a way that there were no "dead-end" educational institutions and all students had equal rights and opportunities to continue their education. A woman could continue her education, whatever the level and time in which she was earlier educated in. It has been estimated that in 1975, 53 per cent of women enrolled at institutes of higher education, 63 per cent at secondary specialised schools and 98 per cent at general education schools attended daytime studies, while the corresponding figures for men were 49 per cent, 53 per cent and 96 per cent respectively. Lately, however the more and more women have been enrolling at evening and correspondence departments (G.P. Sergeyeva, 1975: 82). In this way, the Soviet government had given a great attention to the quantity as well as the quality of education of Central Asian women. In reality, a good education is the soundest support for women's political and economic emancipation and the Soviet regime strengthened this attribute extensively.

Status of Central Asian Women in the Cultural Structure of USSR

To bring enlightenment in Central Asian States, the Soviet state regime had taken the help of cultural outfits and media. In 1928, on the International Women's Day such cultural a invasion took place in Turkmenia, where cultural activists marched into villages with banners, songs and puppet shows. They entered the huts, bathed the children, cleaned the place, and treated the sick. Gifts were distributed in the villages and cultural programmes were organised, highlighting the need for the protection of the childhood and motherhood (Fannina W. Halle, 1938: 162).

Mock trials were conducted during these enlightenment campaigns to highlight the malevolent nature of such prevailing practices as drunkenness, opium smoking, wife-beating and cruelty towards children. Cinema was another medium that played an important role in the emancipation movement in Central Asia. Women films, urging women to throw off their servile status, were made in local languages and were successful to some extent in communicating with their audience (Fannina W. Halle, 1938: 164-67).

The finest outcome that came from this cultural movement was that the male members were mentally prepared to be aware of women's position and side by side involved themselves in improving women's condition in the existing society. Secondly, these cultural activities assisted the Soviet government to a great extent and made it possible to convince the Central Asian masses to accept women related laws in a humble manner. Since, it is generally observed that imposed laws do not sustain for long time. Thus, these cultural movements accomplished a great success because through such development, the Soviet system implemented all these changes in an indirect manner that was more stable and long lasting.

Status of Central Asian Women in the Economic Structure of USSR

The real empowerment of women is not possible without their equal and unhindered participation in the production process. They could have neither real equality nor freedom without financial independence. The Communist theory also supports this concept. The abolition of the private property would destroy the cause of women's dependence on men. V.I. Lenin, the founder of the Soviet Union had eliminated all the traditional laws which kept women in a humiliating position and deprived her of her rights. Lenin said that "of the laws which had kept women in an inferior position not a single one remained." There were some announcement "On equal pay for equal work for men and women" and "On mother and child protection" issued very soon after the revolution (V.I. Lenin, Vol. 27, 1965: 320).

Soviet Union made the first economic change through the land and water reform laws. There were three main land and water reform laws. First land and water reform 1920-21; the second, land and water reform 1925-29. The right of water through marriage was abolished and 3000 Turkmen women, for example, received land and water rights, thousand of widows and landless peasants were given land through these transformations (Fannina W. Halle, 1938: 249-250). The highest form of agricultural reform was collectivisation i.e. public ownership of means of production and collective form of labour which was put into action on a large scale in Central Asia towards the end of 1929 (R.R. Sharma, 1979: 131). The actual massive work on large scale collectivisation began in 1930 and it was completed by 1940.

Table 2.7: Collectivisation of Peasant Households

(in percentage)

Central Asian Republics	1930	1932	1937	1940
Uzbekistan	34.4	81.7	95.0	99.3
Turkmenia	22.8	73.0	95.4	99.4
Kyrgyzstan	29.1	67.4	89.1	98.7
Tajikistan	13.3	41.9	89.9	97.4

Source: R.R. Sharma (1979), A *Marxist Model of Social Change, Soviet Central Asia: 1917-1940*, Macmillan, Delhi, p.135.

For an extensive level of the agricultural collectivisation skilled women force was obligatory and the Soviet government introduced the third five year plan that sought to create skilled women agricultural labour force. In January 1938, the first enrollment as tractor driver's course at Uzbekistan's Machine and Tractor Stations were established. In those training centres 6710 were trainees, of which 3110 were women. By 1938, there were 56 women truck drivers and 23 harvester operators in Uzbekistan (R.Kh. Aminova, 1985: 217-18). Though in agricultural production women's participation was really immense but still her role in manual work was large in number and her involvement in specialised agricultural work was very low as compared to men.

Table 2.8: Women in Specialised Sections in Collective and State Farms in Uzbekistan, 1939-59

Occupations	*Number of women, 1939*	*Number of women, 1959*
Heads of cattle-breeding, fur-breeding and poultry farms	66	129
Field team leaders	1097	453
Cattle-breeding team leaders	48	77
Other team leaders	264	384
Cattle, calf and pig tenders, dairy maids, stable tenders, poultry breeders	4250	21082
Herds women and women shepherds	1374	1543
Orchards, vineyards, vegetable growers, melon growers	1118	1253
Women engaged in irrigated agriculture	72	593
Other occupations without specification of jobs	867200	898380

Source: R.Kh. Aminova (1985), *The October Revolution and Women's Liberation in Uzbekistan*, Nauka Publishers, Moscow, p. 225.

Even in the specialised agricultural work much higher women labour force was available in comparison with the ratio of heads and leaders. In Uzbekistan among field cropping team leaders, only 2.5 per cent were women, among cattle breeding team leaders 3.2 per cent and 5 per cent of other specific team leaders. There were only 0.4 per cent women among the tractor drivers and harvester operators (R.Kh. Aminova, 1985: 226). It was noticed that due to the appropriate use of modern equipments in agriculture sector in 1934, Uzbekistan had a record production of cotton and the cotton growers of the Uzbek republic were awarded by the government. Most legend award, the 'Order of Lenin', given to a woman, Tadzhikhon Shadiyeva, the head of political department of the Fergana Machine and Tractor Station (R. Kh. Aminova, 1985: 213). Thus, by the end of the 1930s, the success in drawing women into social production was significant.

After 1917 revolution there was a great change in industrial policy of the Soviet Union. The nationalisation of large and small scale industry was completed on a large scale. On March 7, 1918, 288 cotton industries were nationalised. By the middle of 1918, over 370 of the major regional industrial undertakings and by March 1919 all transport and banks had been nationalised (R.R. Sharma, 1979: 143-144). The Soviet Union had been transformed from an agrarian country into an industrial power. Industrialisation determined the technical restoration of the national economy. These circumstances allowed women more comprehensively to be active in all leading branches of production. The following table shows the rapid growth of the industrial sector and all this offered women a real assurance of right to work in some way.

Table 2.9: Growth of Small and Large Scale Industries, 1917-1955

Year	*Small scale industry*	*Large scale industry*
1917	71	63
1921	31	21
1926	98	108
1928	132	152
1932	267	352

(Contd...)

1937	588	816
1940	852	1172
1945	782	1085
1950	1476	2060
1955	2723	3900

Source: Nina Popova (1957), "Equality of Soviet Women in the Economic Spheres" in *Equality of Women in the USSR,* Foreign Languages Publishing House, Moscow, p.100.

In Central Asian traditional society, it was very tough to carry women as an industrial worker and in such a situation it was very essential that women should be brought through some traditional industrial work like handicraft industry. In the early days of Soviet regime women's craft societies were established. Till the 1920s a number of handicraft cooperatives played an important role.

Table 2.10: Growth of Women's Cooperative Craft Societies in Uzbekistan

Year	*Number of Cooperatives*	*Number of Members*
1925	8	247
1926	6	572
1927	30	648
1928	50	1558

Source: R. Kh. Aminova (1985), *The October Revolution and Women's Liberation in Uzbekistan*, Nauka Publishers, Moscow, p. 167.

The above table shows the growth of cooperatives and increasing number of members. All these cooperatives belonged to the traditional handicraft works which were from the very beginning measured women's works, for instance, these works were clothes-making, knitting, hosiery-making, embroidery, weaving, silk-winding, silk-spinning, cotton-ginning and card board articles production etc. But in the early stage Central Asian women faced some limitations, e.g. low wages, irregular order and inadequate culture, lack of skilled education and insufficient credits. Because of all these obstacles Central Asian women could not participate in these cooperatives to their full potential and the majority was caught up simply in labour occupations in agricultural or industrial sectors. Only the Soviet government made efforts to bring some change in their lives.

The constitution of the USSR, under which the Soviet women enjoyed equality in all spheres of life, gave many economic and social rights to women. The Article 122 of the constitution explained, "The possibility of exercising these rights is ensured by women being accorded an equal right with men to work, payment for work, rest and leisure, social insurance and education, and by state protection of the interests of mother and child, state aid to mothers of large families and unmarried mothers, maternity leave with full pay and the provision of a wide network of maternity homes, nurseries and kindergartens" (R. Kh. Aminova, 1985: 218).

Such regulations show the steps taken towards equality for women in the USSR. All these facilities provided by the constitution enhanced women participation in national economy. The female labour increased from 27.9 per cent in 1929 to 41.6 per cent in 1939. In 1954, the percentage of women workers in machine building was 44, electrical engineering 47, radio engineering 55, machine tool and tool building 36, transport machine building 40 and heavy machine building 33. In some branches of production their proportion was even greater (V.S. Yazykova, 1975: 104).

During the Soviet Union regime women were given some facilities on humanitarian grounds. For instance, age was not an obstacle to the employment of Soviet women. They could receive old age pensions along with their working status. This was specially related to teachers, physicians and engineers. Besides, married and motherhood status were not any cause of rejection for women employment. Moreover, the Soviet laws harshly treated those people who dishonoured the married women and mothers' rights.

Under the impact of all the above mentioned privileged position provided by the Soviet rule to Central Asian women in industrialisation enhanced their numbers in offices and industries. In 1928 at the beginning of the industrialisation women percentage was 18 among the workers and office employees in Uzbekistan and 7 per cent in Tajikistan. But in 1940 there was a fair hike in women participation in offices and industries in these republics. It was 31 per cent in Uzbekistan and 29 per cent in Tajikistan (V. Perevedendsev, 1975: 9).

Table 2.11: Number of Women as Industry and Office Workers in the Soviet Economy

Year	*No. of women Industry and Office*	*Percentage of Total*
1922	1560	25
1926	2265	23
1928	2795	24
1940	13190	39
1945	15920	56
1950	19180	47
1955	23040	46
1960	29250	47
1965	37680	49
1970	45800	51
1973	50000	51
1974	51200	51

Source: Y.D.Yemelyanova (1975), "The Social and Political Activity of Soviet Women" in *Soviet Women: Some Aspects of the Status of Women in the USSR*, Progress Publishers, Moscow, p. 21.

The Soviet Code of Labour Law (Article 129, CLL) prohibited the employment of women in heavy and harmful work, such as smelting and pouring of molten metal, rolling hot metal, cleaning gas mains. Women were not employed in chemical printing, meat industry, mining industry and railway, sea and local transport services (Nina Popova, 1957: 115). In the USSR women had the same social insurance rights (in case of old age and any disability) as men and had a right to rest on equal terms with men. Men and women both had right of paid leave from two weeks to two months.

All such laws, provisions and services improved the living standard and working conditions of the Central Asian women and provided them great opportunities to participate in social, political, industrial, cultural, educational and professional activities. Nina Popova, the Secretary of the USSR Central Council of Trade Union stated in her report 'Equality of Soviet Women in Economic Sphere' that "Our women are working or seeking to work not only because their earnings add to the family budget or because it makes them economically independent. One of the reasons is that they want to share the common interests of the people and to contribute their share to that great and truly majestic work of construction that the Soviet people are engaged in for the sake of brighter life and their children's happiness" (Nina Popova, 1957: 117).

It means that in the USSR not only much improvement had been seen in the position of Central Asian women but it is quite clear that it had provided an individual identity to women in the region. Especially, it had developed their thinking and given liberty that they could foresee the future of their own and their children. Additionally, it was observed that the position of the Soviet women was far better than its own past as well the position of their counterparts in the other part of the world. The operation of the USSR government was to a great extent successful and could carry women from secondary to equivalent status.

Status of Central Asian Women in Political System of USSR

The Soviet Union had always supported and voted for proposals and recommendations made by the UN General Assembly for a speedy solution to the problem of granting women political rights on an equal footing with men in all countries of the world. Lenin was familiar with this fact very well that only giving rights to women is hardly of any worth unless and until the society and state do not accept those provisions and women can avail them in a free and fearless environment. Such conditions in his opinion would materialize with the establishment of a system for training women masses to run state affairs, their re-education in the very process of social work, the enhancement of their cultural level and their emancipation from the burden of their household works (Y.D.Yemelyanova, 1975: 41-42).

Lenin stated, "We want the working women to be the equal of the working men not only before the law but in actual fact. For this the working women must take an increasing part in the administration of the socialised enterprises and in the administration of the state....by taking part in the administration, women will learn quickly and will catch up with the men." (V.I. Lenin, Vol. 30, 1965: 371-72) Lenin said that every housewife should know how to govern and utterance which gained popularity. The Soviet constitution gave women complete equality with men before law and Soviet government abolished all the law of pre-revolutionary period which had bonded women in unequal chains. The Article 22 of the Soviet constitution the equality to all the citizens of Soviet republics, regardless of sex, race and nationalities and the Article 64 gave women right to elect or to be elected to the Soviets on equal bases with men regardless of race, creed and nationalities (K. B. Usha, 2005: 146).

These constitutional rights initiated the emancipation of women. Delegates Meetings, which were the main part of *Zhenotdel* became the milestone of political advancement of working women and their training for government work. In these meetings women of this or that factory, village, cooperative etc. sent their elected representatives. These women delegates took part in the activities of the various government bodies, and their departments, helping them to improve labour conditions, labour laws, health services, education and upbringing their children, set up nursery schools, kindergartens and promote municipal developments (Anna Pankratova, 1957: 18). The number of women members in Communist parties increased after 1924.

Table 2.12: Men and Women members in Communist Party of Soviet Union, 1924-1926

Year	*Men*	*Women*	*Men per cent*	*Women per cent*
1924	407588	38501	91.4	8.6
1925	664623	76494	89.7	10.3
1926	873682	128807	87.2	12.8

Source: Y.D.Yemelyanova (1975), "The Social and Political Activity of Soviet Women" in *Soviet Women: Some Aspects of the Status of Women in the USSR,* Progress Publishers, Moscow, p. 41.

The growth in the number of women party members was a result of the enhanced political consciousness of women workers and peasants and appearance of their strength in socio-political activity.

The Soviet Union made the constitution of 1936 more democratic where community could play a part. It introduced universal, equal and direct suffrage by secret ballot. All this provided a great opportunity to the Soviet women to participate in government at all levels. The Article 137 of 1936 constitution claimed that women have right to elect and to be elected on equal terms with men. This right gave the Soviet women political participation which was a male prerogative in pre-revolutionary time.

The percentage of women members of commission for election to the local Soviets was impressive. In 1939, when the election to the local Soviets were held under the constitutional electoral system for the first time 34.1 per cent of the total membership of the electoral commissions were women. In 1955, the percentage had gone up to 41.3 of total members. Women were proved good and efficient in administration and public affair. They were elected deputies to local and Supreme Soviet, and decision-making among factory employees, collective farmers, teachers, physicians, engineers, agronomists and others.

Table 2.13: Women Deputies of the Supreme Soviet of the USSR

Year	*Women*	*Percentage of All Deputies*
1937	189	16.5
1952	348	25.8
1958	366	27
1962	390	27
1966	425	28
1970	463	31
1974	475	31.3

Source: Y.D.Yemelyanova (1975), "The Social and Political Activity of Soviet Women" in *Soviet Women: Some Aspects of the Status of Women in the USSR,* Progress Publishers, Moscow, p. 62.

In 1939, the number of women Deputies was 422,362, in 1947-48, the number was 482,000 and in 1950, it was 518,000 at local level.

The total number of women elected to local Soviet since1939 exceeded 2,500,000. In 1956, 348 women deputies were in Supreme Soviet, which was 25.8 per cent of its total membership of 348 deputies (Y.D.Yemelyanova, 1975: 62).

In Central Asian region the Tajik Republic had 25 members in the Soviet of nationalities, of whom nine were women. There were 99 women of 300 deputies to the Tajik Supreme Soviet. Masuda Sultanova, an Assistant Professor at Central Asian State University (an Uzbek woman) and Zaura Omarova, an Engineer at Mine designing Institute in Karaganda Region (a Kazakh woman) were Deputy Chairpersons of the Soviet nationalities of the USSR Supreme Soviet (Anna Pankatova, 1957: 22). Women deputies took part in the work of the permanent credentials budget, legislative propositions and Foreign Affairs Commissions of both chambers of the USSR Supreme Soviet. Nearly one-third of the deputies to the Supreme Soviets of the Central Asian Republics were women.

Besides, women in Soviet rule also participated in various government or administrative offices and to the offices of judges or people's assessors, about half the people's judges were women in Central Asia in 1950s. Women were doing a great deal in the numerous cooperative organisations, the Red Cross and Red Crescent Societies and Sport Societies etc (Anna Pankatova, 1957: 29).

In this way, the Soviet government improved the women's involvement by framing some laws, by giving some constitutional rights and by making some transformations in the social system. The Soviet rule not only favoured their right to vote, but also their active participation in politics and administration. During these changes in the Soviet Union for women emancipation, Central Asian women also benefited from some government sponsored schemes associated to domestic works, child upbringing and household responsibilities etc. As a result, women gave their utmost contribution to the social, political, economic and cultural advancement of the Soviet Union.

But at the same time this fact was also true that what dreams the Communist government had publicised to the Central Asian women were proved fictitious and to some extent were beyond fulfilment and reality. Lenin's policies were a paramount effort to bring men and women to equal height. But the later rulers gave more attention to the country's development. Some critics underlined that women were developed during the Soviet system for the cause of national development rather than for raising women's level from downtrodden conditions. Wherever the women's rights came in the way of the advancement of the Soviet system either they were altered or abolished, whether it was the matter of Zhenotdel or abortion right. The Soviet policies had some drawbacks, the study of all these factors is very important to investigate the status of Central Asian women.

In 1920s, Soviet economic policies raised drastically to number of unemployed women, and this was the major factor behind the growth in prostitution in this region. Some steps were taken very forcefully for women emancipation which proved wrong and in contradictory and worsened the condition of women. For instance, *Kalym* and unveiling campaign pushed many women to death. The *Zhenotdel*, which was meant for women emancipation was abolished in 1930 and it was stated that all necessity for such organisations had been fulfilled. It was the point of view of the government, though in reality it had achieved the target of neither women emancipation nor gender equality.

During the Second World War, a policy was initiated to bear maximum children in the family. Central Asia had a high birth rate as compared to the Russian territory. Stalin approved the title of 'Heroine Mother' and 'Motherhood Medal' to the women and abortion was illegalised during his regime. Additionally, the government had reduced the expenses on public services and maternity services. All this heightened the burden of household work and affected outside professional work of the Central Asian women. Western scholars had termed this position as double burden. In fact, all these policies were just tactical move to promote necessary gender role model and in reality the double burden of the working mother was glorified (Susanne Conze, 2001: 216-243). On the other side, Central Asian women were a great labour force in the Soviet system. The critics observed that in the Soviet Union the Central Asian women were crushed under the combined burden of work with motherhood.

It is visible that the Soviet rulers have favoured these policies, starting with Stalin, who wanted women to work hard to fulfil his plans, but did not assign them to high political offices. Stalin even abolished the Women's Section of the Central Committee of the Party which had been established in 1918. Thus, the equality of the sexes in the Soviet Union meant that to a large extent women were used as beasts of burden in backbreaking occupations from coal mining and foundry work to street sweeping and digging ditches. Men were appointed as foremen over women simply because they were men and not on the basis of higher qualification. In the Soviet Union, women have double tasks. They were expected to work as hard as men in offices, factories, and in the fields. Then after coming home, they had to spend several hours a day shopping, cooking, and cleaning because Soviet men (to preserve their masculinity) refused to help their wives in household duties. There was a lack of respect for women in Russia and Central Asian states (due to the impact of religion). The equality that was promised in the Constitution broke down and the facts of daily Soviet life most sharply detached from Communist ideology (Alice Schuster, 1971: 266).

Bolshevik government had basically failed during the 1920s in providing the day care centres, cafeterias and other community services which were quite necessary to free women from their traditional household works. The new development of the first five-year plan assured further setbacks in women emancipation by eroding their prospects to join in paid labour force. The plan began to transform the Soviet economy in 1929 and in early 1930. The slow-down in industrialisation and resulting unemployment was noticed particularly in the Central Asian region. Men were partially affected but women particularly faced great trouble under such transformations and a huge number of women were unemployed (Thomas G. Schrand, 1999: 1455).

The mid 1930s witnessed the return to more traditional and conservative values in many areas of social and family life, e.g. divorce was made more difficult to obtain in order to bring stability to the Soviet family, and abortion was recriminalised in an effort to boost the birth rate. During the Second World War, in USSR men went off to war while women were active in running industries and civil work. At that time they were given the position of leadership and responsibility. For the first time they became pilots and obtained other male dominate jobs (Melanie Ilic, 2001: 1-8). All this happened under some compelled circumstances and not out of the liberal policies of the USSR for women.

Women's number was very small at high positions as compare to men. Women constituted 73 per cent of those in education; 98 per cent of nursery, kindergarten and boarding school teachers were women. Women continued in such traditional occupations as typists and stenographers (49 per cent); office workers (95 per cent); cashiers (94 per cent). All this confirm that the USSR was more interested in providing traditional jobs to women than power jobs to them (V. V. Vodzinskaio, 1973: 14). The Soviet expression about the equal opportunity to women and the confirmation of their involvement as full citizens of the Soviet states clashed with a publicly approved customary function limited and controlled by men. The declared feminism of the Soviet government and the official equality of women were challenged and resisted by more traditional attitudes and complete narrow-mindedness both within the party and in the population at large.

Artyukhina, a member of Bolshevik women's movement claimed that women were ignored especially in party organisations. The 1936s constitution granted equal right to women in all economic, state, cultural and socio-political areas of life. In reality, the integration of the female labour into the industrialisation process created double burden for Soviet women and they were left with little influence over their role and status in society. Stalin said, "The wife should also be a happy mother and create a comfortable home, but she should not neglect her job because of that, for the sake of community. She must be able to keep everything going at home, and then still keep up with a man's performance at work." (Susanne Conze, 2001: 218) In workplace women experienced harassment and discrimination from men, particularly in male dominated industries. Male co-workers felt threatened by women, male manager did little to promote them or encourage them to raise their qualifications (David L. Haffmann, 1994: 119-124).

Women in Central Asia were still far from having achieved complete parity with men. Despite the comparatively high number of women in labour force, women in all Central Asian Republic formed an extremely high percentage of non-working population of these republics. Women pre-dominated in lower skilled and manual jobs and both disparities were particularly pronounced in respect of women of the indigenous nationalities. In 1975, for example, an estimated 12 to 15 per cent of the able-bodied population of Uzbekistan were working outside of social production, in household and private subsidiary work. More than 95 per cent of these people were women, to whom the vast majority were Central Asian (Nancy Lubin, 1981: 184).

The same situation was with Turkmen and other Central Asian republics. In 1973, only 53 per cent of the able-bodied women in Turkmenistan were workers and employees and less than one-third of these were Turkmen (Nancy Lubin, 1981: 185). As compared to the Central Asian indigenous women, Slavic women tended to dominate the higher skilled positions in industrial and certain other key sectors. The Central Asian women were not only considered inferior to men but they were measured second-rate citizen as compared to the Slavic women. It means that the Central Asian women were facing a great disparity on the gender basis as well as due to the differences that existed among the indigenous and Slavic women.

Women played a significant role in education, but only as teachers in elementary and secondary schools. But at higher educational level the proportion of women was considerably smaller. Among the academic people engaged as teaching-heads of departments, professors, associate professors, instructors, and assistants, the proportion of women was 41 per cent at the end of 1956, and among Heads of Institutions, Deans, and other important academic administrators the proportion was only 15 per cent. In general, the proportion of women in the highest academic positions was very small.

Table 2.14: Women among Soviet Research and Professional Personnel, 1947-1959

(*Percentage of women at the end of year*)

	1947	*1950*	*1955*	*1959*
Degree holder Doctors	29	27	27	29
Professors	5	5	6	7
Associate Professors	14	15	17	17
Senior Research Associates	31	30	30	29
Junior Research Associate	48	48	52	51
All Research and Professional Categories	35	36	36	36

Source: Alice Schuster (1971), "Women's Role in the Soviet Union: Ideology and Reality", *Russian Survey,* Vol. 30, No. 3, p. 265.

The graph presents a picture of the somewhat low skills among women in several of the higher professional and scholarly fields. Although all professions were open to women their prospects for improvement was not very favourable, even though the Soviet educationalists stated that women were just as good as men in all subjects, including scientific and mechanical ones. Some unseen factors were responsible for these circumstances. Obviously the old attitude of male superiority was approved and men obtained more training and acquired better positions. To justify this discriminatory attitude, it was pointed out that women do not dedicate all their energies to their professions because of the disturbance of caring for their families. As a result, argument was advanced that it was reasonably sound to employ only a small percentage of women in higher ranks.

In Soviet Union, Central Asian women were living two dissimilar position at the same time; on one side, women were legally equal to men with the same rights in the field of economics, politics and socially. But on the other side, there was hardly only appearance of female equality even on the part of women themselves. Even women with higher education and good jobs often observed traditional and religious customs within the home and their personal life (K. B. Usha, 2005: 147).

There was very little involvement of women in higher level of politics in Soviet federation. Even in 1957, a long time after the declaration of equal political rights to Soviet women the percentage of women membership in party was 19.5 per cent, in Central committee was 3.3 per cent and Supreme Soviet 28 per cent. This was under Khrushchev, who tried to increase political representation for women. However, in Brezhnev years, the situation was a little bit changed and the share of women in the Deputies of Supreme Soviet varied from 25 per cent to 33 per cent. But the executive and political position at higher level of the government apparatus still remained a male domain (K. B. Usha, 2005: 149-150). There was only one woman in Central Committee while none in politburo in 1980. Women constituted less than 4 per cent of ministers at the union republic level.

Table 2.15: Women Membership in Central Committee, 1917-1971

Year	*Total Central Committees*	*Total Women*	*Percentage of Women*
1917	31	3	9.7
1919	27	1	3.7
1921	40	0	0
1924	87	2	2.4
1927	121	5	4.0
1930	138	4	2.9
1934	139	3	2.2
1939	139	3	2.2
1952	236	7	3.1
1956	254	10	3.9
1961	330	11	3.3
1966	360	15	4.2
1971	397	15	3.8

Source: Gail Warshofsky Lapidus (1975), "Political Mobilisation, Participation, and Leadership: Women in Soviet Politics", *Comparative Politics,* Vol. 8, No.1, p. 110.

The above data reveals that women's involvement in high political positions was nominal. Women were somewhat more likely to be found in ministerial positions in Central Asia, where special efforts had been made to appoint them to prominent positions in public life. Women tended to concentrate in some areas like health, food, light industry, housing, social-insurance and labour reserves. Through allocation system women represented top offices but they were not given the position of responsibility. It means that the status of Central Asian women in the Soviet Union was very much different from the theoretical provisions (a huge disparity in their legal rights and practice).

It is true, during the Soviet period the Central Asian woman was raised from her sub-human status by giving her a number of political, constitutional, economic and social rights. But the major drawback in this whole sequence was that the speed with which the movement was started in the beginning could not maintain its pace later on. Some Western scholars viewed a numbers of limitations in the Soviet period which were not in the interest of women. But at the same time, it does not mean that the status of Central Asian women remained identical to the pre-Soviet period. If the condition of women is compared particularly in both these times then undoubtedly the Soviet period was outstanding in a number of matters and especially, the steps some of which were taken by the Soviet system were far better than the Western world. For instance, the facilities made available to the working women and especially mothers.

The Soviet government was the very first system in the world that was the true saviour of a working woman and a mother. It endeavoured to improve together both the personalities of women. In such a situation woman had to face the double burden but the Soviet regime had made its maximum effort to wipe out all these restrictions. But the number of women in high positions in the various spheres like politics, education and administration was very low. After Lenin, in Stalin era women were not much favoured by the government laws in some respects (Abolition of Abortion right, Divorce was made complicated and other working conditions for women). The dreams which were realised by Lenin administration in 1917 were becoming dim and women emancipation was replaced by national necessity. Empowerment weakened with the passage of time but not entirely disappeared from the sight.

Though from time to time various steps were taken by the Soviet system to improve women's position in the society, it could not attain the desired results and changes immediately in the social structure of Central Asian States; the reasons behind all this were the male favoured culture, influence of religion and traditional social standards that influenced the masses in the region. But this fact is also true that it was the Soviet Socialist regime that brought the Central Asian women from the dark past in such a short span of time. The literacy rate of Central Asian women was enhanced from 2 per cent in 1913 to 99 per cent in 1991 and it abolished the much deep-rooted orthodoxy like *kalym*, *paranjas* and polygamy etc. In this entire episode, the Central Asian woman also played a remarkable role by sacrificing their own lives. The government bodies gave their extreme support to women, without them it was almost impossible for the Central Asian women to comprehend and struggle for their rights. Lastly, it can be stated that the status of Central Asian women was sufficiently good in the Soviet period each and every discipline (Social, Economic, Political, Cultural and Educational) as compared to the pre-Soviet period. But still her position was really secondary to man in the society in many ways.

Chapter - 3

Comparative Positions of Women in Contemporary Kazakh and Uzbek Societies

Since independence in 1991 all five states (Kazakhstan, Kyrgyzstan, Tajikistan, Turkmenistan and Uzbekistan) have faced the huge challenges of nation building, creating new constitution and establishing organs of government. The disintegration of the former Soviet Union and independence in the Central Asian States created conditions reforms in economic, social, and political spheres. It also had impact on religious freedom and on social and economic activities. Under the Soviet system, religion faced restrictions and scepticism was encouraged as scientific viewpoint in the national curriculum. But today religion is again explicitly practiced in these states. In Central Asia the principle of equal rights, liberties and identical opportunities for men and women is approved and set out in a number of legal and constitutional regulations that are continuously being improved to enhance the position of women. However, the current legal framework only provides such egalitarianism and prevents discrimination in theory and not in practice. An interesting and relevant enquiry should find out whether this open practice of religion has affected the status of women in these societies, their changing position within the family, their marital status and fertility.

The five countries of Central Asia – Kazakhstan, Kyrgyzstan, Tajikistan, Turkmenistan, and Uzbekistan – comprised the largest primarily Islamic region of the former Soviet Union. Following independence from Moscow in the early 1990s, these countries opened their markets to global competition but pursued different paths for the development of their economies and human rights. Turkmenistan's natural gas sector provided a large amount of foreign exchange, but the social policies pursued by an egocentric dictator, President for Life Niyazov, led to repressive social policies that set the country apart from the others in its overall development. The death of President Niyazov in 2006 led to a change in government (President Berdimuhammedov), and some positive social changes have been implemented. However, it is too early to determine how open the country will become and the development path that it will follow.

Tajikistan was immediately embroiled upon independence in a civil war based on rivalry for political power. The war ended in the late 1990s, but Tajikistan was far behind the other countries in its post-Soviet development. It needed to focus on recovery from the war and political stability, and the beginning of its adjustment to global market conditions was 6-7 years behind that of the other countries in the region. President Rahmon was last elected in 1999, and his party is firmly in control of the government.

Uzbekistan was a slow reformer and approached development more gradually than Kazakhstan or the Kyrgyz Republic. State enterprises were not closed at the same rate as in the other countries, and the country did not suffer the immediate and often harsh disruption to household income stability. Although the country initially pursued openness towards the press, religion, and opposition to the ruling elite, President Karimov's regime became one of the most repressive in the region in the late 1990s and pursued harsh policies towards vocal opposition often expressed in mosques.

The most open of the five countries and one of the poorest is the Kyrgyz Republic. It is still the most tolerant country towards freedom of the press and speech, but depends on the support of Western donors such as the United States and the European Union for economic survival. The non-violent "Tulip" revolution in 2005 threw out the government of President Akaev and replaced it with the government of President Bakiyev who was alleged to be as corrupt as the former president. However, the economy is open to foreign business, and it has experimented with new, innovative social policies to redress the large wealth inequality within the country.

The largest and wealthiest country in Central Asia is Kazakhstan. With its large reserves of oil and natural gas, it has become a major player in the international oil market and has enough foreign exchange to pursue the most advanced social policies in the region. It has been innovative in the development of the state pension system, although this has not been without criticism or corruption. It has recently focused on education as one of the keys to long run economic development. The Bolashak programme, for example, sends hundreds of students to the West for college and post-graduate training. The press is relatively free in Kazakhstan, but the government is tightly controlled by President Nazarbayev, and corruption in government, education, and other sectors has been a significant problem. Because of its wealth, the poor are well-off compared to those in other states, and Kazakhstan has become a net importer of immigrant (legal and illegal) labour from other countries in Central Asia (Kathryn H. Anderson and Charles Becker, 2008: 1-2).

The Central Asian States have, by and large, left in place the Soviet legislation regulating family matters. However, the traditional practices of bride-price, bride kidnapping, polygamy and so on, which never ceased during Soviet era, are now practiced openly. In Kazakhstan, for instance, the groom gives a vigorously negotiated amount of livestock to the bride's family in return for the bride's hand. The extended family remains powerful in all the Central Asian States. Newly married woman is likely to be young and to have little income generating power of her own until she has produced her first child. She is at the bottom of the familial hierarchy and her parents-in-law are likely to be the ultimate authority to decide about her life. They will determine whether she goes out to work or she can study and how often she sees her own family. Though the law of the state gives her autonomy, they are often trampled by the unwritten laws of the community (Charles Foster, 2007: 2).

Arranged marriages are still common throughout Central Asia in both rural and urban communities and a significant minority of brides do not know their husbands before the wedding day. In all the Central Asian States, the revival of pre-Soviet traditions can be noticed easily, for instance, the customs of marriages, the least rights of women in divorce matters or to be given an equitable financial settlement after divorce. The pattern is of reversion to the old patriarchal values and practices: in Uzbekistan women whose husbands do not consent to divorce have sometimes been debarred from all claims to the matrimonial assets (Charles Foster, 2007: 3).

Following the Soviet pattern, all the former Soviet states acknowledge the mother's rights to custody of the children, give paid maternity leave of varying lengths, (often, even considerably longer than under the Soviet regime) and pay the mother allowance in relation to each child, whether legitimate or not. If the biological mother is not primary carer the benefits can be transferred to whoever is. Increasingly these benefits are causalities of the economic pressures on Central Asia. For instance, paid maternity leave, government creches and kindergartens have been dramatically curtailed. This pattern is likely to be repeated throughout the region and child and maternal support are getting pushed even further downside in the list of national priorities (Kathryn H. Anderson and Charles Becker, 2008: 70).

Muslims comprise the majority of the population in all the Central Asian States. In Kazakhstan the proportion is about 50 per cent, in Kyrgyzstan 65 per cent, in Uzbekistan 76 per cent, in Tajikistan 84 per cent and 88 per cent in Turkmenistan. The proportion may well grow in the future. There are some indication of Islamic orthodoxy is growing too. In the history, Central Asian States were witnessed to the influence of Islam under the regime of a number of rulers that devalued the position of women in these societies time and again. The veil is commonly seen in Uzbekistan and Tajikistan. The Islamist groups, especially in Tajikistan, are advocating voluntary seclusion of women. Gulf oil money pays for splendid mosques and Islamic schools throughout the region.

At the state level all Central Asian states have declared secular intention. However, the leaders in power in all these state disowned their communist past and professed Islam. All these states have established links with Islamic oriented states in varying degrees. In this way, somewhere Islam is influencing the government policies and society norms indirectly. As Kathryn H. Anderson, Principal Investigator, NCEEER (the National Council for Eurasian and East European Research) observes the religious outlook of masses towards women's behaviour in certain situation in Central Asian states.

Table 3.1: Religion and Attitudes towards Marriage, Children, and the Role of Women

(In percentage)

	Not Religious	*Muslim*	*Orthodox Christians*
Ideal number of children	2.94	3.71	2.78
Disapprove of a woman as a single parent	42.6	75.8	41.6
Woman needs children to be fulfilled	82.6	94	91
Working woman can have warm relationship with children	86.4	82.4	84.7
Husband and wife should both contribute to family income	79.4	75	70.7
Men have more right to job than women	38.2	54	28.2
Divorce never acceptable	22.2	53.9	14.3
Average divorce	48.7	28	54.7
Abortion never acceptable	41.6	64.2	32.1
Average abortion	36.8	22.1	41.2
Homosexuality never acceptable	67.8	86.4	56.6
Average homosexuality	24.3	14.9	28.3

Source: Kathryn Anderson H. and Charles Becker, (2008) "Religious Affiliation and Family Formation in Post-Soviet Central Asia" a project report from *The National Council for Eurasian and East European Research*, April 25, p. 20.

The above table presents a comparison of attitudes towards marriage, children, and the role of women by religious practice. It reveals significant differences in the attitudes of the average respondent across the three religious categories. On average, Muslims want more children than Russian Orthodox or non-religious respondents. Muslims are more likely to feel that a man has more right to a job than Orthodox or the non-religious. The differences in attitudes towards homosexuality are also quite different across groups and only Muslims to a relatively large extent think that homosexuality is never acceptable.

It is a truism that women living under Islamic are visibly the most suppressed. At the same time some analysts believed that the mobilisation by conservative clergies has not gained much impetus: Post-Soviet Muslims feel closer to a moderate enlightening Islam. The reason of this moderate Islam is the secularising effect of the Soviet past when a modern ideology was imposed in the entire Soviet Union i.e. curbing all religions equally. Moreover, Central Asian States had little linkage with Islamic states of Middle East and significantly Central Asian women rejected their Pre-Soviet status even though they do not reject religion as a whole (Anuradha M. Chenoy, 1996: 517).

In all Central Asian states, Islam is making a disheartening influence on the status of women and one can observe its utmost negative influence on Uzbek women and least on Kyrgyz women. Islamic revival is taking place in the background where the state has been secular for almost a century. That the revival has a negative impact can be seen in reports of the practice of checking marriage sheets to ensure the virginity of the bride in Tajikistan and Uzbekistan, alongside practices of bride price and bride stealing. Polygamy is also allowed in Uzbekistan as long as the wives are not living in the same household. Such women's lives are increasingly difficult which is borne out by high female suicide rate, which some suggest are connected to high level of violence against women including domestic violence; a significant numbers of women attempt suicide through self-immolation. The practices of honour killings or crimes are also being revived in some regions thus justifying wrongdoing, and there is a discussion of honour suicides in Tajikistan following rape during the civil war (ECPAT International, 2002).

Rapid social change in transitional societies might lead to social upheaval. In the case of the former Soviet societies wide ranging changes in social stratification is likely to occur. The impact of these changes will first be felt by women both at work place and home. The main reason behind the disintegration of Soviet Union was the economic crisis and as a result, all the Central Asian states faced that stiff situation in the same manner. Privatisation and structural adjustment led to cuts in social outlays. The share of public expenditure for basic social services like education, health, pension, child allowances, unemployment benefits, pre-school institutions, kindergarten, mid-day meals were the first to be cut by the governments of these states. All this made a very negative impact over women's employment and efficiency. Besides, unemployment affected women more than men and their working future has become more uncertain (Central Asia Human Development Report, 2005: 158-159).

Like the rest of the Soviet Union, women in the Central Asian states have been the first to be laid off. As many as 70 per cent women were unemployed and that was upto 90 per cent in some areas in 2001. During the Soviet era, women's wage averaged 70 per cent of men's and now this figure has dropped to 40 per cent (Anuradha M. Chenoy, 1996: 518). In Tajikistan an average working woman earns just over half what an average man takes home. The girls are half as likely to be enrolled in higher education as boys and just only half pregnant women receive any form of prenatal care, resulting in very high mortality rate. In Central Asian States, especially Kyrgyzstan's, written law allows women full right to land, but customary law dictates that in the case of divorce or death, the land reverts to male heirs or their husband's family (Disparities between Men and Women in Transition Countries of Europe and Central Asia, 2002).

In Central Asian States, especially in Kyrgyzstan, Tajikistan, Turkmenistan and Uzbekistan the maternal mortality rate is swiftly increasing. The statistics produced by the UNFPA and the Population References Bureau, 100 women died for every 100,000 live birth in Tajikistan in 2008. As in the other part of Central Asia, most deaths occur in rural areas where normally deliveries take place at home. Reducing maternal mortality is not a priority for Tajik authorities and those with financial resources seek treatment from private physician or travel to neighbouring Kazakhstan and Russia for medical care (Maternal Mortality in Central Asia, 2008).

The public health department of Turkmenistan was badly disturbed by former Turkmen president Niyazov. He ordered the closure of all the hospitals outside the capital, cut the state's healthcare budget and fired 15,000 experienced healthcare workers and replaced them with untrained army conscripts. After the death of Niyazov, public health officials began to think optimistically about Turkmenistan's future. The rising maternal mortality rates in Kyrgyzstan and Uzbekistan are fuelled by the increasing numbers of medical workers who are leaving these countries for better paid work abroad, particularly in Russia. Officially statistics put the maternal mortality ratio for Kyrgyzstan at 110 and for Uzbekistan at 24 per 100000 live births and Kazakhstan 45.6 per 100000 births (Kazakhstan Country Analysis, 2008).

However, both international and local public health experts doubt that these numbers give an accurate estimate. It is clear that the increasing emigration of medical workers is a serious threat to preserving the health of women in difficult labour as well as that of other citizens of Kyrgyzstan and Uzbekistan. Thus, the healthcare facility created by the USSR in the Central Asian republics is rapidly declining especially in the case of women in these states. The present governments systems are not taking the health issue as priority.

Women Education in Contemporary Central Asia

After independence, enrollment in basic education declined in Central Asia, and school attendance and completion rate fell. In Tajikistan and Turkmenistan, generally secondary enrollment roughly halved between 1989 and 2001. However, three other countries – Kazakhstan, Kyrgyzstan and Uzbekistan – have overcome to a certain extent transitional constraints and reached pre-independence enrollment level in the early 2000s.

The official data on school attendance possibly do not reflect the actual situation in rural communities. A UNICEF and UNESCO survey in Kyrgyzstan revealed that the problem of low school attendance and the number of missed classes is significantly higher than the officially registered data. A number of factors have caused the lower attendance rate, poverty and the rise of child labour, limited access to safe transport, heating problems and increasing schools formal and informal expenses and fees (Central Asia Human Development Report, 2005: 150).

There are two other worrisome developments which are proving to be big blockade in achieving education for women, first, the earlier well structured pre-school system in the region has broken down, which affects children at a critical age and also limits women's involvement in social and economic life. On the whole noteworthy drop in pre-primary enrollment (about three quarters) took place in Kazakhstan and Kyrgyzstan. Even in Kazakhstan, which is considered economically stronger than the other Central Asian countries, after 1990 more than 80 per cent of kindergartens were closed. Second, there is a grim weakening in vocational and technical secondary education over the last decade. In Kazakhstan, Kyrgyzstan and Tajikistan enrollment among the groups aged 15 fell by half. In Turkmenistan, it dropped to one-fifth and in contrast, Uzbekistan successfully handled this catastrophe and vocational and technical secondary education enrolment has already reached it pre-independence level (Central Asia Human Development Report, 2005: 151).

When the Soviet rule was introduced in pre-dominantly Muslim areas, a long campaign was made, to draw women out of their homes so that they could study and work. Central Asian women gained an identity and considered the right to education and full employment as the norm, at least in the urban areas. Once the economic down fall hit the region in the mid-1990s, women were the first sufferers of the widespread unemployment. They were encouraged to stay at home because many men found it difficult to accept a competing economic partner at home at a time when their own jobs were threatened. A more customary view of the role of women has been revived; marriage is yet again becoming the main concern over education and work. As a young Tajik female student explained: girls are now brought up in anticipation of their life after wedding, which for them it is the only opportunity to see another house beyond their four walls. So they are happy about it, though out of ignorance (Youth in Central Asia, 2003: 3-4).

Such traditional outlooks are particularly widespread in rural Tajikistan, Uzbekistan and Turkmenistan. In Tajikistan two-third more boys completes schooling than girls (Tajikistan: Human Development Report, 2003: 84). In Kazakhstan and Kyrgyzstan, society has better understanding of the economic power of education and encourages girls to finish school and university. A UNICEF survey conducted in collaboration with Tajik Ministry of Education in 2003 revealed the increasing number of girl student leaving school even before reaching grade nine. Further, the survey concluded that there are three main factors behind girls' dropping out of school: poverty, family spending priorities and gender socialisation. The poor families explained that the withdrawal of the girl child from school was partly due to lack of resources, and partly because of insecurity i.e. the distance of the school.

If the above limitations do not exist, even then the girls are kept at home to help the mothers in household works or they are removed from the school out of fear and revolt of a father or an elder brother in the family. As for gender socialisation, according to the report the drop out of girls from schools is based on two characteristics of traditional Tajik culture. The first is that of different role imposed upon girls and boys. Traditionally, the focal sphere of girls' and women's lives has been the house work, child bearing and rearing and family maintenance (Youth in Central Asia, 2003: 5).

Education is the first step as far as the women empowerment is concerned and this most important base is profoundly harmed in Central Asian States in post-USSR period particularly. Only Uzbekistan has only made sincere efforts to recover it; even Kazakhstan has stayed behind in achieving educational goals as used to be in USSR times. Besides, education does not mean primary education only but it means that on the basis of education one can make his or her own choice in life independently. There is a dire lack of such notion in Central Asian States generally. Unless and until these features are taken care of in favour of women, one cannot imagine an empowered woman in this region.

Women's Political Participation in Contemporary Central Asia

The Central Asian Republics claim to be based on parliamentary system and all have adopted constitutions after attaining independence. The degree of democratisation and political participation varies across the republics: Kazakhstan has over 25 registered political parties while formal opposition to the one party state in Turkmenistan is illegal. The percentage of women in parliament ranged from a high of 26 per cent in Turkmenistan to 7 per cent in Kyrgyzstan and Uzbekistan in 2005 (Liz Kelly, 2005: 18). During the Soviet period women's participation in central and local governments was high by international standards. The constitutional and legal system favoured equal representation of all genders in the machinery of government, the party and the state enterprises. However, in reality men dominated the key decision making positions but there were some place for women in decision making or political sphere.

Recently in some Central Asian States, there have been some measures, including quotas to increase women's political participation. In Kyrgyzstan 30 per cent of political party candidates must be women, even Uzbekistan has similar quota of women in political parties. Women's share in government at ministerial level was 12.5 per cent and women in lower house of parliament 25.6 per cent in 2005. Despite of the lack of political training for women and funding for women campaigns, such measures have increased the number of women in politics, including in the national parliaments mostly through party lists. Still it is difficult to achieve true participation and real equalities of opportunities and it is not clear whether these numbers are resulting in substantive realisation of women rights (Liz Kelly, 2005: 18).

Women's economic dependence on men prevents them from taking important stand in politics, as voters and as officials. The small percentages of women who do participate in politics face discriminatory attitude and practices and obstacles to their own effectiveness and advancement. Many male state officials hold patriarchal attitudes about women's role in society, most legislative processes do not take into consideration issues of gender inequality; and budgeting process rarely result in any financing for women's empowerment – political or otherwise. The participation of rural women, poor women and single women is negligent in political area (Liz Kelly, 2005: 18).

The Millennium Development Goals (MDGs) indicator of seats in parliament held by women varies in all countries of Central Asia, and may actually cloud the real extent of political participation. For instance, in Kazakhstan, members of women representatives in the upper house of parliament was very nominal, 2 out of 42 i.e. 4.3 per cent (Women in Parliament in 2008, 2008: 5). In 2004, in the Turkmen parliament women comprised 26 per cent of the members compared with 9 per cent in Kazakhstan and 7 per cent in Kyrgyzstan, even though it is likely that women actually have less ability to influence what happens to them in Turkmenistan than in the other two countries, due to the greater degree of political control in Turkmenistan. In March 2005, parliamentary elections in Kyrgyzstan only male deputies were elected because women were displaced at an early stage in the electoral process by male candidates (Central Asia Human Development Report, 2005: 158-159).

Still it is difficult to achieve true participation and real equality of opportunities. For example, in Uzbekistan the position of deputy Hakim (Governor) and deputy Prime Minister for women's affair have been reserved for women. This may represent progress but as some local women's advocates have pointed out, this could also serve to restrict the access of women to governor or minister positions (Central Asia Human Development Report, 2005: 158-159). In Tajikistan, in 2000 parliamentary (Majlisi Oli) election campaign, only 17 out of 365 registered candidates were women i.e. 5 per cent and a total of 181 deputies were elected of whom just 5 were women i.e. 3 per cent. Following the abandonment of quotas for women which ensured the representation of women at all level during the Soviet period within government, in 2005 there were only 2 women ministers (Jane Falkingham, 2000).

Women have limited access to decision-making position in both the executive and legislative branches except in the healthcare and social protection sector. Some women's NGOs advocate a restoration of the quota system for parliamentary representation as a way of ensuring women's political participation but all this is not a guarantee that it will make women empowerment possible. The most significant factor inhibiting Central Asian Women's ability to participate in public life, including in the cultural sphere, is due to discriminatory values and religious belief, lack of social service and men's failure to share the tasks associated with the household and care and raising of children. Patriarchal attitudes confine women to the private sphere and exclude them from active participation in public life (Central Asia Human Development Report, 2005:158-159).

Throughout the Central Asian region women complain about the humiliating treatment they receive when attempting to access government structures since many women get discouraged by bureaucracy, rude and unresponsive officials. For example, Kazakh women who have managed to overcome all the obstacles that were created for her, but once she has done it, she was invited to visit the head of the local municipal government who offered her a place in one of the political parties, where by his words she could continue her political activity. But it was an offer for an exchange to withdraw her candidature from the elections. The situation of women's political opportunities in the rural areas is much worst as one can anticipate. In these areas strict traditional idea about women's place in the society and public affairs are much stronger than those in urban areas, local officials often have the cynic opinion about women's involvement in governance.

In many cases the role of wife and mother is reported to be so inflexible that women who fall outside this category are detested by individuals and are discriminated against by state institutions.

Women faces disgrace by the society when trying to enter public sphere has the reason to try to drive away these woman back to family and socially expected frames and try to pursue to fit social norms (Ismagilova Nuria Rifkatovna, Women in Politics and Gender-based Corruption in Central Asia: Realities and Responses).

Women cannot participate in public life because they do not afford it. They actually do not have property, are not documented as the person who can decide what to do with their assets need to get permission from husbands or other male relatives such as father or brothers in order to go out or work and have little contact with representatives of the state or with community leaders. All the Central Asian States have adopted anti-discriminatory conventions and have worked out plans for raising political status of women, but social practice will not change without supportive changes.

Economic Status of Women in Contemporary Central Asia

The initial decline after the disintegration of the Soviet Union is a major factor behind Central Asia's dismal trends in human development, poverty and inequality. The initial sharp collapse in economic output and incomes resulted in cumulative losses in measured GDP that ranged from about 20 per cent in Uzbekistan to almost 70 per cent in Tajikistan between 1990 and 1996, with intermediate losses of about 40 per cent for Kazakhstan, 45 per cent for Kyrgyzstan and 50 per cent for Turkmenistan. All these states suffered from serious rise in inflation, budgetary deficits and excess borrowing as governments tried to adjust to the collapse of output transfer from Moscow and the Soviet financial settlement system (Central Asia Human Development Report, 2005: 43-44).

Table 3.2: Growth in Real GDP, 1989-199

(in percentage)

Year	*Kazakhstan*	*Kyrgyzstan*	*Tajikistan*	*Turkmenistan*	*Uzbekistan*
1989	0	8	-3	-7	4
1990	0	3	-2	2	2
1991	-13	-5	-7	-5	-1
1992	-3	-19	-29	-5	-11
1993	-9	-16	-11	-10	-2
1994	-13	-20	-19	-17	-4

(Contd...)

1995	-8	-5	-13	-7	-1
1996	1	7	-4	-7	2
1997	2	10	2	-11	3

Source: Richard Pomfret, "Central Asia after Two Decades of Independence", *World Institute for Development Economics Research,* Working Paper No. 2010/53, May 2010, pp. 3-4.

Table 3.3: Inflation (change in consumer price index), 1991-1997

(in percentage)

Year	*Kazakhstan*	*Kyrgyzstan*	*Tajikistan*	*Turkmenistan*	*Uzbekistan*
1991	79	85	112	103	82
1992	1381	855	1157	493	645
1993	1662	772	2195	3102	534
1994	1892	229	350	1748	1568
1995	176	41	609	1005	305
1996	39	31	418	992	54
1997	17	26	88	84	59

Source: Richard Pomfret, "Central Asia after Two Decades of Independence", *World Institute for Development Economics Research,* Working Paper No. 2010/53, May 2010, pp. 3-4.

Fortunately, all Central Asian economies have achieved relatively high growth rates since 1999, pushed along by a combination of recovery reforms, high mineral prices and the positive spill over effect of rapid growth in neighbouring countries.

Table 3.4: Growth in Real GDP, 1998-2008

(in percentage)

Year	*Kazakhstan*	*Kyrgyzstan*	*Tajikistan*	*Turkmenistan*	*Uzbekistan*
1998	-2	2	5	7	4
1999	3	4	4	17	4
2000	10	5	8	19	4
2001	14	5	10	20	4
2002	10	0	9	16	4
2003	9	7	10	17	4
2004	10	7	11	15	8
2005	10	0	7	13	7
2006	11	3	7	11	7
2007	9	8	8	12	10
2008	3	8	8	10	9

Source: Richard Pomfret, "Central Asia after Two Decades of Independence", *World Institute for Development Economics Research,* Working Paper No. 2010/53, May 2010, pp. 3-4.

Table 3.5: Inflation (change in consumer price index), 1998-2008

(in percentage)

Year	*Kazakhstan*	*Kyrgyzstan*	*Tajikistan*	*Turkmenistan*	*Uzbekistan*
1998	7	11	43	17	29
1999	8	36	28	24	29
2000	13	19	33	8	25
2001	8	7	39	12	27
2002	6	2	12	9	27
2003	6	3	16	6	12
2004	7	4	7	6	7
2005	8	4	7	11	10
2006	9	6	10	11	14
2007	11	10	13	9	12
2008	17	25	21	12	13

Source: Richard Pomfret, "Central Asia after Two Decades of Independence", *World Institute for Development Economics Research,* Working Paper No. 2010/53, May 2010, pp. 3-4.

The five economies gradually became more differentiated as their governments introduced national strategies for transition to a market based economy. Kyrgyz republic introduced trade liberalisation and extensive privatisation and then President Akayev fostered the emergence of the most liberal regime in the region, in July 1998, the Kyrgyz republic became the first Soviet successor state to join the World Trade Organisation. Kazakhstan had similar transition indicators to the Kyrgyz republic; with less complete trade liberalisation but a better functioning financial sector and more reformed infrastructure. Moreover, the country's substantial energy and mineral resources held great potential; the oil reserves were about to be tapped by the Chevron-Tengij project under the largest foreign investment agreement in post-Soviet territory (Richard Pomfret, 2010: 7).

In Tajikistan the civil war destroyed the planned economy and effectively privatised economic activity. Institutions, such as security of contact, crucial to efficient operation of market economy were under developed. After the 1997 peace agreement Tajikistan pursued reforms with liberalisation of trade and financial sector policies, but institutions remain weak. Uzbekistan's financial sector remained dominated by state-owned banks and financial institutions. In rail transport and in some utilities, the government gradually allowed some market forces to operate. Overall, Uzbekistan became a market oriented economy but with substantial government direction (Richard Pomfret, 2000: 733-748). Turkmenistan established the most personalised and autocratic regime in Central Asia, pursuing a policy based on neutrality and economic independence with minimal economic reform (Nancy Lubin, 1991: 61-78).

The government kept tight control over the farm and energy sectors. Outdated agricultural policies and poor management led to cotton yields falling and the production of energy declined drastically during the 1990s. However, after 2000 some good signs were seen from both direction (Agriculture and Energy) and export is gaining at satisfactory level. Finally, it can be observed that presently all Central Asian States are on the road to economic recovery after the drastic collapse of 1990s. If all the rise and fall of this period are minutely explored then the largest sufferer and affected section are the women of these states. Out of economic compulsions the governments of all the Central Asian States have withdrawn the economic incentive provided in the USSR period.

Women were steadily ruined by unemployment and privatisation. They are now really under the triple burden of life, which comprise of the burden of the household work and upbringing of children, professional work and exploitation done by the private companies at their work places. Under such circumstances, women's life is made miserable, blood and soul was sucked by the manipulative systems and the social surroundings. Women were really under helpless conditions where neither the government was there to help out nor any NGO or body that could raise some voice for them. Besides, the traditional forces are enhancing pressure over women about their social behaviour in the region. For example, the influence of Islamic forces is dragging women particularly in higher education sphere and further makes them incapable to acquire good positions. They are compelled to be dressed in the traditional costume especially in the rural areas of Central Asian States.

For example, in Tajikistan 482 private enterprises and farms those are member of the association of small and average business only 16 i.e. 3 per cent are headed by women. According to a survey by the business women association of Khudjand women occupied 25 per cent of legal and senior management posts in 2000 (Jane Falkingham, 2000: 36). In Central Asian States there is a low representation of women in senior economic positions and it is the result of discrimination, direct and indirect, combined with the traditional views about the appropriate roles for men and women in society. Even women themselves may also act as barrier to their own advancement.

Central Asian women in employment are highly concentrated in the lowest paid sectors of agriculture, education and health where wages are approximately 2.5 times lower than those in traditional men's sectors which are mining, building, transport, communications and distribution of electric power, gas and water. In Kazakhstan, only 3.5 per cent of heads of government bodies, managers of all level and heads of organisations were women in 2009. While 76.7 per cent of workers at lower level are women. The economic growth in the country creates a hope that this situation will improve. Women increasingly become involved in business and according to official statistics around 40 per cent of Kazakh women in 2009 had their own business (Anita Seibert and Ewa Pintera, 2009: 32).

Migration to more prosperous regions of the country is an important factor impacting the economic situation of women in Kyrgyzstan, Uzbekistan and Turkmenistan. Women who migrate in search of work predominantly work in agriculture and in sale in the market. But in most cases their work is unregistered, they are still poor, they have no homes and do not have access to healthcare and other services, for instance, their children usually do not attend school (Anita Seibert and Ewa Pintera, 2009: 34).

Though after 2000 a boost in the economies of Central Asian States has been recorded and a sense of hope is generated for improving the economic status of women in the region, it seems that contemporary time is really tough for women in economic context, where liberalisation, privatisation and traditional social structure are continuously mounting their troubles. Besides this women are also facing a number of problems which are directly or indirectly distorting their personality.

Alcohol and Drugs

The vodka culture is part of the everyday life of young Central Asia. Still available at very low subsidized prices or brewed at home, hard liquor remains an easily affordable escape for many young people both male and female. Across the region, bored or depressed youth get together, start drinking and act in a state of drunkenness that is the prelude to most violence and crime. A young Kyrgyz woman acknowledged that "The main problem is that all men here drink terribly. They work very hard in summer and autumn but in the evening and in the winter all they do is drink and then get into fight" according to International Crisis Group report (ICG Interview with Rural Youth, 2003).

According to a World Bank report in 2002, alongside alcohol abuse, drug abuse and its most immediate consequence, the spread of HIV/AIDS are having a terrible impact. While HIV prevalence remain under 1 per cent according to official figures, it is rising faster in the former Soviet union than anywhere else in the world seems likely to go up even more sharply in years to come. Most infection is the result of injecting drugs, a practice that has developed fact with an estimated half million injecting drug users in the region, of whom 70 to 80 per cent were likely to become HIV infected (World Bank Report, 2002).

In Kazakhstan, the most affected country, over half of HIV-infected persons are aged 20-29, and most are unemployed young men. Hard drugs used there are mostly heroin that is either inhaled or used via needles. Prices have goneup dramatically. One gram of heroin cost US $60 i.e. three times the average monthly salary. The economics of drugs thus explain a boom in drug injection, which has been accompanied by a predictable rise in HIV cases. About 80 per cent of HIV patients in Bukhara were injecting drug users (IDUs). Officially in 2002, there are 820 hard drug addicts in Bukhara itself, but in fact of the real figure are around 5000 of which 40 per cent are IDUs (ICG Interview with Medical Specialist, 2002).

Many factors are responsible for the explosion in drug consumption in Central Asia, the important being the malfunction of the institutions of family and state. Children and young people often receive little respect and attention at home from parents who have little time, energy and money to spend on them. The state proved as a complete failure in providing the right to education, employment and a hope for secure future to its youth. The family values are in trouble due to the economic problems. As a result, the young generation attracted towards drugs as a shelter from all anxieties in life. The state and parents are often hesitant to recognise it as a problem. The parents refuse to admit or even recognise drug addiction within their family; they fear if such information will be released to public knowledge about addiction then it would create a bad impression for the whole family. The social shame is emotionally involved in the matter and in such a situation; the prevention for drug addiction becomes more difficult. This situation makes young women very vulnerable to the dangers of drug, abuse, manipulation, prostitution and sexual diseases. For the poor, the only way to continue buying drugs is to get involved in crime, to force wives or children into prostitution (Youth in Central Asia, 2003: 26-27).

Besides, drugs and narcotics are also affecting the Central Asian Women in another way. The young women in the region are easily targeted for smuggling drugs couriers by the drug mafia for drug trafficking. The young women arouse least doubt; they can easily hide narcotics with their body and can deceive the security system without any difficulty. But whenever they are arrested in such offences then situation is really painful. Consequently, the police treat with them as criminal; the legal proceedings and lastly rigorous imprisonment make their lives worst. Economic and family obligations transform a simple girl to a criminal. Such numbers of prisoner are continuously increasing in the region and these women are harassed by the family, drug mafias and the legal structure of the state. Additionally, the drugs enhance the domestic violence in the families and the prevalent victim of all this are women and children alone. Though the governments of Central Asian States are familiar with drugs menace in the region they are not fully prepared to deal this crisis and especially Uzbek government is very slow in dealing with such matters.

Kyrgyzstan and Kazakhstan have adopted more realistic and courageous policies by recognising the problems and allowing a number of pioneering programmes that were later extended to Uzbekistan and Tajikistan such as methadone use and needle exchange programmes. Still the Uzbek government has not implemented any concrete step towards the root of this problem i.e. unemployment, drug mafias and drug trafficking and any positive step to bring the drug patients again into the mainstream.

Human Trafficking

Human trafficking is a form of modern day slavery and victims of trafficking are exploited for commercial sex or labour purpose. Traffickers use force, fraud, coercion to achieve exploitation. After drugs, human trafficking is tied with illegal arms trade as the second largest criminal industry in the world and it is the fastest growing in Central Asian States. The UN protocol requires that trafficking cases contain three elements: recruitment, transfer and transportation, harbouring or hosting a person; improper means like force, coercion, fraud, deception, abuse of power/position of vulnerability or the giving/ receiving of payment to control another person; and an intention to exploit (Liz Kelly, 2005: 7).

According to the IOM (International Organisation for Migration) report 2005, Central Asia is a growing region of origin for trafficking in women. Approximately 10,000 young women from Central Asia are becoming trafficking victims being "bought, sold and transported and kept in slave like conditions" every year (Liz Kelly, 2005: 20). At this stage the main country of origin is Kyrgyzstan followed by Uzbekistan and Tajikistan. Kyrgyzstan is also a popular transit country for trafficked Uzbek and Tajik women due to the close geographical position within the Fergana valley. The town Osh has become the famous transhipment point of trafficking women from where they are further transported to far abroad.

Map of Kyrgyzstan (Osh Port)

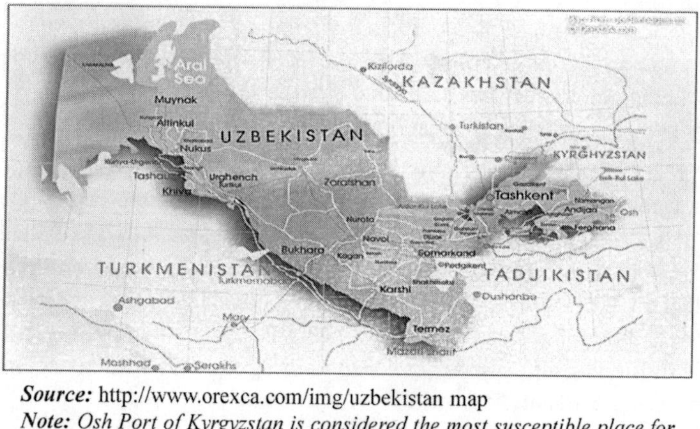

Source: http://www.orexca.com/img/uzbekistan map

Note: *Osh Port of Kyrgyzstan is considered the most susceptible place for Women Trafficking in Central Asian States.*

No official statistics on trafficking in persons in Central Asia are available. According to some sources shed light on the gravity of the problem throughout the region. Some statistics about 5000 victims are trafficked annually from Kazakhstan (Kazakhstan in Country report on Human Rights Practices 2002). Between 3000 and 4000 victims are trafficked from Kyrgyz republic and between 1000 and 2000 women are trafficked annually from Tajikistan to foreign countries. The problem may well be growing given the recent worsening of the economic situation. For instance, there were reports that a number of young girls aged 13 to 14 years old were provided with false passports and sent to various countries for prostitution (International Women Rights Action Watch report, Uzbekistan).

In Turkmenistan, there are no official or confirmed cases of trafficking; however, there are anecdotal reports of women to Turkey and the United Arab Emirates to work as prostitutes, some of whom may have been trafficked (Kazakhstan Today, 2003). Foundation for women, a Thai NGO reported increased presence of Uzbek women who were subsequently found to have been as trafficked. In Thailand, 2695 women arrived in 1999 that increased by almost half to 5017 in 2000, and 228 were detained in 2002 by immigration police. Most detained women were from Samarkand or Tashkent. Similarly large populations of imprisoned women in UAE for prostitution offence are from Uzbekistan (Liz Kelly, 2005: 20).

The main destination country for women and children trafficked from Central Asia is the United Arab Emirates, although many victims are also sent to Albania, Cyprus, Greece, Germany, Iran, Israel, Italy, Kosovo, Malaysia, Pakistan, Russia, South Korea, Syria, Thailand and Turkey (Mohamed Y. Mattar: 151). Trafficking in persons from Central Asia takes many forms. Sex trafficking, or trafficking for commercial sexual exploitation is the most common. But there is also trafficking for forced labour in Central Asia and these victims are mainly from rural areas. According to various reports Kazakhstan appears to be the major destination country for trafficked labour from other Central Asian Republics.

Human Trafficking in Central Asia

Trafficking for childbearing and marriage is also prevalent in Central Asia; women from Tajikistan are trafficked to Austria for the sole purpose of giving birth to a child, who is then taken away from the mother. "Marriage Agencies" in many Central Asian countries arranged for women to be trafficked elsewhere for forced marriage. Finally, there have been reports for trafficking for organ donation. While this form of trafficking appears to be rare in Central Asian countries, it nevertheless exists. For example, two such cases have been reported in Uzbekistan: one involves a woman who sold her daughter to unknown people who killed her to take her organs (Alisher Taksanov, 2003). The problem of child labour is prevalent in most countries of Central Asia with the exception of Kazakhstan. In the Kyrgyz republic child labour is widespread in the industries of construction, prostitution, narcotics, tobacco, cotton, rice, cattle-breeding, heavy industries, gasoline, sales, car-washing, shoe-cleaning and work involving pesticides and chemicals etc (Liz Kelly, 2005: 154).

Any analysis of trafficking in persons in the context of Central Asia should consider the underlying causes of trafficking infrastructure in the region. Among the key factors that make women and children in Central Asia particularly vulnerable to trafficking are low incomes, gender, age, ethnic factors, labour market, information access to markets and employable skill learning. These factors fall into economic, political and cultural vulnerability. There are some social, political, economic and religious grounds behind the trafficking of women and children in Central Asian countries.

Economic vulnerability is one of the most apparent contributing negative factors. The extreme poverty, high employment rates and elimination of social protection services previously provided by the Communist governments became widespread. In addition, most trafficking victims are young women usually with no higher education and no job prospects (Liz Kelly, 2005: 159). Political vulnerability is another factor present in the majority of the post-Communist transition state. The transition in each state from communism to a quasi-democratic form of government and the accompanying weaknesses of the new political institutions have created a favourable environment for organised crime and corruption to thrive out of the five Central Asian countries. Tajikistan is perceived to be the most corrupt, according to the 2003 Corruption Perceptions Index (CPI) calculated by Transparency International. Tajikistan has ranked 124th out of 133 countries surveyed and the corruption there is perceived to be pervasive. Kazakhstan's stand deteriorated from 88th to 100th in the overall ranking and Uzbekistan and Kyrgyzstan are ranked 100th and 118th respectively. Such an extreme level of corruption is certainly an instrument in helping the traffickers with trafficking in Central Asia commonly "involves highly organised and well connected criminal syndicates" (Transparency International Corruption Perceptions Index 2003).

Besides, traditional social-environment is also accountable for the trafficking of women in this region. The nature of the societies in Central Asia is of strong conventional patriarchy and secondly, it is under the impact of Islam. These factors are again distressing the legal status of women and customs like arranged marriages, polygamy and bride-price etc. are yet again visible in the region. All these have really harmed and devalued the social life of women in this region.

According to Uzbek NGO activist, "prostitution is on the rise because women who divorce from forced marriage have no skill and cannot feed their children. There is a human marketplace where women stand and get into cars.... Sometime those women never reappear" (Youth in Central Asia, 2003: 28). Finally, it has been suggested that the geographical location of the Central Asian States can be viewed as yet another factor contributing to the increasing levels of trafficking in persons. In particular, the location of these countries between the main destination countries in East Asia and Middle East makes them an ideal recruitment area for traffickers (Liz Kelly, 2005: 164).

Lastly, it can be observed that the problem of human trafficking is continuously increasing in Central Asia and particularly trafficking of women and children. There is no uniform terminology used for trafficking in Central Asian States nor all these states treat human trafficking as a crime. There is hardly any law existing against such violations in this region. In Turkmenistan, the laws only criminalize actions involving someone in prostitution. In Uzbekistan, the legislation only prohibits hiring people for sexual or other forms of exploitation, through fraud and coercion. At the same time, there are a number of articles in the criminal code of Kazakhstan that can be used to prosecute the cases of trafficking in persons. Similarly, until August 2003, the Kyrgyz criminal code prohibited the purchase or sale of children and the recruitment of people for sexual or other types of exploitation (Mohamed Y. Mattar: 176-177).

So far as the problem of women's trafficking is concerned in Central Asian States a number of measures are required in this direction and mass awakening is needed to tell people about its ill-effects. Beside it, to improve the social, economic and political status of women is urgently needed in the region. In these states, religious rigidity and orthodoxy are dragging women onto the back foot and creating odd circumstances for women, such effects should be sorted out for women to progress.

Bride Kidnapping

Bride kidnapping is another problem of Central Asia, which shows women are still treated like domestic animals. Though this problem was largely controlled in Soviet period but in the post-USSR period especially in the mountain areas of Kyrgyz and Kazakh the problem is again reviving and such cases are frequently increasing in these regions. This problem is against the law but people are doing it without any hesitation and fear, there is no action against the people who are involved in this sort of action and bride kidnapping is somewhere socially acceptable. In Kyrgyzstan, bride kidnapping is one of the most common form of forced marriage and is becoming more admired. Human Right Watch found in 2006 that approximately 40 per cent of women in cities had been victim of bride kidnapping while 60-80 per cent of rural community women had been victims (Human Right Watch, 2006: 90).

Historically, bride kidnapping in the eighteenth and nineteenth century has been used by consenting couples who would not otherwise be able to marry due to financial difficulties or social constraints. In modern times, consensual "pretend abductions" still occur to avoid financial and social restrictions. A description of non-consensual kidnapping of women by a stranger or acquaintance for forced marriage is summarised by Human Right Watch report on Kyrgyzstan: "Kidnapping of women and girls some as young as 12 years old for forced marriage are carried out by group of men who capture a woman through physical force or deception and take her to the home of intended groom. The abductor's family then exerts psychological and sometime physical pressure to coerce the young woman to consent to marry. In some cases the young woman is raped soon after being taken to the abductor's house, so that she will feel shame and unable to return to her parent's home; other time the kidnapped woman is coerced to have sex or in some cases is raped on her wedding night after a marriage ceremony is performed" (Human Right Watch, 2006: 2).

Bride kidnapping is a violation of human rights and deprives women of other fundamental rights. Even if she is not raped, her virginity will forever be questioned after being abducted. Women have hardly any option except to agree to such marriage due to the traditional force, lack of education, economic dependency and other social pressures on her. Even if the woman does escape the abductor she often faces disgrace and is detested by her own family and community. The women who are kidnapped can suffer physically as well as psychologically and emotional trauma (Human Right Watch, 2006: 114-119).

In Tajikistan, girls are often forced into marriage before they reach the minimum age of 17. In Uzbekistan, people sometime do not realise that forced marriage is a crime and police have indicated that in practice local tradition has taken precedence over the law. In Kyrgyzstan, the government officials sometime contend that bride kidnapping is a tradition and often consensual. In this way, many times government bodies, authorities and police ignore such crimes and somewhere promoting them indirectly.

Domestic Violence

Violence against women and the threat of violence are main barriers to women's empowerment and equal participation in society. However, they often go unnoticed and undocumented and therefore unresolved. When stress and violence increase in society in general as they have in the transition countries women's safety at home, workplace and community is often seriously affected. The UN declaration on violence against women adopted in 1993 defines violence against women as encompassing "any act of gender based violence that result in, or is likely to result in physical, sexual or psychological harm or suffering to women, including threats of such acts, coercion or arbitrary deprivations of liberty, whether occurring in public or private life" (Combating Gender Based Violence, 2005: 6).

Violence against women in Central Asia are existing in many forms, for example, bride-kidnapping, bride-price, trafficking of women for sexual exploitation, religion that curtails the legal rights of women and polygamy. All such problems have already been discussed in this chapter earlier. But domestic violence against women is again a serious problem that is rapidly increasing in contemporary Central Asian society. Domestic violence is not a new phenomenon in Central Asian states but after gaining independence the rate of this evil has gone up. It is a sort of violence that takes place at home or within the family. It presumes a close relationship between the victims and the offender. It includes emotional abuse and neglect as well as sexual and physical violence.

In Kazakhstan, there is no specific law on domestic violence; however it may be addressed under assault and battery provisions of the criminal code. There is no law that specifically prohibits spousal rape. The maximum sentence for wife beating is three years. The national commission for women and children was established in December 1998 by the Decrees of the President of Kazakhstan to ensure the necessary conditions for the participation of women in the political, social, economic and cultural life of the country. A special parliamentary group on family and a special chamber of the parliament on the issues of women, family, youth, tourism and sport has been created. But violence against women including domestic violence remains a serious problem in Kazakhstan.

Over 60 per cent of women have suffered from physical or sexual violence at least once in their lifetime. According to the Municipal Department of Internal Affairs, in Almaty alone 8561 crimes against women were committed in only six month in 2002, of these 1405 were related to family and domestic relations (Merrill Morrow: 58).

In Kyrgyzstan, the family law specifically prohibits domestic violence and spousal abuse. Gender analysis council has been established and as a result of the Council's work, the National Gender Policy Council had been created in the office of the President in July 1998. The council is monitoring the national implementation of international human rights treaties and agreements including the Convention of the Elimination of all forms of Discrimination against Women. But even after this there has been alarming increase in the crime of violence against women. In 2001, Interior Ministry Statistics indicated that there were approximately 2600 crimes of all types against women reported (Radhika Coomaraswamy, 2003: 196).

Violence against women remains a serious problem in Tajikistan also. According to figures from the regional branch of World Health Organisation, about 50 per cent of the women in the country in 2002 had been exposed to physical violence and 47 per cent to sexual violence. Women also faced verbal abuses and humiliating treatment often from husbands. Given their economic dependency on husbands abusing them, some women saw no other way out of violent situations than suicide with self-burning as an extreme form (Radhika Coomaraswamy, 2003: 215).

The constitutions guarantee equal right to women. However, due to the norms and people's attitudes prevailing in society women were often in weak position. In Turkmenistan, domestic violence against women was common, but no statistics were available. The subject is not usually discussed in society, and the majority of victims of domestic violence keep silent, partly because they are unaware of their rights, or because they are afraid of more violence from their husbands and relatives. There are no programmes addressing domestic violence, except for one project on advocacy that conducted seminar on women's rights and domestic violence. In Uzbekistan there are currently no specific laws dealing with domestic violence in place, neither in the penal law nor in the civil law. Violence against women in the family is widespread. It occurs across all ethnic and religious groups and social classes (Radhika Coomaraswamy, 2003: 196).

Such cases usually are handled by family members or elders within the community (*Mahalla*) and rarely come to court. When women turn to the criminal justice system in cases of violence against them, the crime is often reportedly not effectively addressed. On the one hand, the legal system also focuses on reconciliation, which means in practice that the police, prosecutors and judges refer cases of family violence to the Mahalla for settlement. In fact, cases of domestic violence are often only receiving attention when the victims commit suicide. The number of female suicide rate is increasing in Uzbekistan. However, the government has created the committee of women in Uzbekistan with branches in various regions in the country (16 Days of Activism against Gender Violence, 2002: 26).

Although the committee of women has the status of an NGO, it is a governmental organisation and reportedly does not play a substantive role in the formation of policy. After analysing all this it can be observed that more or less domestic violence exists in all Central Asian States. The government organisations, International Human Rights Organisations and NGOs are still away from finding any solution to this problem. The existing religious culture, patriarchal customs and rigid traditions are creating great obstructions in according the deserving honour to women in the region. To change all this system is not an easy game because somewhere government is also having some soft corner for traditions and customs.

Homicide is also a form of violence that is commonly recognised as a crime, easily defined and usually reported. These cases are rapidly increasing in this region and if the numbers are analysed from 1989 to 1997, such cases have been mounting particularly in Kazakhstan, Kyrgyzstan and Tajikistan while in Turkmenistan and Uzbekistan homicide rate is stable. The sharpest increase has been noted in Tajikistan i.e. around four-fold since it got its independence in 1991 (Liz Kelly and Linda Regan, *http://www.britishcouncil.org/waw.pdf*).

The problems of women in Central Asian states are worse in post-USSR period but it does not mean that the government bodies are not aware about these worries in the region. All the states in this region have given an equal place to men and women in their constitutions. Additionally, if any woman is victim of abuse like rape, prostitution and trafficking, there are enough legal provisions to protect her position. All the Central Asian States have sanctioned the founding document of the international women's human rights movement is the Convention on Elimination of all forms of Discrimination against Women (CEDAW).

CEDAW came into force in 1979 and has been signed and ratified by 185 countries. CEDAW is a binding legal document that addresses such rights as access to healthcare and family planning service, education and freedom from discrimination in employment and political representation (among many rights). This treaty also demands that signatory governments remove barriers to gender equality and actively monitor the situation of women and girls in their respective countries (Global Justice Now, *http://globaljusticecenter.net*). In Central Asia, Kazakhstan (1998), Kyrgyzstan (1996), Tajikistan (1993) and Uzbekistan (1995) have approved CEDAW. States that have ratified

CEDAW are largely obligated to take steps to respect, protect, promote and fulfil the rights of women (Merrill Morrow: 56).

Kazakhstan, Kyrgyzstan and Tajikistan have also ratified the optional protocol but awareness of optional protocol to CEDAW is not high. In Kyrgyzstan, there are no known examples of women having used it. The government has not taken measure to provide information and training to the population on the complaint process. As a result, not a single registered application has been made through any individual complaints mechanism from Kyrgyzstan to any of the UN committees of treaty bodies. The situation was reported to be similar in Kazakhstan and Tajikistan. All Central Asian countries have established special National Action Plan for achieving gender equality and ensure to prevent women human rights (Radhika Coomaraswamy, 2003: 192-221).

The National Action Plan was prepared with the participation of NGOs, based on the Beijing platform for action priorities and included several progressive actions. But all these government and non-government programmes do not prove promising as they were expected. The major lack in the whole episode on the part of government was to train judicial, legal, medical, social, educational, police and immigrant personnel in dealing with violence against women. Most of the training that exists is carried out by women's NGOs, but it is limited because of resource constraints faced by these organisations (Merrill Morrow: 56). In fact, all the local NGO are active only with support from foreign funds or own funds. The constitution and the legislations prohibit any financial assistance to the non-governmental organisations from the government.

Besides, some government laws also raised women's disparity. For instance, women in Kazakhstan are prohibited from driving large automobiles and buses carrying more than 14 passengers. Moreover, new discriminatory laws have come into force following CEDAW ratification. A new Labour Law (2000) in Kazakhstan revoked many privileges earlier granted to women with young children. Women are no longer entitled to break, which previously was included as paid time, for feeding children who are under 18 months of the age. Maternity leaves has been reduced and this law also does not include a direct prohibition on the dismissal of women who are on pregnancy or maternity leave, does not provide individual working hours schedule and part time jobs for women as stipulated by CEDAW. The new law also prohibits men from going on leave to take care of children.

Thus, the Central Asian woman is struggling herself for identity, freedom, liberty and equality in contemporary times. She has to make her own efforts to free herself from the rigid customs like *paranja* (veil), polygamy, early and abducted marriages in the society. The communist USSR government had made its utmost efforts to establish literacy and complete employment for women but the same goals seem beyond reach under the ruling of capitalist governments of Central Asian States.

Structure of Kazakh Society

To reveal the status of women in Kazakh and Uzbek societies is the main focus of this study. Though both states have a common historical inheritance but there are structural (i.e. economic, political, social and cultural) differences between the Kazakh and Uzbek societies. Further it is intended to investigate in this chapter as to what sort of variation exists in the status of women in these two states.

Kazakhstan is the largest country in economic and geographical terms in Central Asia. It shares the longest borderline with Russia and its size is 2,717,300 sq. km. with the average population density of 5.5 persons per sq. km. and recorded a total population of 15.9 million (in 2008). The term Kazakh means a nomad. Kazakhs as nomads distinguish themselves from other settled Muslim communities, mainly Uzbeks, Tartars and Uighurs. Kazakhs identified themselves primarily by genealogy, i.e. membership of a particular clan. Genealogy or clan membership always indicated the regional affiliation or identity of the Kazakh in question (Bhavna Dave, 2004: 2).

Nomadism was a product of a given ecological setting, a means of adjustment to the ecological conditions by its inhabitants in a pre-technological age. The customary natural geographical settings, lack of water or irrigation facilities and impossibilities of developing agriculture made pastoral nomadism the only possible means of survival. Nomadic lifestyle required the maintenance of balance between the available water resources and the size of the population, low population density was a common attribute. In 1926, only about a fourth of the Kazakhs led sedentary mode of life, while most were dependent on the livestock economy and seasonal agricultural farming. As part of collectivisation policies implemented by the Soviet state in the late 1920s, the Stalinist regime argued that an immediate settlement of the nomads was the only means of increasing agriculture production. The forced settlement of Kazakhs led to the perishing of almost 90 per cent of all cattle – the only source of livelihood for nomads. The subsequent famine resulted in a terrible human loss (Bhavna Dave, 2004: 3).

The depopulated land of Kazakhstan soon became the dumping ground for deportation of various "enemy" nationalities as well as for convicts sentenced to hard labour during World War II. By 1949, Kazakhstan had become the home to at least 820,165 deportees which included 444,000 Germans, 302,526 Chechens and Ingush, 33,088 Karachai, 28,130 Poles, 28,497 Meskhetian Turks, 17,512 Balkars and numerous smaller nationalities (Bhavna Dave, 2004: 3). The virgin lands campaign inaugurated by the general secretary of the Communist party Nikita Khrushchev during 1954 to 1956 led to the arrival of about 640,000 settlers from the Slavic and Baltic republic. The 1959 census unveiled a totally transformed ethnic profile of the republic with the Kazakh share reduced to a mere 29 per cent of the population and the Slavic and European nationalities together forming nearly 60 per cent of the total. The Slavic influx into Kazakhstan had slowed considerably by 1970 with the economic downturn in Central Asia. For the period 1966 to 1979 the number of arrivals to Kazakhstan from the republics decreased by 60 per cent and the number of persons from Slavic and German nationalities in Kazakhstan decreased by 940,000 between 1970 and 1989 (Bhavna Dave, 2004: 4).

Kazakhstan's ethnic composition has undergone a radical change over the first decade of its independence as a result of immigration of Russian and other Russian-speaking groups mainly Germans. Kazakhstan's ethnic German population dropped sharply, from 946,900 people in 1989 to 353,400 in 1999. Overall, nearly two million Russian-speakers have left Kazakhstan over the last decade.

Table 3.6: Ethnic Composition in Kazakhstan, Census Data 1959-1999

(In percentage)

Nationality	*1959*	*1970*	*1979*	*1989*	*1999*
Kazakh	30.0	32.6	36.0	40.1	53.4
Russian	42.7	42.4	40.8	37.4	29.9
Ukrainian	8.2	7.2	6.1	5.4	3.7
Belorussian	1.2	1.5	1.2	1.1	0.8
German	7.1	6.6	6.1	5.8	2.4
Tatar	2.1	2.2	2.1	2.0	1.7
Uzbek	1.5	1.7	1.8	2.0	2.5
Uighur	0.6	0.9	1.0	1.1	1.4
Korean	0.8	0.6	0.6	0.6	0.7
Combined Turkic/Muslim	39.7	42.7	45.5	50.2	61.0
Combined Slavic/European	60.3	57.3	54.5	49.8	39.0

Source: Bhavna Dave (October 2004), "Minority Rights: Cultural Diversity and Development in Central Asia", *United Nations Office of the High Commissioner for Human Rights*, Bishkek, p. 5.

Table 3.7: Proficiency in the State Language Kazakh, and in Russian in the 1999 Census among Major Nationalities.

(In percentage)

Nationality	*Proficiency in Language*		
	Of own nationality	*Of other nationality*	
		Kazakh	*Russian*
Kazakh	99.4	—	75.0
Russian	100.0	14.9	—
Ukrainian	16.1	12.6	99.5
Belorussian	13.5	9.0	99.4
German	21.8	15.4	99.3
Uzbek	97.0	80.0	59.2
Tatar	37.1	63.6	96.9
Uighur	81.3	80.5	76.1
Korean	25.8	28.8	97.7

Source: Bhavna Dave (October 2004), "Minority Rights: Cultural Diversity and Development in Central Asia", *United Nations Office of the High Commissioner for Human Rights*, Bishkek, p. 5.

Most ethnic or cultural communities in Central Asia did not see or imagine themselves as members of a distinct nation or state, or as belonging to a specific ethno-linguistic group before the advent of the

Soviet rule. The Soviet rule, by contrast, forged a strict correspondence between ethnicity and language as it transformed the fluid ethnic linguistic difference within the agrarian and nomadic communities into territorialised "nations" possessing their own distinct language and scripts. Soviet territorial administrative structure and socialist ideology have played a pivotal role in shaping collective and personal identities. In Soviet term, nationality is synonymous of ethnic membership and is distinct from citizenship. Nationality was recorded in Soviet passports, as well as in all major official documents.

In Kazakhstan, despite of the existence of diverse identity of various ethnic groups, no ethnic conflict and clash was observed. The vast majority are Muslims although not in any extremist or fundamentalist type that have practices such as requiring women to be veiled. The remaining are either Russian orthodox, some other religion, or simply not religious at all. The Kazakh-Uyghur people have a long history of living in the region, originally as nomadic, clan-based families and enjoyed many mixed marriages (Evelyn Zellerer and Dmitriy Vyortkin, 2004: 447).

Tradition, Culture and Family

Kazakh culture is traditionally a patriarchal one, with much respect being given to men. While years ago it was common for women to marry very young, times have changed; education has become much more important for both genders and marriage for people in their mid-twenties are becoming more common. Marriages are not arranged by the parents but are usually formed through dating and courtship. Inter-racial marriage is rare but tolerated. Three aspects of traditional Kazakh culture still occasionally affect marriage. Today in Kazakhstan marriage is forbidden to any couple related over the past seven generations. In additional, the male should be older than the female. Finally, the nomadic tradition of stealing a bride is still practised, although rarely. Kazakh weddings are a three-day event and highly expensive for both sides (groom and bride) (Culture of Kazakhstan: 16). Divorce is not uncommon, especially in urban areas, though it is not considered good in social norm but is acceptable in Kazakh society. There are no formal rules for who gets what when a marriage breaks but women usually keep children.

The Kazakh and Russian families have enough disparity in their family structure in Kazakhstan. Basically, Kazakhs tend to have more children than Russians. The Russian couples have only one or two children, while Kazakh families five or six children usually. Men exercise the most representative authority in both Kazakh and non-Kazakh households. Men will often lounge on large pillows or stand outside and smoke while women prepare food or clean up after a meal. Men do work around the house, but it is usually with the houses, garden or car. But there are many strong women and powerful matriarchs who wield all practical control (Culture of Kazakhstan: 16).

After independence, the revival of religion has been observed in all Central Asian states, including Kazakhstan. It enhanced the expansion of Islamic traditions in these societies. One can observe the impact of Islam in social customs (marriage, divorce etc.) of Kazakhstan but this impact is not all the same so far as the urban and rural societies are concerned. Undoubtedly, it has harmed women's position in society. But at the same time, the combination of multi-ethnicity, nomadism and European culture made Kazakhstan a better society than its neighbouring states i.e. Uzbek and Tajik where one can find the hold of Islamic fundamentalism.

Kazakhstan witnessed a great decline in the birth rate from 1990 to 1999; the reason behind this was the small number of marriages and economic difficulties. Nationally, the marriage rate went down from 10.1 marriages per thousand populations in 1991 to only 5.8 in 1999, it was a 43 per cent decline (Charles M. Becker and Ai-Gul S. Seitenova, 2005: 5). In reality, marriage and economic position are inter-connected; from both perspectives husbands and wives are likely to be reluctant to enter into the institution of marriage under uncertain economic conditions. In Kazakhstan, especially in urban areas, marriage ceremony can be a costly affair. As a result, during economic crisis, only a fewer families would be capable to pull on the expenses of marriage.

However, the marriage rate and child birth rate are universally higher among entire Kazakh population. There is a greater demand for children among ethnic Kazakh due to stronger social tradition. According to Kazakh tradition, the purpose of women's lives is to marry and produce children. Other factors like education, employment and career for women are secondary. This tradition is strongly favoured in rural Kazakhstan. In urban regions this trend is weak because of the economic and livelihood struggle (Charles M. Becker and Ai-Gul S. Seitenova, 2005: 7).

It means that Kazakh ethnic society even today is following the nomadic culture and in such culture women are considered simply a mother of warriors and men are measured as the breadwinner in society. But whatever Kazakhs got from the multi-ethnicity and Soviet legacy only diluted the nomadic culture rather completely end it. In fact, Kazakh women (especially in rural areas) are happy and satisfied with their stereotype image if they have no economic crisis in their lives. The current economic transition has broken down the traditional gender roles, which required men to keep up the role of the main bread winner. In new conditions the number of women undertaking the role of breadwinner has increased and created unprecedented problems for themselves and society. But it is true that radical changes to the economic and political landscape, especially the absence of necessary infrastructure for a capitalist market have had negative effects in Kazakh society, including spiralling unemployment, poverty and crime rates (Evelyn Zellerer and Dmitriy Vyortkin, 2004: 445).

Mother, Childcare and Education

Child birth in Kazakhstan occurs in a hospital under the care of a doctor whenever possible. Every district in the country has a hospital and medical care is free; patients only pay for drugs and specialised test and care. Babies are well cared for and cherished by all groups in Kazakhstan. Independence and access to market have brought improved access to infant care products. According to the official statistics, the level of infant and child mortality is steadily decreasing. In particular, infant mortality has reduced from 26.4 cases per 1000 new born in 1990 to 14.1 in 2006. However, even these indicators of infant mortality in Kazakhstan are considered by the WHO to be one of the highest compared to European countries. In most cases i.e. 62.1 per cent children died in early neo-natal period, 20.5 per cent during the post-neo-natal period (Mussiraly Utebaev, 2008: 82).

Furthermore, starting on January 1, 2008, Kazakhstan used criteria of viability valuation, live birth and dead birth, recommended by the

WHO. As per the statistics of the WHO, maternal mortality is higher in Kazakhstan than the European countries. A negative impact on the health of children and women is caused by limited access of vital infrastructure, in particular, to pure drinking water, heating system and road. The Kazakh government aimed for 2015 to reduce 65 per cent child mortality and 75 per cent reduction in maternal mortality. In this direction all the preventive measures have been taken by administration. For instance, reforming efforts on decreasing neo-natal mortality, improvement of an efficient pre-natal assistance system and further improvement of the system of public health services and improvement of the social welfare of the population of the republic is necessary (Mussiraly Utebaev, 2008: 82).

After privatisation, a great decline has been observed in the pre-school facilities in Kazakhstan. Such facilities were available to 47.9 per cent of the children in 1990, and the same declined upto 27.6 per cent in January 2007. In total, more than one-three of children in the Kazakh republic are not in position to attend elementary school, about 80 per cent of children of pre-school age with limited abilities do not have the opportunities to complete physical and mental development during the most important period of their lives (Mussiraly Utebaev, 2008: 81). Shrinking in public services is actually hampering women's growth in society. it is not only making an ill-effect over children but over women also extensively. Women are really under a great deal of pressure with household chores and other responsibilities and when public services are not available in the surrounding, it really holds back women from their desired place.

A similar situation exists in regard to comprehensive schools. The reduction has occurred basically, within rural schools. The proportion of children trained during the second shift increased from 30.9 per cent in 1995 to 35.6 per cent in 2006. The proportion of children trained during the third shift increased from 0.46 per cent to 0.8 per cent. In total, the country lacks more than 153 thousand places for student (Mussiraly Utebaev, 2008: 81). In Kazakhstan, free education in public educational institutions is guaranteed to all citizens, but higher education is expensive. Hardly 8 per cent people are able to access higher education.

Table 3.8: Dynamics of Human Development Index Components and HDI Disaggregated by Gender in Kazakhstan, 1998-2000

Description	*1998*	*1999*	*2000*	*2001*	*2002*	*2003*	*Increase*
Life Expectancy Index	0.757 0.567	0.767 0.588	0.768 0.587	0.772 0.592	0.775 0.595	0.775 0.592	0.018 0.025
Education accessibility Index	0.925 0.915	0.932 0.922	0.939 0.929	0.945 0.935	0.954 0.940	0.959 0.942	0.034 0.027
Income Index	0.600 0.687	0.602 0.696	0.586 0.731	0.619 0.753	0.643 0.670	0.661 0.788	0.061 0.101
HDI	0.761 0.723	0.767 0.735	0.764 0.749	0.779 0.760	0.790 0.769	0.797 0.775	0.036 0.052

Note: numerator – women, denominator – men

Source: National Human Development Report for 2004, Education for all: the Key Goal for a New Millennium, *UNDP Kazakhstan,* 2004, Almaty, p. 29.

In general, there is no gender disparity in access to education. At the end of 2003, the level of education accessibility for women was 0.959 which was slightly higher than that of men i.e. 0.942. Despite the fact that women had lower income than men by 0.127 in the index. But there is existing stereotype of gender role in Kazakhstan society. Young girls choose the field of education for career (86 per cent) whereas young boys choose Electrical Engineering (94 per cent). The women are quite less in number at higher positions, e.g. in 2004, professors in higher educational institutions were 18.6 per cent women and 81.4 per cent men, and even today there is hardly any change in the condition (CEDAW, Monitoring of Implementation of Recommendations, 2006: 5).

Healthcare

The Kazakh government provides free healthcare facility to its society. However, bribes often are necessary to obtain required care. The quality of healthcare which remained entirely under state control till 2006 has declined in the post-Soviet era because of insufficient funding and loss of technical experts through immigration and lack of government funding. The most common diseases are respiratory, cardiovascular condition and tuberculosis. Since 2000, the incidents of Human Immuno-Deficiency Virus (HIV) have been increasing and higher than its four neighbouring countries combined. Vulnerable groups include intravenous drug users (IDUs), commercial sex workers, prisoners and youth. The 70 per cent of HIV infected persons are aged from 15-29 and injecting drug user represent 83 per cent of HIV infected people. In 2003, an estimated 23,000 citizen had HIV. An outbreak of juvenile HIV was caused by improper hospital techniques gained national attention (Kazakhstan Profile, *http://www.ifrc.org/../05AA075profiles.pdf*).

The pregnant women have poor knowledge about specific HIV transmission from mother and child and do not know about the means of reducing such infections. That is why, in recent year efforts have been made to cover all pregnant women with full prevention services and the mother to child prevention is a big part of the Kazakhstan HIV programme. The wide expansion of tobacco and alcohol consumption is also affecting the health condition of the population which is rapidly deteriorating. Today, in Kazakhstan every fifth woman smoke and every seventh woman take alcohol. Free surgeries on abortion decreased women's death rate from home abortion; in 2000 it was 713 while in 2002 it went down to 173 (CEDAW, Monitoring of Implementation of Recommendations, 2006: 5). So far as such cases are concerned now the nationwide situation is improving satisfactorily.

In Kazakhstan, a woman is given the right to decide for herself the issue of motherhood. In order to protect women's health, modern method of contraception can be used by her consent; surgical sterilisation can be carried out only by her consent if there are medical indication and her will. It is obvious that the first item includes discriminative aspect in respect to men in the area of family planning. It sometimes happens in Almaty when men turned to the Centre of Family Planning to have surgical sterilisation, but they are refused and instead are asked to bring a medical certificate about their psycho-health conditions. According to the law, only men have right for surgical sterilisation in the republic and motherhood in the republic of Kazakhstan is protected and encouraged by state (CEDAW, Monitoring of Implementation of Recommendations, 2006: 34).

Therefore, even after providing many rights to women and laws have been structured in favour of women in the Kazakh system, there is an evident disparity existing in the status of men and women and it seems that men are enjoying the dominant position in Kazakh society. It does not mean that position of women is deplorable in this country, but at the same time it is also a fact that the current position of women in Kazakhstan is no better than the Soviet regime. It is essential to know the problems of Kazakh society simultaneously with its structure of family, education, health and customs etc. All these factors are directly or indirectly related with women in society. The problems of domestic violence, prostitution, unemployment, bride kidnapping and drug addiction etc. have already been discussed in this chapter.

Kazakhstan is a diversified liberal society; yet the legacy of Islamic influence and Nomad setting preserves several customs which are not at all favourable to women in the country. Such a context is favourable to a patriarchal social order. But at the same time the impact of European liberalism and Nomadic freedom prevent it not to be a rigid society. Besides, it is also true that after independence all Central Asian states had to undergo a social transition and this common shift mostly influenced women in these countries. But women were helped a lot by the Soviet legacy (i.e. literacy, awakening for women's rights, abolition of dogmatic customs and economic independence) to sustain their own condition in the society. Women are really in a better position if an evaluation has to be made regarding her position in society overall from 1991-2000 and 2000 onwards.

Structure of Uzbek Society

Uzbekistan is the most populous country in the Central Asian region with an area of 447,400 sq. km., the population of Uzbekistan is five times that of Kyrgyzstan or Turkmenistan; currently standing at 27,600,000 people (in 2008), 37 per cent of which is urban, while 63 per cent are rural population (80 per cent of population is Uzbeks, 5.5 per cent Russians, 5 per cent Tajiks, 3 per cent Kazakhs, 2.5 per cent Karakalpakas, 1.5 per cent Tatars and 2.5 per cent Other Nationalities). Uzbekistan is a multinational country; there are more than 25 representatives of different nationalities and ethnic groups. But Uzbek ethnicity is in majority in Uzbekistan. Over 60 per cent of the population lives below the poverty line.

After independence, there was a surge of interest in Islam, including the emergence of political Islamic groups seeking to the challenges secular nature of Central Asian States. The heavy handed repression of early manifestations of political Islam led to violence, and the appearance of extremist and terrorist groups in Uzbekistan society. Many Islamists fled first to the Tajikistan and then to the Afghanistan where they formed the Islamic Movement of Uzbekistan (IMU). In Uzbekistan, there is an another radical group Hizb-ut-Tahrir which seeks the overthrow all secular states in the region in favour of a single Islamic Caliphate, although it claims to be committed to non-violence (ICG Report "Central Asia: Islam and the State", 2003: i).

In Uzbekistan, the government strengthened its anti-Islamist propaganda and took steps to interdict Islamist individuals, literature and financial resources coming into Uzbekistan from Pakistan and Middle East. In 1997, when Islamist movement reach its peak, sources estimated that Uzbekistan had more than 4200 mosques of which 2433 operated in Ferghana valley. In 1998, the government endeavoured to limit extremist tendencies imposing rigorous restrictions on the establishment and operation of unregistered religious educational institutions and mosques. As a result, in 1999, official statistics reported the existence of only 1566 registered mosques and official Muslim schools (Alisher Ilkhamov, 2001: 45).

The revival of Islam also speeded up and recharged all Islamic rituals and traditions in the country which were completely banned during the Soviet period and it really affected the women's position in the state. Presently, many young women can be seen in *Hijab* at public places, at the same time one can find veiled women working in kiosks and restaurants in both semi-rural and urban settings. While the majority of Central Asian women have worn headscarf at some point in their lives, there is a new way many Uzbek women are wearing them today. Though a national dress code has been decided for women in Uzbekistan in which a patterned scarf wear on the head and tied at the back of the neck, leaving the face open unlike what is regarded as an Arab or Islamic dress – a dark coloured scarf clasped in front or cover the face. The latter style of dress is not acceptable because it does not conform to Uzbek tradition. In Uzbek education system, schools and university claiming that such form of public display are evidence of Muslim extremism, fundamentalism or Wahhabi sentiment and threaten the state's commitment to secularism and because of that these educational institutions have been expelling female students who cover their face and do not confirm to the Uzbek standards of dress (David Abramson, 2006: 6-7).

The influence of Islam has enhanced the polygamy culture in Uzbek society. Women like to be the second wife rather than live as a single woman. As per the law polygamy is an illegal act and further it is subject to criminal penalty. The law envisages either a fee reaching 50-100 times the minimum salaries, or penal labour and imprisonment upto three years; everything depends on a specific case (Uzbekistan: Polygamy in Central Asia, *http://www.wluml.org*). Despite all these legal provisions, the practice of polygamy continues to remain socially acceptable and does not result in punishment.

The radical Islam is having a negative impression due to terrorism and Uzbek society is not attracted to this phenomenon. In March 2004, the blast in Chorsu market of Tashkent is an evident example of a fanatic movement and was carried out by a woman suicide bomber. A nineteen years old girl, Dilnoza Holmuradova, exploded herself killing at least 47 people, including 10 policemen. Dilnoza came from an educated middle class family, was well educated and joined the Tashkent police academy in 2001, having competence in 5 languages. After dropping out of the police academy she started studying religious literature in 2002. The religious leaders she encountered during the meetings appeared to have left a deep impression on the teenager. In 2004, she and her sister left home without a word to their parents taking their Islamic literature in the house with them. The central police department in Tashkent says Dilnoza and her 22 years old sister Shahnoza were active members of a radical Islamic groups and that both had received training in some unspecified country. Her recruitment by the Islamic Jihad Group, a radical off shoot of the Islamic Movement of Uzbekistan, likely resulted in her decision to carry out the operation (Farhana Ali, 2006: 24).

Another woman who is said to have blown herself up was 26 years old Zahro Turaeva – again a woman with good prospect who had graduated from the University of Technology and was employed in a government office for architecture and construction. It is necessary to understand the circumstances in the society which prompted Dilnoza, Shahnoza and Zahro to blow themselves up and what sort of impact all such activities have in the society. One thing common in all these episodes was that women especially religious ones and those wearing scarves are suspect in the eyes of security forces. According to Human Right Watch, hundreds of women have been rounded up, beaten, harassed and intimidated and even raped. The whereabouts of several women are not known, many women being held in custody following the suicide attack are those whose husbands or brothers are in jail (Sudha Ramchandran, *http://www.atimes.com/../FD28Ag01.html*).

At this moment one can observe more fatal conditions in Uzbekistan where more suicide attacks can be expected in the coming years and in all likelihood, the bombers will be women. Women suicide bomber are less likely to be detected and they can be easy targets of radical Islamic groups. The crisis of terrorism and extremism are crushing a number of innocent people in Uzbek society. Among those whom the government has targeted are not only member of extremist groups such as the Islamic Movement of Uzbekistan (IMU), but also outfits like the *Hizb-ut-Tahrir*, which though Islamist has been moderate in its method so far. What is more, many of those who have been rounded up and tortured are just devout Muslim with no links to terrorism. According to Human Right groups 6000-7000 Muslim men have been jailed in recent years on charges that they are trying to overthrow Karimove's secular government. Many of them are missing, perhaps killed during torture in custody (Sudha Ramchandran, *http://www.atimes.com/../FD28Ag01.html*).

The women who are associated with these personnel all the time live their lives under the gloom of uncertainty and fear. Thus, the religion that was trying to offer an identity to Uzbek society after 1991 is harming negatively in contemporary times. All such pressures are directly and indirectly making its own negative impacts not only over her social but economic, political and religious life too.

Tradition, Culture and Family

In Uzbekistan, a New Family Code was developed in consultation with the public and adopted in 1998. The marriage, childcare, spouse rights and duties and property rights all are determined by the same family code in Uzbek society. Marriage is based on the willing consent and forcing women to marry or obstructing marriage is prohibited. The age for entering into marriage is 18 for men and 17 for women (Article 15 of the Family Code). If an individual wishes to enter into marriage at an earlier age, in exceptional cases, local administration may lower the marital age by a maximum of one year. The marriages registered by civil status registration bodies are legally valid (Article 13 of the Family Code) and marriages entered into by a religious ceremony is not legally recognised and a woman marrying by a religious ritual, unlike the legal wife cannot claim her share in jointly procured property, child maintenance etc. Marriage is not permitted between individuals if one is already married or if parties entering into marriage are to direct relatives.

In Uzbek society both men and women have equal rights to instigate a divorce but the family code contain a provision, prohibiting husband to divorce his wife during pregnancy or within one year from the birth of the child (Article 39 of the Family Code). The childcare and rearing as well as all family matters are joint responsibility (Article 21 of the Family Code). The unmarried mothers are not given a rightful honour in the Uzbek society that pushes women to be the second wives easily. The polygamy is very common and can be observed anywhere though the family code has sanctioned only one marriage in Uzbek society. The family code also regulates spouses' property ownership relations. It stipulates that spouses enjoy equal rights to mutual owned property even in the case when one of them is engaged in housekeeping, childcare or other activities preventing him/her to be gainfully employed. But this does not apply to the couples living together without formal matrimonial registration (Gender Briefing Kit, The Legal Framework, 2004: 2).

Nevertheless, women's high legal status does not reflect women's real status on the ground. Women's legal rights are frequently infringed upon. There is gross under-reporting of discrimination and violence against women, particularly when it occurs in the family. The report on the status of women in Uzbekistan (1999) noted that women are the first to lose their jobs, especially women with many children. The forced early marriage and the refusal to allow women to work outside the home also violate the rights of women. The family prefers to deal with or is more likely to be quiet on domestic and sexual violence against women and children. This makes it more difficult for authorities to prosecute and emphasises the role that culture and lack of legal literacy play in the continuing violation of the rights of women and children in Uzbekistan.

The self-immolation and suicide rate is rapidly increasing in Uzbek society, the reason behind this is that women are unable to adjust themselves in this transitional period (i.e. women are caught between the liberal Soviet legacy and the rigid traditional revival). There is a great anxiety in the families because of the parents' intolerance about the desires and aspirations of their daughters. In one such family, a young girl committed suicide by jumping from the ninth storey of a building. In other case, a daughter died as a result of severe cuts following a fight over whether she should be allowed to cut her hair. Her parents were categorically against this before her marriage (Wendy Mee, 2001: 17). There are many cases where husbands do not allow their wives to work outside the home or when religious fanatics demand that young women cover their face in the presence of men in public places. Young girls are sometime forced into early marriage, thus posing a serious threat physically and psychologically. There are a number of examples in Tashkent when disabled women or women with many children were refused employment and those who are working in private sector being prohibited to have children.

Women also face discrimination in courts. In one case the court made a decision in favour of the husband in setting a divorce dispute. In this case, he was awarded ownership of their jointly owned house, and asked to pay the wife financial compensation of 15,000 sum (about US$ 30-40 at the time). In another case, a woman with two children was actually deprived of her right to her share of property. The main reason for the discrimination against women is that a few women have a sound understanding of their legal rights. According to a survey conducted by Centre of Sociological Research, only 26.4 per cent of women had good understanding of their legal rights; 60.1 per cent women said that they know something of legal law; and 13.5 per cent responded that they know nothing (Wendy Mee, 2001: 18).

On an average, women in Uzbekistan considered more than three children ideal. Rural women wanted more children than urban women, and women with primary and secondary education wanted larger families than women with vocational and higher education. The ideal number of children was higher among Uzbeks than among women of other ethnicities (Among Uzbekistani Women, 1998: 43). A desire to have large families and many sons is still customary, particularly in rural areas. A survey carried out by the Women's Resource Centre in Tashkent region in 1995 found that 70 per cent of women with four children still wish to have more and more sons. The traditional Uzbek family is regarded as complex based on patrilocal residence and patriarchal authority structures on the basis of seniority and gender. In such families, the father is the head of the family, followed by his wife, and then by their sons in order of seniority, and finally by the son's wives in order of seniority (.Wendy Mee, 2001: 29).

Most births (94 per cent) take place in a hospital. However, if the mother was 35 or older or if the mother had three or more births, the birth are more likely to have occurred without prenatal care. About 19 per cent of children under three are underweight for their age, and 5 per cent were severely underweight. The infant mortality rate fell from 70.8 in 1993 to 34 in 2008 at per every 1000. The maternal mortality rate also reduced and it was only 24 in 2008 for 100,000 live births. However, both international and local public health experts doubt that these numbers give an accurate estimate. Moreover, data collection is especially difficult in Uzbekistan where the local definition of maternal mortality does not correspond with international definition. Despite challenges in gathering an accurate statistics it is clear that the increasing immigration of medical workers is a serious threat to the health of women in difficult labour, as well as other citizens of Uzbekistan (Maternal Mortality in Central Asia, 2008).

Healthcare in Uzbekistan

The condition of child mortality and maternal mortality is not good in Uzbek society. The current data associated with maternal death in Uzbekistan indicates the presence of higher proportions among the 21 to 24 age groups. The major cause of the high rate of maternal mortality is related to the social, cultural and legal guidelines supporting the early marriage of women. Furthermore, the existing gender disparities in education also play an important role in women's and children's ability to protect themselves. Education affects women's capabilities to maintain not only their children's health but also their own. The high level of anaemia, poor nutrition and frequency of child birth, all contribute to increasing vulnerabilities of during child birth (Gender Briefing Kit, Gender and the MDGs, 2004: 7).

In Uzbek society poverty has become more feminised. Women are usually paid less because they represent the majority in the area such as education, medical service, social activities, culture etc. where the salary scale is lower. Women are often offered less prestigious and lower paid jobs from the very beginning because of their low level of education. The constitution has given equality and many other supportive provisions on economic ground to women but in reality women's income is significantly less than men (women's wages are approximately 2/3 of men's) (Gender Briefing Kit, The Legal Framework, 2004: 3).

Even after all such huge social denial towards women in Uzbekistan, the life expectancy is more than men in the country (i.e. 72 for women and 68 for men). The centrally planned health system has its advantages, as is evident from the basic health indicators of the population of Uzbekistan. Healthcare is widely accessible in both rural and urban areas; the number of healthcare facilities and professionals in relation to the size of population is high. The health system possesses an abundance of resources, but fails however to use those resources efficiently. In Uzbekistan, the problems of developing world e.g. infectious diseases and high infant and maternal mortality are combined with high rates of diseases associated with comparative affluence – cancer, coronary heart diseases, transmitted disease and accident cases are the primary problematic zones in the health sector in Uzbekistan. The key reason for all these health problems are the lack of hard currency for procuring medicines, low salary for health care workers and increased consumption of cheap and low valued food products (National Human Development Report, 1995: 7).

HIV/AIDS has become a serious challenge in Uzbekistan. From 1987 to 1999 there were only 76 registered HIV cases but the number has been constantly increasing since 2000.

Table 3.9: Registered Cases of HIV/AIDS in Uzbekistan from 2000-2007

Year	*Registered Cases*
2000	154
2001	549
2002	981
2003	1836
2004	2016
2005	2010
2006	7600
2007*	16000*

*Children, HIV and AIDS in *www.avert.org/children.htm*

Source: Djamoliddin Fazylov and Galina Smirnova, "The Development of Education: National Report of Uzbekistan", 26 September 2008.

Among HIV infected women's percentage is 18.4 per cent while children's is 1.5 per cent. The major causes of HIV infection are Injected Drug User, sexually transmitted infection, commercial sex workers and blood transfusion. Besides, there is a lack of mass awareness about this disease. In August 1999, law of the Republic of Uzbekistan on the prevention of diseases caused by HIV was adopted. There are 15 AIDS centre, 230 anonym centres and 10 NGOs working in sphere of HIV/AIDS prevention and support for vulnerable groups of population. A number of UN agencies, World Bank and other

International Organisations are working in the field of HIV/AIDS averting programmes (Gender Briefing Kit, The Millennium Declaration, 2004: 14). One of the main objectives of the education sector is to publicise healthy lifestyles among students and pupils. Additionally, Iodine and Ferrum deficiency, struggle against drug addiction, alcoholism and smoking are other active problems which are affecting health of the citizens in Uzbek society.

Women and Education

Uzbekistan is a country with high rate of literacy and this rate is 99.1 per cent. According to the Constitution of the Republic of Uzbekistan in Chapter 9, Article 41 it is stated, "Everyone shall have the right to education. The state shall guarantee free secondary education. Schooling shall be under state supervision." The pre-school education is the first stage of continuous education system. It ensures the formation of healthy, developed children, arouses their inclination to learning, preparing them for systematic study. The pre-school education in Uzbekistan is provided in the national language along with languages of other ethnic groups. Now a days, there are 6232 pre-school education institutes which cover 554,171 children, 2346 pre-school institutions are in urban areas cover 296,807 children, 3886 per-school establishments are in rural areas and cover 257,364 children. At the same time, there are 72 Non-governmental pre-school institutions which cover 4000 children (Djamoliddin Fazylov and Galina Smirnova, 2008: 4).

During last 10 years the coverage of children of pre-school age increased from 18 to 22 per cent. The ministry of Public Education in cooperation with UNICEF is conducting a project on pre-school upbringing in the family. In the last few years the number of children enrolled in pre-school education has increased to 1991 but the real percentage of children in pre-school education has declined as compared to 1991. In 1990, there was 70 per cent enrollment recorded in pre-primary institutes in Uzbekistan but the same was reduced to 28 per cent in 2006. The main causes that are obstructing the pre-school education system are shift to home or family – based upbringing of pre-school age children, reduction of subsidies provided by the state and therefore, increased fee paid by the parents. Further, the unemployment of women made them stay at home and take care of their children (Djamoliddin Fazylov and Galina Smirnova, 2008: 5). All this has enhanced the pressure of family responsibility on the Uzbek women and as a result her public life is critically distorted.

The nine years general secondary education in Uzbekistan is compulsory and free. All children of school age attend general and specialised (for children with special need- physical and mental) primary school. The primary education covers 100 per cent of children of the respective age groups. Secondary specialised vocational education became compulsory from 2009. The objective of secondary specialised vocational education is not only intensive intellectual development and in-depth study of general subjects, but also preparing graduates to join the labour market and providing them with professional skills. Secondary specialised vocational education is provided on a full-time basis, in two types of education establishments i.e. academic lyceums and vocational colleges. There is a slight difference in the enrollment of male and female students in secondary level education 92.2 per cent and 90.7 per cent respectively (Education Statistics: Uzbekistan, *http://www.childinfo.org/files/CEECIS_Uzbe...*).

Higher education is expensive, limited and provisioned quota with entrance exam in Uzbekistan. Now there are 66 higher educational institutes, 22 of which are universities, 42 institutes and 2 academies. The share of girls amongst in higher education is low (40 per cent) as compared to boys. In 2007-08, the percentage of boys and girls studying in schools was almost equal i.e. 51 per cent for boys and 49 per cent for girls. But the ratio of boys and girls studying in academic lyceums was 64 per cent and 36 per cent, in colleges it was 53 per cent and 47 per cent (Djamoliddin Fazylov and Galina Smirnova, 2008: 5). The reasons behind the less involvement of women in higher education are family problems and economic constraints. This trend parallels social and cultural ideas that support girls being kept at home to assist in domestic works and in some cases to work in the family farms and in other form of informal employment.

The concern in the area of gender and education can also be discussed in relation to the family code of Uzbekistan, and to specific provisions which allow for men and women to be married at 18 and 17 years of age respectively. The code also allows for the possibility of marriage at an earlier age. The relevance of such provisions relates directly to the probability of men and women to be married at early ages, at the cost of completing school (Gender Briefing Kit, The Millennium Declaration, 2004: 10).

It can be observed that Uzbek society is a patriarchal, traditional and stable one. Being a society with such characteristics it could neither assume the transformation in its social structure nor could it sustain all this for longer time. Because the culture of a stable society is developed over a very long period, it cannot be changed from outside. The recent example in this regard is that all the forcible changes (ban on polygamy and veiling, equal rights to women etc.) made by the USSR are getting eroded with the passage of time though they were very favourable for a progressive society.

In Uzbekistan, Muslims are in majority and that is why Islamic customs and traditions are quite admired in this society. On the other hand, Uzbekistan is also experienced the impact of the Soviet legacy. As a result one can view high literacy rate in the state and the Uzbek government is very anxious and wants to bring an end to the revival of all the societal practices which were prohibited by the Soviet system. But still women are far behind in terms of equality in the state. The revival of Islam is flourishing many social customs which are fatally harming women's position in the society. The Uzbek population is also increasing constantly but at the same time the government facilities and other welfare schemes are not rising in that proportion. Additionally, the rural society is facing many problems as compared to urban setting. There is a lack of fundamental needs like water, sewerage and transport. The structure of family is also quite large. Women's low economic and political status is directly related to their heavy domestic responsibilities.

Finally, all this denotes that after 1991 like other Central Asian states, the responsibilities (of homecare, childcare, self-education, self-employment, to improve economic condition of the family and adjustment within the family) on Uzbek women also increased and that aggravated her position in the society. The Uzbek women are countering a large amount of complex trends like prostitution, polygamy, suicidal bomb, religious extremism, poverty and domestic violence. The domestic violence is sanctioned by the society and families or at least seen as a private matter.

Kazakhstan and Uzbekistan got their independence in 1991, with a rich legacy of USSR. Both states are religiously Muslim dominated, patriarchal and agrarian in nature. Both are having almost 100 per cent literacy rate and faced an economic crisis after attaining sovereignty, equally having socialist values and authoritarian political background. But at the same time, as far as the positions of women are concerned, both societies have great disparity. Kazakh is a nomadic society but Uzbek society has a stable structure. Over many centuries and being immediate neighbours, it seems that the social characteristics of these societies are overlapping each other. For instance, agriculture and heterogeneity are the features of a stable society that can be viewed easily in Kazakhstan and homogeneity, bride kidnapping and polygamy which are considered nomadic characteristics have become the identity of Uzbek society.

If a comparison has to be made of women's position in these two different societies, then Kazakh women are living a better life in some terms, equal in some way and worse in few matters to the Uzbek women. The Kazakh women are having a sound footing in higher education, employment, family liberty, maternal and child health security, divorce and marriage provisions, social security and less rigidity of Islam than the Uzbek women. In social customs, wages and participation in political and public decision making women in both societies are facing a great disparity to men. Both are equally facing the problems of polygamy, bride-kidnapping, prostitution, drug addiction and trafficking, malnutrition, domestic violence and economic crisis in transition period. But over some issues Kazakh women are facing much difficulty than Uzbek women, e.g. women and drug trafficking, prostitution, drug and alcohol addiction and victim of HIV/ AIDS.

If the impact of Islam is measured then Uzbek society is much religious. In Kazakhstan there has been much less interest in ideologies that challenges secularism. In Uzbekistan, this has been oppressive in the extreme. But both states, however, have two aims: first, to control any appearance of political Islam whether moderate or extreme, since they are considered a threat to the constitutional order; secondly, to use Islam as a channel to promote their own ideology and campaigns, in general as a tool of the state.

Thus, it can be said that there are two specific differences between the Kazakh and Uzbek societies presently. First, Kazakh one is a multi-ethnic society with a fair number of Russian, Ukrainian, German population which are considered a liberal group of people, while Uzbek society is having a large majority of Uzbeks i.e. about 80 per cent and remaining 20 per cent are again dominated by Tatars and Tajiks and a very limited number of people of liberal mindset. All such factors are making Uzbek a traditional and rigid society. Second, the Islamic influence can be seen to have a strong presence in Uzbek society. The Uzbek government seeks to domesticate Islam by using it as a part of the nation building process, while putting limits on Islamic form of expression. It thus, brings religion into politics, but tries to subordinate it to national priorities. On the other hand, Kazakh government made its national identity on the basis of Kazakh language, Kazakh ethnicity, secular and liberal values. Religion is merely a personal subject and not a nationalised programme. The Uzbek women is toxically affected by both the internal social problems (customs, traditions and religion etc.) and external problems (drug and women trafficking, economic crisis, and global issues etc.) but the Kazakh women is much affected by external problems and less with internal troubles.

Chapter - 4

Changing Position of Women in Market Economy: Comparison of Kazakh and Uzbek Women

A market economy is a type of economic system in which the trading and exchange of goods, services and information takes place in a free market system. A market economy is therefore also known as a free market economy. The phrase is typically applied to countries or administrative regions that follow this approach. Since free markets are governed by the law of supply and demand, the marketplace itself will determine the price of goods and services, and this information will be made available to all participants. Business can decide which goods to produce and in what quantity, and consumers and businesses can decide what they want to purchase and at what price.

Additionally, a market economy requires an effective financial sector. Private banks, created through privatisation of state-owned banks, as well as encouraging the emergence of new banks and establishment of foreign banks, are necessary for investments and important for the privatisation process in general (Gros and Steinherr, 2004: 297). In contrary, a planned economy is where the government decides what to produce, in what quantity and to be sold at what price. The mixed economies are a merge of market and planned economies, meaning that the government will have some role in regulating the market, but all other activities will be driven by the decisions of buyers and sellers.

Since the government will always have some level of regulatory control, no country operates as a free market in the strict sense of the word, but it is generally said that the market economies are those in which governments attempt to interfere as little as possible; while the mixed economies include the elements of both capitalism and socialism. The main characteristics of a market economy are its flexibility and decentralised nature. This type of economic system is more suitable to cope up with ever changing market trends making it faster and more reactive. Regardless of the government's role, decisions made in free market economy are primarily made by the invisible hand of the market forces and not mandates issues by the government.

Women in Kazakh Economic System

Since independence, in late 1991 all the Central Asian countries were forced with break down and the centrally planned economies during the Soviet era followed the market economy. Despite some similarity of economic structure, they have pursued differing development strategies. The Central Asian Republics' (CARs) role in the Soviet division of labour was as producers of raw materials. The Kazakh Republic's higher living standards reflected a more diversified economy with grain exports and a variety of minerals and energy resources. The Uzbek Republic's economy was dominated by cotton, as were neighbouring parts of two other republics. Turkmenistan had experienced a boom in natural gas production during the closing decade of the USSR, while the mainly mountainous Kyrgyz and Tajik republics had fewer exploitable resources. The Central Asian Republics were almost totally unprepared for the rapid dissolution of the Soviet Union in 1991. As new independent states at the end of that year they faced two major economic shocks: these were the transition from central planning and hyper inflation. Dismantling the centrally planned economy created severe disorganisation problems, which lead to output decline everywhere in Central Asia, and attempts to maintain existing trade, commercial and political links by retaining a common currency fuelled hyper price increases (Richard Pomfret, 2001:185).

The current chapter discusses the effects of market economy over Kazakh and Uzbek women. Firstly, in this regard the condition of Kazakh women has been examined; Kazakhstan- a large country, larger than all the other Central Asian states with a small population, a country rich in natural resources, adopted the market economy with full vigour. It is prodigiously rich in oil, gas and mineral deposits and also it is the major source of non-ferrous metals like Zinc, Lead, Titanium, Magnesium, Chromium Iron and Gold (Amy L. Chua, 1998: 80). Kazakhstan had a better base for creating a market economy, given its higher living standards and human capital endowments, and it too was initially viewed as one of the more reformist Soviet successor state. Although macro-economic control was attained more slowly than in the Kyrgyz Republic, with an annual inflation rate of 50 per cent in 1996. Kazakhstan did more fairly quickly with price liberalisation and enterprise reform.

The privatisation process, or more specifically the policies towards energy and mineral rights, has however been associated with wide spread corruption, and a sense of "casino or crony" capitalism. Such practice in a country with poor institutions is ideal for corruption to occur. Corruption is associated with lower investment, lower economic growth, misallocation of resources, and increased income inequality and poverty (IMF, 1999: 74). The Kazakh government has eagerly embraced IMF reforms, adopted over 130 market-friendly laws, expanded trade vigorously, privatised most of its industrial giants, including the country's major oil and gold facility and signed dozens of multi-million dollars international deals (Sander Thoenes, 1996: 4).

The Kazakh government swiftly began to implement reforms that would make the nation increasingly attractive to foreign interest, while avoiding the more severe consequences of the financial *shock therapy.*[1] Kazakhstan was the first to pay off its debts to the IMF in 2000 following economic reconstruction (seven year ahead of the schedule), the first to obtain a favourable credit rating, the first to implement financial institutions approaching Western standards of efficiency and reliability, and the first to develop and introduce a fully funded nationwide pension programme. Besides, rising oil revenues, one of the key elements in Kazakhstan's economic success has provided it ability to attract foreign investors. The EU formally recognised Kazakhstan as a market-based economy in October 2000, while Washington accorded Kazakhstan similar recognition in March 2002 (John C.K. Daly, 2008: 7).

By and large, these market economy measures have been successful; most international observers today regard Kazakhstan as the wealthiest and the most politically stable in all the

Central Asian Republics. The economy of that country has been growing by 10 per cent for the last ten years between 1999-2009 and its GDP is larger than that of all remaining Central Asian countries combined. As for GDP per capita, it has grown from US $ 400 in 1991 to US $ 6500 in 2007. The Foreign Direct Investments (FDIs) exceeded US $ 60 billion in 2007. In 2008, the FDI inflow was recorded US $ 14.5 billion. The FDI stock grew from US $ 10 billion in 2000 to US $ 58 billion in 2008, thereby contributing 44 per cent to Kazakhstan's GDP (UNCTAD, 2009: 250).

Secondly, Kazakhstan alone attracted almost 80 per cent of all FDIs to Central Asian States. Currently Kazakhstan is a net exporter of capital; the Kazakh entrepreneurs had already invested by 2007 more than US $18 billion in foreign economies, among them US $ 5.3 billion is made in European Union (EU) countries. International experts estimate the potential of Kazakh companies to invest abroad at over US $ 40 billion. At present the Kazakh investors are encouraged to actively enter foreign markets through buying shares of successful companies overseas and participating in large scale projects and thus acquired a footing in prospective role of the world economy (Kairat Umarov, 2007).

As a result of government's comprehensive economic reforms and due to the continued exploitation and trade of its rich mineral resource, Kazakhstan has become one of the economic leaders of the former Soviet Union. In recent years, the country has experienced an extraordinary economic boom followed by a combination of high world oil prices; expanded domestic production, increased investment, strong domestic consumption and balanced macro-economic policies. As an outcome of all this, the Kazakh GDP is rapidly growing 2000 onwards, only in 2008, 3.3 per cent growth was recorded in GDP due to the decline in oil prices and global economic downturn.

Table 4.1: The Constant Growth in the Kazakh GDP, 2000-2007

Years	*GDP Growth in per cent*
2000	9.8
2001	13.2
2002	9.2

(Contd...)

2003	9.5
2004	9.4
2005	9.2
2006	10.6
2007	8.7

Source: Maarten van Klaveren et al. (May 2010), "An Overview of Women's Work and Employment in Kazakhstan" Working Paper 10-93, *Amsterdam Institute for Advanced Labour Studies (AIAS)*, University of Amsterdam, pp. 21-22.

Kazakh agriculture suffers from environmental problems, but prospects for export of both livestock products and crops are good. The long-term prospects of agriculture in contemporary Kazakhstan's market economy system seem well. The financial indicators for the economy are strong but the country's manufacturing base remains weak. The price hikes in the everyday commodity, particularly in recent years have enabled the extra-active industries to modernise, but other sectors are being left behind. The area of oil, gas, mining and metals directly account for 35 per cent GDP and giving exposure to nearly 80 per cent of industrial output, and more than 80 per cent of exports and able to generate new jobs. After initial gains from aggressive economic reform, productivity has remained stagnant in other sector since 2001. The agriculture sector is considered one of the sustainable and reliable sectors in the economy of any country. While the agricultural labour productivity has been falling for more than a decade, the employment in agricultural jobs had increased to 35 per cent in 2003.

Table 4.2: Agricultural Labour Productivity and Percentage of Women Employment in Agricultural Sector in Kazakhstan

Agriculture Sector	*1998*	*1999*	*2000*	*2001*	*2002*	*2003*
Labour Productivity ($ per worker)	1309	1178	738	833	838	894
Employment (per cent)	22	22	31	35	35	35
Women Employees (per cent)	25	24	24	24	26	29

Source: World Bank (2005), *Getting Competitive, Staying Competitive: The Challenge of Managing Kazakhstan's Oil Boom.* Washington, DC.

As the above figures suggests, women employment in agriculture sector had more than doubled from 3.384 million (25 per cent of the total) in 1998 to 7.095 million (29 per cent of the total) in 2003 despite the low returns on their labour, because of the lack of other job opportunities in rural areas (ADB, Kazakhstan, Country Gender Assessment, 2006: 27).

Because of the boom of economy due to oil revenue Kazakhstan halved its poverty rate in just five years, which fell from five million or 39 per cent of the population in 1998 to three million or 20 per cent in 2003, the lowest poverty rate among the Central Asian States. However, according to UNDP 2005, a low aggregate income of the majority of people stands out as an important cause of poverty in Kazakhstan. The poverty in the country affects both men and women, employed and unemployed and urban and rural people. Most of the people are living their lives below poverty line, mainly to be found in rural area where a de-modernisation of the economy and society have taken place despite the growth of the oil and gas industry. There are significant regional disparities due the fact that economic reforms and economic growth have affected the regions differently. The southern agriculture *oblasts* (administrative territorial divisions) have traditionally high poverty indicators. In the western *oblasts*, such as Atyrau and Manghistau industrial production (oil and gas) is high. However, it is not being distributed to the population leading to high poverty among the rural people of these *oblasts* (Marie-Carin von Gumppenberg, 2007: 27).

To large extent, with the help of rich resources and the market economy system, the Kazakh government was able to prevent the country from very high levels of poverty and unemployment. But it was estimated in 2003 that 17.2 per cent of the country's population lived below the common UN income poverty measures of US $ 2 a day, and for 2004 this share was estimated at 10.4 per cent. In 1996, 5.0 per cent of the population was computed to live below the US $ 1.25 a day standards for extreme poverty and for 2004, 1.2 per cent population was estimated to live below this yardstick (Maarten van Klaveren, 2010: 33). Also in 1996, 34.6 per cent lived below the national poverty line, a share that had declined to 15.4 per cent in 2002 but increased to 16.1 per cent in 2004, when the national poverty line was 5427 Tenges (Kazakh currency) per month (UNDP 2008; UN MDG Indicators).

There are two basic forms of poverty in Kazakhstan, first is housing infrastructure conditions and the second is lacking of primary education. The more serious problem of the two is of housing and poor basic infrastructure. In 2002, an estimated 43 per cent population suffered from at least one form of poverty which 58 per cent in rural and 30 per cent in urban areas was recorded. By 2002, the pension system was the main mechanism for preventing poverty among the elderly citizens. But under the pension reform the level of benefits declined significantly below the 2002 level. The overall decline is driven by the steep decline in the value of women's pension due to the more direct relationship between wages and years of work in new system. According to the World Bank, "the significant reduction of pension benefits could lead to a greater prevalence of poverty among the elderly, especially women." (World Bank, 2004: 37)

Due to the booming economy, in major cities migration within and immigration from outside of Kazakhstan have increased decisively over the past years. Economic migrants have been attracted by the prospects of low skilled jobs in the growing construction and service sectors. There are a large number of migrants, mostly from under developed rural region in southern and western parts of Kazakhstan which are attracted by the concentration of new wealth in cities like Astana and Almaty. At the same time illegal migrants from neighbouring countries are floating the cities, working either temporarily or permanently in the country.

As a result, shack towns have sprung up on the outskirts of Astana, Almaty, and other cities creating social pressures and new lower class. The Almaty city administration has made several attempts in last few years to clear away these townships that have sprung up around the edges of the former capital in the recent years but has encountered stiff resistance from residents. As a result, tensions increased and protest actions began cumulating into the bloody clashes on 14 July 2006 (Marie-Carin von Gumppenberg, 2007: 27).

In the global perspective, Kazakhstan is located in the lower rank of human development. In 2006, the country ranked 71 in Human Development Index (HDI). The estimated earned per capita income for man was US $ 11782 and for woman US $ 8039 (UNDP, 2008), women in the country earning about 32 per cent less income than men.

This is quite a low rate indicator for the position of Kazakh women in the field of work and employment. During the period of 2001-2008, the number of male employees improved by 28 per cent and the number of female employees by 42.5 per cent. Each year female employment grew slightly more rapidly than male employment but such increase in total employment was a bit unpredictable (Maarten van Klaveren, 2010: 24).

The period from 2001-2008, the official unemployment rate of Kazakhstan gradually fell from over 10 per cent to below 7 per cent. Although the absolute gap between the male and female unemployment rate fell somewhat (in 2001 nearly 14 per cent of women were unemployed, against 10 per cent of men), but the female unemployment rate had elevated up to three times more than the males in 2008. During the period from 1991-2000 and 2001-2008, if a comparison is made in reference to general employment and especially women employment then the overall situation relatively improved in the later period.

Table 4.3: Employment in Various Industries and Total labour Force in Kazakhstan, 2008

Category of Industries	*All*		*Male*		*Female*	
	x1000	*Per cent*	*x1000*	*Per cent*	*x1000*	*Per cent*
Agriculture, Forestry, Fishing	2370	30.2	1250	31.1	1120	29.2
Mining	200	2.5	149	3.7	51	1.3
Manufacturing	573	7.3	360	9.0	213	5.5
Utilities (gas, water, electricity)	165	2.1	115	2.9	50	1.3
Construction	549	7.0	418	10.4	131	3.4
Wholesale and Retail	1150	14.6	470	11.7	680	17.8
Transport, Storage, Communication	589	7.5	434	10.8	155	4.0
Restaurants and Hotels	103	1.3	32	0.8	71	1.8
Finance	96	1.2	37	0.9	59	1.5
Real Estate, Renting, Business	378	4.8	182	4.5	196	5.1
Public Administration and Defence	375	4.8	206	5.1	169	4.4
Education	754	9.6	195	4.9	559	14.2
Health, Social work	347	4.4	82	2.0	265	6.9
Other Community Services	205	2.6	88	2.2	178	4.6
Total	**7857**	**100**	**4018**	**100**	**3839**	**100**

Source: Maarten van Klaveren et al. (May 2010), "An Overview of Women's Work and Employment in Kazakhstan" Working Paper 10-93, *Amsterdam Institute for Advanced Labour Studies (AIAS)*, University of Amsterdam, p. 38.

As the above data suggests, Kazakh women have an excellent presence in sectors like agriculture, forestry and fishing and record a very nominal participation in mining, utilities (gas, water and electricity) and construction. Women's participation is better than men in wholesale and retail trade, restaurant and hotels, education, health and social work while in all other categories women are lacking behind to men. In 2008, the total men labour force was 4,018,000 and women were 3,839,000 i.e. 48.9 per cent women's share in total work force and it gives a reflection of a legitimate participation at various workplaces in Kazakhstan.

Table 4.4: Employment in Various Occupational Groups and Total Women Labour Force in Kazakhstan, 2008

Various Occupational Groups	*x 1000*	*Per cent*
Legislators, Senior officials, Managers	194	38.3
Professionals	683	67.9
Technicians, Associate Professionals	467	65.4
Clerks	124	72.9
Service, Shop, Sales workers	717	66.6
Skilled Agricultural, Fishery workers	624	48.7
Craft and related trades	169	22.9
Plant & Machine operators and assemblers	77	10.8
Elementary occupations	777	47.8
Total	**3839**	**48.9**

Source: Maarten van Klaveren et al. (May 2010), "An Overview of Women's Work and Employment in Kazakhstan" Working Paper 10-93, *Amsterdam Institute for Advanced Labour Studies (AIAS)*, University of Amsterdam, p. 40.

The above figures reveals that women are principally involved in low paid jobs like the occupational groups of professionals, technicians, associate professionals, clerks, services, shops, sales workers and their number is quite low in power jobs where one has the power of decision- making in their respective professions. It means that the market economy has just provided woman an opportunity to work in Kazakhstan and their involvement in numbers at workplaces are improving primarily. There is a positive shift in the position of Kazakh women where they are making a move from working to an empowered position; a position where she could drive her thoughts in running the system. Yet, generally, the decision-making positions are still occupied by the males.

Table 4.5: Average Monthly Earnings in the Various Industries by Gender in Kazakhstan, 2008

(in Tenge)

Category of Industries	*Male*	*Female*	*Male/Female Gap in Per cent*
Agriculture	34084	24698	27.6
Fishing	30714	22428	27.0
Mining	117867	82517	30.0
Manufacturing	73457	48764	33.6
Utilities (gas, water, electricity)	60346	46423	23.6
Construction	83407	61985	25.7
Wholesale and retail	66094	51208	22.5
Transport, Storage, communication	87342	73749	15.6
Restaurant and hotels	90832	52137	42.6
Finance	178649	116749	34.7
Real Estate, Renting, Business	97807	84616	13.5
Public Administration and Defence	51670	40540	21.5
Education	37255	33506	10.1
Health, Social Work	39384	34952	11.2
Other Community and Personal Services	75816	47914	36.8
Total	**63441**	**43501**	**31.4**

Source: Maarten van Klaveren et al.(May 2010), "An Overview of Women's Work and Employment in Kazakhstan" Working Paper 10-93, *Amsterdam Institute for Advanced Labour Studies (AIAS)*, University of Amsterdam, p. 45.

The above statistics make one thing very clear that first of all, the male in each industry are earning more than females in terms of average income. In Table 4.3 and 4.4, it is clearly explained that in some occupations women are leading in number and it seems that they have an outstanding footing in some sectors but the amazing thing is that still even in those specific sectors their average income is lower to their male counterparts. Even the education level of women surpassed their male colleagues in their professional lives.

Apart from this, it is a global fact that women take their work and duty more sincerely and seriously. The average income gap between male and female grew from 30 per cent in 1990 to 38 per cent in 2002 (ADB, Kazakhstan, Country Gender Assessment, 2006: 28), and in 2008 this difference in income was 31.4 per cent. The things are shocking at this point, first, though the Kazakh GDP is improving the conditions of women income is no better than at the time of independence. Secondly, there is discrimination towards women in their professional life; the worst kind of discrimination being, the males employing men predominantly in key and high salaried positions in all relevant sectors. Sometimes women are not even equally paid for the same services compared to a male counterpart.

Besides, the wages varied largely across sectors, occupational categories and gender. They also vary widely across the urban and rural regions. In 2002, the average wage in rural areas (i.e. US $ 380 per year) was significantly lower and less than half of the average urban wage (i.e. US $ 797 per year). Further, this difference was more in some of the oblasts in Kazakhstan ranged from US $ 443 to US $ 1221 per year in 2002 (World Bank, 2004:18). The major factors behind this disparity are the agricultural employment and lack of education in rural areas. In addition, women who are living in rural areas are facing more hardships and there is a complete lack of basic necessities of life.

The negative impact of market economy increases their vulnerability to poverty and losses to the economy of highly educated workers. The wage gap sometimes is a disincentive for women to seek employment, especially when little childcare facility is available. Women would not be interested to improve their skills when they may not be promoted and given power posts. Women hold only 3 per cent of management positions despite being just under almost 50 per cent of work force. Most notably, with the public service, 77 per cent of lower positions are held by women despite their higher education.

In this way, they are facing vertical segregation in the market economic system. The women participation in Kazakhstan is basically in stereotyped jobs, for instance, education, social and healthcare, wholesale and retails, hotels and restaurant sectors but not in the sectors of high growth such as industry and processing. The Feminised sectors tend to have lower average salary, which contributes to the overall average wage gap between male and female. In that situation they are suffering from the horizontal segregation of market economic system (ADB, Kazakhstan, Country Gender Assessment, 2006: 28).

Due to all the above given reasons Kazakh women make up 51.2 per cent of all self-employed people. About 42 per cent of all women rely on self-employment compared with 36 per cent of men;

in rural areas 64 per cent of women are self-employed in low skilled agricultural activities. After the decline of social welfare facilities in Kazakhstan women have to bear family responsibility, while worrying their family financial conditions. So they do not have as much time for extra skilled training. Further, there is a complete lack of the availability of better training centres in rural areas. Without any other support, such as business training or access to markets for products or services, it is complicated for many women to expand self-employed activities into possible business enterprises. Thus, self-employment may not offer them a reasonable return on their labour as compared to men (ADB, Kazakhstan, Country Gender Assessment, 2006: 30-31).

Moreover, there is another effect of market economy on women in Kazakh society. After introducing that system there was a decline in marriages and low fertility rate is observed in that society. Though all the Central Asian states witnessed such decline after 1991 but the Kazakh society seems largely affected by this phenomenon. Nationally, the crude marriage rate declined from 10.1 marriages per thousand populations in 1991 to only 5.8 in 1999, a 43 per cent decline (Tatibekov, 2004: 8). The primary reasons behind this entire episode are that firstly, the market economy has enhanced the economic competition among the country's general population; secondly, women's involvement in such rivalry was also recorded.

Consequently, Kazakh women are not able to give rightful consideration to family and marriage. Therefore, such primary institutions like marriage and family are now at back foot and losing its grip in Kazakh society in contemporary times. On the other hand, there is a great influence of Europe over Kazakh society, as a result of which women are more concerned with their career and higher education. Subsequently, it has increased the age for marriage and simultaneously a drop in fertility was also noticed.

In 1988, the Total Fertility Rate (TFR) in Kazakhstan was recorded 3.16, it dropped to 1.76 in 2000; 2.16 in 2003; 1.89 in 2004; 1.89 in 2005; 1.89 in 2006; 1.89 in 2007; 1.88 in 2008; 1.88 in 2009 and 1.87 in 2010 (Kazakhstan, Total Fertility Rate, *www.indexmundi.com/kazakhstan/total_fertility_rate.html*). The fertility rating after 2003 is not satisfactory and is rather low; such index is not at all favourable for a healthy society. The total fertility rate may widely differ between population groups in regions also; in 1999, the TFR for ethnic Kazakh was 2.5 and that for Russian was less than 1.4; in the southern Kazakh the TFR was high on the other hand, while in western region it was quite low. The market economy has raised the rate of emigration and most emigrants are young adults of marriageable age, which also has a negative effect on fertility (Charles M. Becker and Ai-Gul S. Seitenova, 2005: 12-13).

Gender inequality is one of the structural socio-cultural causes hampering development in Kazakhstan. Such dissimilarity stems from the legacy of the past along with factors such as a traditional culture with weak democratic values, paternalistic relations in society, peculiarities of economic activity, dependence on mining industries, weak infrastructure, regional disparities, and unsustainable use of environmental resources. These causes lead to insufficient participation of women in different sectors of society, their exposure to various risks, and a growth in discrimination and sexism. Kazakhstan has the potential to achieve gender equality by 2015. The issue now is how this potential will be developed and used, how deep the institutional and cultural changes in the society will go, and whether new threats to equality might arise (Kazakhstan: Achievement, Issues and Prospects, a Perspective by the United Nations. 2004: 50).

The Kazakh society is still far from that ideal position where women are treated as equal to men. But it is true that the market economy has given women a better strength in their national economic system, their position is far better than many other countries in the region and the world in this respect. On the other hand, the present market economy system has snatched all the facilities which were provided by the Soviet Union to women, made it tough for women to work. In reality, now Kazakh women are lingering in the hardships of working women, family liabilities and the exploitive policies of MNCs. In brief, they are confronting the triple burden; however, their involvement and contribution is remarkable in making the present market economy system a success.

Women in Uzbek Economic System

The Soviet period the economic system of Uzbekistan was imbalanced. Overemphasis on cotton cultivation led to the dependence of the republic for food grains on other republics. The lack of agro-processing facilities turned the state mainly into a supplier of raw materials to the Soviet Union. All such situations had its impact on the future. But it does not mean that at the time of Soviet disintegration there was no industry available in Uzbekistan. The Uzbek economy had several branches of industry which were fairly well developed. They were electricity generation, steel processing and non-ferrous metallurgy, precious mineral industries particularly gold and silver and well developed silk industry. There was an aviation industry in the republic. However, the major branches were processing and agro-based industries and the agriculture sector remained the major source of income for the republic.

In 1991, after independence, the Uzbek minister for Local Industry, Victor Chizhen, reported that there was a huge storage of consumer goods due to the inefficiency of the mechanism and because of the Soviet economic legacy the Uzbek republic was not able to meet the local needs for many daily necessities such as soap, matchsticks etc. (R. G. Gidadhubli, 1994: 294). After attaining independence, the main objective of Uzbekistan has been the transition from socialist economy to market economy with the creation of multi-sector economy, competitive environment and gradual price liberalisation. With that in view, Uzbekistan has taken several measures to develop its economy on market principles. Several laws have been passed with regard to the ownership rights; entrepreneurship, decentralisation, privatisation and leasing etc. (R. G. Gidadhubli, 1994: 295).

All these laws facilitate the development of a legal basis for the formation of market infrastructures. Similarly as per a decree of the President of Uzbekistan, enterprises, organisations and private farmers can now make and exercise their own decisions. During the period of 1992-94, 54,000 former state enterprises and establishment were privatised. Out of these, 18,000 are privately owned, 26,000 are shareholding companies and 9100 are under collective ownership (R. G. Gidadhubli, 1996: 212). The average wage growth turned positively after adopting the market economy system, in 1995 to 2000 it was 12.50 per cent and in 2001 to 2007 it was 35.17 per cent. All this has had a very positive effect over the GDP of Uzbek economy, the annual growth average was 3.07 per cent from 1995 to 2000 and the same growth was extended to 6.27 per cent from 2000 to 2007 (ILO, Global Wage Report 2008/09, 2008: 81 and 103).

In place of Branch Ministries and Departments, new institutions have been created in the form of associations and concerns particularly with regard to certain key sectors of the economy such as food industry, consumer industry and gas industry and so on. Even in the rural sector new economic relations are being introduced. The peasant farming is gaining momentum and family farming is being encouraged to cater to the market needs of the society. Private enterprises have also been set up.

Islam Karimov, the President of Uzbekistan, is well familiar with the fact that in this changed scenario to bring political stability, the first and the foremost requirement is make a shift from socialist economy to free market economy. But at the same time he had an example of Russia's shock therapy. Karimov has noted that one should not demolish one's home before building a new one. In other words, Uzbekistan will make efforts to introduce changes in phases rather than bringing about an abrupt total change.

In this regard, it is claimed that the Uzbek model is substantially different from the approach of some other CIS republics. In particular, Uzbekistan does not propose to introduce shock therapy. It is true that the Uzbek government has introduced free market economy but they are of the firm opinion that the state should not totally give up the management of the economy. The state should remain the main reformer. It should set priorities and the sequence of phases in which transition could take place. This is in contrast to the approach of Kazakhstan (R. G. Gidadhubli, 1994: 295).

In fact, this policy was a requirement of the social setting of Uzbekistan and it had a positive effect on the GDP and production of the country. In the field of agriculture, more than 2.5 million subsidiary peasant farms have been set up. The yields in these farms are reported to be three times higher than on state farm land. After observing all this the Uzbek government has took the decision of converting all *sovkhozes* (state farms) and *kolkhozes* (collective farms) into private units. But the majority of farmer community was not in favour of all this. In consequence, this entire job was decided to be done in installments of 20 per cent-20 per cent. Hence, Uzbekistan's agriculture was stated to be moving towards market relations step by step (R. G. Gidadhubli, 1994: 295).

As low salary is paid to government employees in Uzbekistan many foreign firms are prevented from paying their workers as much as they like. Labour market regulation in Uzbekistan is similar to those of the Soviet Union, with all right guaranteed but right unobserved. Unemployment is growing and the number of people looking for jobs in Russia, Kazakhstan and South-East Asia is increasing every year. According to the official Ministry of Labour estimates around 10,000 citizen of Uzbekistan work abroad. Prices and monetary inflation was approximately 50 per cent in 2002 (R.G. Gidadhubli, 1994: 297).

The liberalisation of the trade regime, however, is a prerequisite for Uzbekistan to proceed to an IMF financial programme. Uzbekistan is a member of IMF, World Bank, Asian Development Bank and the European Bank for reconstruction and development. It has an observer status at the World Trade Organisation, is a member of World Intellectual Property Organisation and has publicly stated its intention to accede to the World Trade Organisation; it is a signatory to the Convention on Settlement of Investment Disputes Between States and Nationals for Other States, the Paris Convention for the Protection of Industrial Property, the Madrid Agreement on Trademarks Protection and the Patent Cooperation Treaty (Economy in Uzbekistan, *http://www.world66.com/../economy*).

In the changed economic environment Uzbekistan has benefited significantly from the boom in Kazakh and Russian economies, especially in the construction industry through remittances from its labour migrants. The labour migrants from Uzbekistan are mainly employed in the construction sector due to the high demand for labour. According to official statistics there are approximately 25,000-30,000 labour migrants from Uzbekistan. Some other sources assess it to be about 1-1.5 million. The primary destination countries are Russia where an estimated 70 per cent and Kazakhstan where perhaps 10-15 per cent Uzbek citizens make a move. For the last ten years, the economic well being of the Uzbek population has been steadily increasing. The official data illustrates a considerable increase in GDP as well as increase in average income, spending and saving. This is partially due to the remittances of labour migrants, who send money after the end of a working season (Umida Hashimov, 2009).

According to the Central Bank of Uzbekistan, only over the 2002-2006 periods the annual inflow of official transfer of funds to the country increased five-fold, reaching almost US $1.4 billion or 8.2 per cent of GDP in 2006. As data from the Centre for Economic Research (CER) for 2007 suggests that the overwhelming portion of money was transferred from Russia (78 per cent), Kazakhstan (5 per cent), the US and Korea (3.3 per cent), which account for most of the transfers (Umida Hashimov, 2009).

Remittances sent to Uzbekistan directly or indirectly increase the national and currency income and improve the balance of payments. Labour migrants also help to keep the unemployment rate relatively low because labour migrants vacate jobs in the internal labour market. It is important in a densely populated country like Uzbekistan, with an excess of workforce in the labour market. In other words, remittances have been a significant contributor to the economic growth of the country. But after the global financial crisis has moved the real estate and construction sector. As a result, construction activities are decreasing considerable in both Russia and Kazakhstan.

The labour migrants from Uzbekistan as well as from other Central Asian States are recently losing their jobs. Some of the migrants have started returning home as the demand for manual labour has dropped dramatically while the number of workforce has not. The income that was coming from outside, almost stopped. Simultaneously the migrants were returning back to their own country. All this has added to the problem of income and unemployment in Uzbekistan. Women had to face much difficulty in this situation than men. Despite Uzbek culture and custom, the women in the country made a channel for education and employment but the problem of unemployment has curtailed this opportunity.

Women are returning to their native place to be unpaid family labour, which seem surprising, taking into account the relatively high level of education of Uzbek women and their experience of salaried work and wage income. An indication of the subordinate position of women within families is the high number of children they bear, and the restrictions placed on their movement. It is not seen as appropriate for younger women to go to local market; men or older women in the family do so. Taking into account their heavy workloads at home and also in the household farm, perhaps women's unwillingness to take more responsibilities in reasonable (Susanna Lastarria Cornhiel and

Zoraida Garcia-Frias, Gender and Land Rights: Findings and Lessons from Country Studies).

The condition is also a result of how state policies currently and in the past have focused on granting certain benefits to women and not on attaining gender equality. While the socialist state promoted policies that benefited women, the objective these policies was to protect women as mother and as workers, but did not address the question of women's equal rights. Under the capitalist market policies, the focus is still on women as family workers and much of the rhetoric refers to women as representing traditional values. The institutions that support the market economy play a significant role in determining land rights. The market economy is generally based on rights to private property and the marketability of those rights. Land, like any other asset, is usually acquired through the market (leasing or buying or selling) at market values.

In Uzbek society where customary practices and traditional social structures dominate, land rights tend to be determined by socio-cultural or religious norms. As an outcome, no special steps were taken by the state with reference to the property and economic rights of women in Uzbekistan. This inaction in Uzbekistan has meant that largely men are in a position to acquire rights to land during privatisation, a process that is facilitating the renaissance of patriarchal land rights (Susanna Lastarria Cornhiel and Zoraida Garcia-Frias).

A former republic of the Soviet Union, Uzbekistan is undergoing a relatively gradual transition from centralised to market based property ownership and production. While maintaining state ownership over most farmland, management of agricultural production and land is being privatised in the sense that responsibility is shifting from the state to rural households. Agricultural collectives have ceased to function as production enterprises, the land has been divided and leased out to families through a number of schemes and unpaid family labour has largely replaced wage labour and machinery (D. Kanddiyoti, 2003: 225-256.).

At the beginning of the privatisation process, all members of a collective were given leases for specific parcels of collective land. Most of these parcels were very small because of high population density. A recent development in the way that state enterprises lease

such new sectors and that has raised their participation in the national work force.

Besides it, wage discrimination is forbidden by law, in that men and women are guaranteed equal wages for equal job categories and qualification levels. The problem overall is that women have a trend to be concentrated in the lower status sectors and the lower job categories within the branches. This occupational segregation leads to women being in low wage jobs. In agriculture, women tend to do the low productivity manual work such as cotton picking. This type of work is also often seasonal in rural areas. It is estimated, for instance, that unemployment by 50 per cent in the April-June period (Uzbekistan Country Gender Assessment, 2005: 31).

The childcare facilities, which were previously provided by state enterprises and collective farms, could no longer be maintained. The social support systems for the elderly also suffered. All this led to an increase in the time-burden for women, who took more unpaid work in the form of caring for young and elderly family members. The closing of state enterprises and former collective farms meant losses of jobs in the formal sector for men and women, which the emerging private sector has not been able to compensate. In the formal sector, women's rights to maternity benefits and leave were retained, making women less attractive than men to private sector employees. Economic hardship meant that women could not on the whole just withdraw from the labour force. Instead they tend to look for income generating possibilities in the informal sector where they are more vulnerable and lost their social protection rights (to pension, maternity leave, sick leave etc.) (Uzbekistan Country Gender Assessment, 2005: 7).

In rural area, the collective farms were replaced first by *shirkats* (joint-stock farming companies) and more recently by private farms which employ far fewer people than the collective farms and *shirkats*. As stated earlier, rural women already had limited opportunities in the Soviet period. In the transition period the opportunities have become even more restricted and women have been more and more squeezed into household or small plot production. Although rural women tended to do low skilled seasonal work on collective and state farms and suffered from low wages and pensions, they did benefit from the social support services offered by collective farms. In the transition period, they have lost this social support system, without benefiting from new jobs in the private sector (Uzbekistan Country Gender Assessment, 2005: 31).

A combination of economic hardship and a conscious change of government policy with regard to demography and fertility rates have led to a decrease in birth and fertility rates. In the late Soviet period, the number of birth in Uzbekistan was 30,000-40,000 annually, whereas in 2003 the number had fallen to 20,800. Annual population growth fell from 2.2 per cent to 1.2 per cent in the period from 1991-2002. Before transition, Uzbekistan received the equivalent of 20 per cent of its GDP in the subsidies from the central Soviet government (Uzbekistan Country Gender Assessment, 2005: 31). With the loss of these subsidies, the country had to struggle to maintain expenditure on social services. This together with the drop in the real value of salaries in the health-care and education sectors meant that the quality of the services deteriorated. Life expectancy has also fallen, especially for men; maternal and infant mortality figures and the incident of infectious diseases have increased.

All of these consequences of market economy have increased economic vulnerability and led to a drop in capabilities. Uzbek women have become more vulnerable to exploitation in the informal labour market and also have become more vulnerable to human traffickers. This economic system has also demised the previous Soviet quota system, which promoted women's representation in top economic positions. In Uzbekistan women's economic status has been affected by the shrinking and financial squeezes faced by state and non-state enterprises experience during the post-Soviet period. Enterprises are no longer subsidised or integrated with the all Soviet economy. The cut in state subsidies has placed great difficulty on enterprises in term of maintaining output and covering production costs. In response, enterprises have either closed or carry a larger number of hidden unemployment (i.e. employed workers on unpaid leaves).

Another common tactic has been the withholding of wages, sometimes upto a year. Wages arrears encourage women to go on unpaid leaves, rather than work for nothing. As a result, wherever possible working women look for other types of employment. However, here women find themselves up against employers' preference predominantly in the private sector for male workers who are more mobile and can dispose of their time more freely than women.

The current labour legislation grants working women a number of benefits that make employer reluctant to employ them except for certain female type jobs. It is no surprising then that although women comprise 42 per cent of the labour force, they account for 63 per cent of the registered unemployed (Wendy Mee, 2001: 31).

As a result of the above changes, there are two worrisome trends regarding women's economic and employment status in Uzbekistan. Firstly, the transition to a market economy has rendered women less competitive in the employment market, particularly in the private sector. Secondly, there is concern that poverty is undergoing a process of feminisation. The labour force participation rate has dropped since independence from 80 per cent in 1993 to 73 per cent in 1997. In addition, the share of women in the labour force declined during the mid-1990s but has improved slightly since then.

Table 4.7: Share of Women Labour Force in Uzbekistan

(In percentage)

Years	*1989*	*1992*	*1993*	*1994*	*1995*	*1996*	*1997*	*1998*
Share of Women	46.5	46.5	43.3	43.4	42.7	43.7	44.0	44.1

Source: UNDP, *Human Development Report* (Uzbekistan 1999).

The above table shows that this change is not a revolutionary one that could improve the economic status of women. Labour force participation is lowest in rural and other deprived areas. According to the government, economic activity grew significantly during 2007 and 2008 and GDP grew by 7.3 per cent and 8.1 per cent respectively. These claims, however, are not supported by indirect indicators such as living standards and the fact of massive out-migration. Economic output has improved due to significant export growth in machinery, chemicals and metals (Dinara Alimdjanova, 2009: 2-3).

More than half of female workers are concentrated in the non-productive sectors of education, healthcare, insurance and culture. Women account for 75 per cent of workers in healthcare, 44 per cent in insurance, 61.5 per cent in education and 53 per cent in culture and arts. Men on the other hand are concentrated in construction (90 per cent), transport and communications (84 per cent) and authority positions (76 per cent) (Dinara Alimdjanova, 2009: 5). The concentration of women in education and public health has implications for women's income level of slavery and future employment prospects.

On the whole, such jobs are found in the public sector, which has been most vulnerable to erosion of real wages.

Table 4.8: Distribution of Female Labour Force in Uzbekistan by Sector, 1998

Sectors	*Percentage*
Education	34
Public Health	19
Industry	14
Agriculture	11
Trade, Catering, Supply, Sales and Procurements	6
Transport and Communication	3
Construction	3
Culture and Arts	2
Others	8
Total	**100**

Source: Bureau of Gender and Development and the State Department of Statistics (1999), *Women of Uzbekistan: Statistical Collection*, Tashkent, p. 80.

However, in these sectors with considerable female employment the average monthly wage is lower than the average national level. For instance, in the healthcare and social security branch the average monthly wage in 2001 was 61 per cent of the national average. In education the average wages 67 per cent of the national average and 43.1 per cent in pre-school educational facilities. The monthly average wages in agriculture, where female employment is also high, was 52 per cent of national average and 41 per cent for those involved in crop growing. Overall, women were paid on average 30 per cent of less than men (Wendy Mee, 2001: 33).

In general, the transition has resulted in a considerable fall in the living standards for most of the population. The transition period has been accompanied by first, a decline in production; second, an increase in unemployment; third, high inflation; fourth, decreasing standard of living, and lastly, increasing income differentiation and inequality. According to the Ministry of Macro Economics and Statistics, the annual inflation rate for 2000 was 26.5 per cent and it is one critical factor in Uzbekistan. Using the Family Budget Survey (FBS) and official poverty line as 1.5 times the official minimum wage, about 14 per cent of the population and 11 per cent of households were considered poor in 1999. But in Soviet era, poverty in Uzbekistan was estimated at 44 per cent of the working population (Nurollo Khalmurzaev, 2000: 287-288). At surface, it seems that the flames of poverty were grim in the Soviet period than the market economic system of Uzbekistan.

However, there is reason to be suspicious of such estimates. Firstly, during the Soviet era, the majority of population considered poor did not suffer from absolute poverty. Most of them had jobs or other sources of incomes, had adequate housing and enjoyed free healthcare and education. The decline in the level of government services such as childcare, health and education over the last ten years has in fact made the experience of relative poverty far worse than during the Soviet era.

Secondly, the official relation between the minimum wage and poverty does not acknowledge the fact that minimum wage level does not cover the actual cost of living. There are also concerns over the underestimation of the real level of poverty. For example, in 1998, 26 per cent of the population received allowances. However, according to the Household Budget Survey done by the Ministry of Macro Economics and Statistics, in the first half of 1999, 40 per cent of the population of Uzbekistan should have been identified as poor and hence, received allowances (Wendy Mee, 2001: 11). The concept of poverty is also affecting the lives at the smallest units of a society where it appears that women are more affected by this curse than men. Further, in the present economic system the gender income gap is increasing, the rank of Uzbekistan was 36 in 2006; 41 in 2007 and 55 in 2008 respectively specified in the Gender Gap Index (The Global Gender Gap Report 2008: 162).

Table 4.9: Gender Indicators of Income Generation in Households in Uzbekistan, 2008

Category	*Share of Households having income, Per cent*		*Share in income Structure, Per cent*	
	Women	*Men*	*Women*	*Men*
Non Agricultural sector	17	55.8	5.5	39.8
Agricultural sector	6.8	20.3	1.6	6.9
Old age Pensions	17.5	9.8	4.3	3.7
Disability Pensions	5.8	5.8	1.2	1.8

Source: Dinara Alimdjanova (2009), Gender Aspects of Agricultural and Rural Employment: Application for Uzbekistan, Gender Study Centre, Uzbekistan, p. 7.

Even the ratio of women is bigger than the men population in Uzbekistan, but the above Table 4.7 shows that men benefited more in all categories barring the old age pensions income. In this way, it seems that women are largely affected by poverty in the country. Such poverty has made a negative impact directly and indirectly on Uzbek women. Coupled with increasing expenditure associated with education has meant that parents are less likely to invest in girl's education. In the longer term, this is leading to loss of capabilities, limiting women's employment choices, reducing their right to work, related social security benefits, and giving them less authority and ability to affect decisions in the family and dependence on parents and husbands, coupled with ignorance about their legal rights, and lack of access to legal aid and increase women's vulnerability. Besides it, poverty also had a negative effect over women's share of nourished diet and health. Generally, women do not compromise on their husbands' and children's health. In such a situation she is absolutely trapped and always occupied by such compromises in her day-to-day life to save her family at the stake of her own health.

On whole one can observe that Uzbekistan suffered a decline in most economic and social indicators in the first years of transition (1991-1995). However, the decline in economic output was less severe than other Central Asian States. The levels of social transfers were kept relatively high and subsidies on basic goods were removed gradually. Since 1995, the country has had a positive economic growth, but practically it was at low levels. But all this has not enhanced the economic and employment status of women at large. While the country has been victorious in achieving self-reliance in energy and wheat, the policy to develop industry has been less successful, and has not helped to improve living standards.

The general economic problems coupled with unemployment and low salaries are compounded by insufficient and expensive provision of services and utilities. For example, since independence the size of the healthcare budget has been gradually slashed. People now pay for most health services whereas such service were free or nominally charged during the Soviet period. Problems such as the irregular supply of gas, electricity and water, and the high cost of health services and education are prevalent. The cost of basic services such as transport, energy and heating are still subsidized by the government and the price of wheat still controlled. However, the amount spent on subsidies overall has declined from more than 16 per cent of government expenditure in 1994 to only 3 per cent in 2000 (Wendy Mee, 2001: 14).

It means that more and more people have to bear the cost of utilities and services which were earlier subsidized. In addition, the occurrence of bribe taking has added to the cost of living for the majority of people. In a situation where wages are not paid in time and further do not cover the costs of living, bribe taking has become common for getting a job and ensuring satisfactory healthcare is a distant dream for an average citizen. Uzbek women are facing a terrible setting to live a respectful livelihood in the society.

If an analysis is made of the effects of market economy over women then it is a fact that market economy creates economic growth and more economic opportunities for women. Women's economic activity in the formal sector has increased in many of the Central Asian States. Market economic system (Globalisation) reduces gender segregation and inequality. The increase in economic activity and labour force participation rates seem to support the argument that gender segregation is declining as women take their place in the economic arena. The liberal market system depends on free competition that forces nations to improve their human capital through educating women.

But on the other side market economy perpetuates and increases the gender division of labour and allows for the exploitation of women by Multi-National Companies (MNCs). Women still face discrimination and barricades on their work place due to a gendered division of labour and also face a great disparity in wage rates compared to her male counterpart. Market economy system may provide more jobs for women and thus greater economic participation but those jobs are at significantly lower rates of pay than similar work held by men and thus the globalisation pushes women to an informal sector of employment. Women are expected to discharge all the duties of the home and they are seen as incompetent to take on additional management and administration duties.

The market economy has its own pros and cons but it is observed that the Uzbek women faced largely the negative impacts of market economy. Though the Uzbek government has adopted the market economy system very slowly and step by step, it has vitally failed in protecting women from its ill effects. Besides, if a comparison is made regarding the position of women between a period from 1991 to 2000 and after 2000, then the positive effects of market economy can be observed and the condition of women is improving gradually. But all such changes are in its beginning and there is a long journey in achieving the golden period for women like in the Soviet times.

Moreover, if a comparison is made between the Kazakh and Uzbek economies, then Kazakhstan is a more liberalised economy and has far outpaced that of neighbouring Uzbekistan, which remains hostile to private wealth. Both states have followed very different roads since independence, especially, in the pace and degree of economic liberalisation. The gap has narrowed somewhat as Kazakhstan and Uzbekistan both took drastic measures to mitigate the effects of the economic crisis, but the essential differences reach far beyond the sphere of economics. Uzbekistan began seriously to implement a nationwide privatisation process that included major industries only in 2007, far behind Kazakhstan where this state in national economic development began soon after independence from the Soviet Union in the early 1990s. Today, the Kazakh economy far outpaces that of the Uzbek, the most populous nation of the former Soviet Central Asian Republics. Kazakhstan with a population of 15 million has GDP nearly five times greater than Uzbekistan. In global ranking index, Uzbekistan was placed in low income category with 55th rank. On the other hand, Kazakhstan's position was in upper middle income category with 45th rank in 2008 (The Global Gender Gap Report 2008: 14).

The key reason for such major distinctions is that Kazakhstan possesses 3.2 per cent of known world oil reserves, Kazakhstan ranks among the world's 10 largest copper producers, 10 largest wheat exporters and the number one producer and exporter of uranium. Uzbekistan although less blessed with natural resources, has its own substantial underground wealth, particularly in gold and natural gas. But unless the economic freedom is expanded and conditions for private business thoroughly liberalised, it's likely that the country's economy will continue to lag behind (Kazakh and Uzbek Economic Diverge, 2010).

Uzbekistan adopted a cautious and gradual approach to market reform and Kazakhstan followed a more aggressive strategy of liberalisation. But while Kazakhstan may have achieved a better policy environment, its economic performance has not been better than Uzbekistan. The extent of the decline was much smaller in Uzbekistan and the subsequent rate of recovery also higher. Consequently, by 1999, Uzbekistan's GDP had recovered to 96 per cent of its 1991 level as compared with 63 per cent for Kazakhstan. In fact, in five years between 1995-1999, Uzbekistan saw a cumulative 10 per cent real economic growth at a time when Kazakhstan's economy shrunk by 9 per cent (Asad Alam and Arup Banerji, 2000: 2).

If a comparison is made about the effect of market economy over the Kazakh and Uzbek women then undoubtedly Kazakh women are in a better position. The involvement of Kazakh women are more in the national work force and a result their average income is largely ahead of their Uzbek counterpart. In 2008, it is estimated that the average earning of Kazakh women was US $ 8831 and for men US $ 13080, the ratio of female to male income was 0.68 per cent. At the same time, the average income of Uzbek women was US $1891 and for men US $ 2694 and this ratio was female to male was 0.64 per cent (Human Development Report, 2009). Whether it is a matter of skilled employment or of high positions in some sectors, the Kazakh women is yet again in a better position to Uzbeks in working conditions. Though Kazakh women are also facing problems, certainly the Uzbek women are facing the problem of unemployment more severely. The fertility rate is also largely affected in Uzbekistan while the Kazakh position in this regard is stable.

Kazakh society is having a European culture in its society where women are largely considered equal to men. The career and higher education are the primary issues for the Kazakh women. On the other hand, Uzbek women's main concerns are family and upbringing of children. In such a situation she could not cross her limitation at the cost of her priorities. In general it can be observed that the both the Kazakh and Uzbek women are affected by the negative effects of market economy but such effects are more noticeable in reference to Uzbek women. Kazakh women have adopted the market economy system and as part of it they are also enjoying the benefits of such system while it will take more time when such changes would be seen in Uzbekistan.

Notes

1. *Shock therapy* advocates of a radical reform programme emphasise a rapid reformation of the market. The market economy of the industrialised countries is the model, and transition countries should develop such an economic system through rapid and comprehensive liberalisation, stabilisation and privatisation in order to "shock" the market (Johan Fredborn Larsson, 2010: 11).
2. ***De jure*** (in Classical Latin ***de iure***) is an expression that means "concerning law", as contrasted with *de facto*, which means "concerning fact". The terms *de jure* and *de facto* are used instead of "in law" and "in practice", respectively, when one is describing political or legal situations. In a legal context, *de jure* is also translated as "concerning law". A practice may exist *de facto*, where for example the people obey a contract as though there were a law enforcing it, yet there is no such law. A process known as "desuetude" may allow *de facto* practices to replace obsolete laws. On the other hand, practices may exist *de jure* and not be obeyed or observed by the people. (*Source: http://en.wikipedia.org/wiki/De_jure*)
3. ***De facto*** (English pronunciation: Latin expression that means "by the fact." In law, it often means "in practice but not necessarily ordained by law" or "in practice or actuality, but not officially established." It is commonly used in contrast to *de jure* (which means "concerning the law") when referring to matters of law, governance, or technique (such as standards) that are found in the common experience as created or developed without or contrary to a regulation. When discussing a legal situation, *de jure* designates what the law says, while *de facto* designates action of what happens in practice. It is analogous and similar to the expressions "for all intents and purposes" or "in fact." (*Source: http://en.wikipedia.org/wiki/De_facto)*

Chapter - 5

Gender and State Policies in Kazakhstan and Uzbekistan

The gender and state policies are intensely inter-connected. If the state guidelines are in favour of gender and keen to eliminate gender discrimination then definitely there would be non-existent gender issues in that society and men and women can make their equal participation in the making and development of the nation. The basic principles of the gender policies are based on equal rights and freedom for women and men that are formally assured in the constitution of the Republic of Kazakhstan and the Republic of Uzbekistan.

The gender policy should deal with the following tasks: achievement of equal participation of women and men in decision-making structures; the realisation of equal opportunities for economic sovereignty; the development of business and career promotion; conditions for equal realisations of rights and responsibilities for family; and freedom from gender based violence. It is essential to examine the state gender policies to analyse the status of women in Kazakhstan and Uzbekistan.

In this regard, first of all it is essential to scrutinize the constitutional and legal position of women in both states, what sorts of rights have been offered to them, whether men and women are equal in constitutional point of view, and how much legal and social security has been provided to women in these states. It is also necessary to find out the attitude of the government of these states towards the conventions and other women welfare policies run by UN and which state is adopting all such guidelines in a proper manner, and especially, the women's status in reference to the institutional frameworks within the country.

The freedom for women NGOs and their success rate is also to be studied to evaluate the state policies of both countries in the direction of minimising gender discrimination and the efforts for development of women. Subsequently, it is also to be measured in terms of the changes in women policies after attaining independence and the impact of these changes on Kazakh and Uzbek women. Thus, the focal point of this chapter is to analyse the status of Kazakh and Uzbek women in the constitutional, legal, institutional and international frameworks and the policies of present government towards women.

Kazakh Women in the Constitutional Framework

The basic framework of Kazakhstan in which the government protects the rights of women and promotes the gender equality is the constitution of 28 January 1993, which guaranteed equality of rights and freedom irrespective of sex and prohibited all forms of discrimination (Article 1). Article 14 of the constitution of Kazakhstan upholds the legal equality for all citizens. The Article also explains, "Everyone is equal before the law and courts and no one can be subjected to any discrimination on the ground of social background, office and property status, sex, race, nationality, language, relation to religion, convictions, place of residence or other circumstance" (Gender Equality: Legal and institutional Framework on Women's Rights and Equal Opportunities, Kazakhstan: 220).

The Criminal Code in force before 1998 considered the prevention of women from taking part in public, social, cultural activities or any other actions violating the equality of women with the use of violence, threats, economic or any other dependence, as a crime punished by imprisonment from one to three years. In the new Criminal Code (1st January 1998) the violation of women's right to equality is no longer considered separately. Instead the violation of any citizens' right to equality (Article 141), including gender based discrimination, shall be punished either by detention for upto three months or imprisonment for upto one year, or a maximum fine of hundred monthly salaries (Women's Social and Economic Rights, Kazakhstan: 222).

The Kazakh legislation guarantees equality for men and women in the sphere of education and the June 1999 "Law on Education" affirms this to be a major principle of state policy. The constitution also guarantees to all citizens compulsory free primary and secondary education in state-run educational institutions. No religious or cultural influences hamper the approach to sex equality or religious or cultural diversity. The Labour Code of Kazakhstan gives some special rights to women to protect their womanhood and facilitate them to be good mothers with their working career.

Article 191. Limitation to the abrogation of labour agreement on the employer's initiative. After expiry of a term of the labour agreement for pregnancy for twelve or more weeks, the employer must on her written request prolong the term of the labour agreement for nursing a child till a child reaches the age of three years.

Article 195. No full working time for women and other persons having the family commitments. The employer on the written request of a pregnant woman or woman having children (upto three years of age) wave full time working regime.

Article 196. Limitation to the application of stipulated working time regime for the pregnant women. Application of the stipulated working time regime for pregnant women is not allowed when the duration of a working day (working shift) exceeds eight hours.

Article 198. Guarantees for women paid annual leave. Before the leave on pregnancy and birth or immediately after it or in the end of the leave on nursing a child the woman on her wish is provided for paid annual working leave.

Article 201. The leave without paid wages for nursing children based on the parents' choice – to the mother or father of a child; to parent – nursing a child by oneself; grandmother, grandfather, other relative or guardian, actually nursing a child (The Republic of Kazakhstan, 2007: 41).

The new Labour Law of 2000 abolished special norms existing before and aimed at maternity protection, particularly paid leave for nursing a baby and to women who have children under a year and a half. Such norms were stipulated in the Convention on Maternity Protection adopted on June 4, 1952 that was in effect on the territory of Kazakhstan till 30 August 1995. Taking into account the date of adoption of the convention as well as 95 recommendations on maternity protection of June 28, 1952, it is possible to assert that Kazakhstan has made a 50 – year step back in the area of maternity protection (Alternative Report, 2006: 19).

The new Labour Law (1 January 2000) prohibits any discrimination in the sphere of labour relations, including on grounds of gender. However, Article 17 of the current Law on Labour Protection, adopted by the Supreme Council in 1993, actually dictates employers to apply unequal criteria upon employment of men and women: "All women as well as persons under 18 years are to be hired only after a prior medical examination, and women upto the age of 45, and (minors) up to the age of 18 must undergo a medical examination annually." With the growth of competition for work places, discriminatory tendencies in terms of the employment and dismissal of women, particularly regarding women with young children and women over 40 years of age, are increasing (Women's Social and Economic Rights, Kazakhstan: 222).

Besides, Article 24 of the Constitution states that "Every person has a right to conditions of labour in accordance with safety and hygiene requirements, to be rewarded for work done without any discrimination, as well as to social protection from unemployment." The average salary of women differs considerably from that of men: in 1998 women received 75.8 per cent of men's average salary and the average wage for educational workers, the vast majority of whom are women, was 80 per cent of the national average wage. In the same period, the average wage of those engaged in the construction industry, which employs mainly men, was 120 per cent of the national average wage. According to the Civil Code of 1st July 1999, there are no restrictions on women's right to own, use or inherit property and this law makes no distinction on the basis of gender on inheritance rights (Women's Social and Economic Rights, Kazakhstan: 223).

In Kazakh constitution, women are given the right to participate in political and public life. According to the constitution, citizens have the right to take part in the administration of public affairs directly or through their representatives, to elect and to be elected in governmental bodies and local self-administration, and to take part in republican referendums etc. The Constitutional Law on Elections secures the right of all citizens to vote upon reaching the age of 18, regardless of background, social, office or property status, sex, race, nationality, language, religion, convictions, place of residence or any other condition.

The government has repeatedly called for the representation of women at all levels of decision-making, but both the government and the President have expressed their opposition to introducing a quota system, as demanded largely by women's NGOs, and committees and commissions. NGOs made disagreement over the fact that despite of the formal equal access to public service and electoral rights, there remains only one women minister and few women MPs in Kazakhstan (Women's Political Rights and Participation in Public Life, Kazakhstan: 227).

Women's participation in politics and governance structures in Kazakhstan is rather low. In 2009, there were two women in the 47 seats of Senate, i.e. 4.3 per cent and 19 women in the 107 member *Mazhlis* about 17.8 per cent. From 2000 to 2007, women occupied eight seat in the then 77 members parliament, or 10.4 per cent. In 2009, there was one woman in the cabinet and one chaired a national agency. The US Department of State (2010) remarks, the traditional attitudes may hinder women from holding high office or playing active roles in political life. Although no legal restrictions on the participation of women and minorities in politics are in existence (Maarten van Klaveren, 2010: 18).

In Kazakhstan, there are some laws about sexual abuse towards women. In Kazakh legislation, rape is defined as sexual intercourse with a person of the female sex, using physical violence, threats or taking advantage of the helplessness of the victim. The punishment for rape and attempted rape is more severe if it results in bodily injuries, causes or terminates pregnancy, or results in HIV infection or any other serious disease or the victim's suicide (Violence against Women, Kazakhstan: 229).

According to Article 120 of the 1998 Criminal Code: [1] Rape: shall be punished by imprisonment from 3 to 5 years. [2] Rape: (a) committed by a group of persons, group of persons with prior collusion or by an organised group; (b) accompanied by the threat of murder and committed with particular brutality towards the victim or other persons; (c) resulting in infection with venereal disease(s);

(d) committed repeatedly by a person, or by a repeat offender; (e) intentionally towards an underage girl, shall be punished by imprisonment from 5 to 10 years. [3] Rape: (a) resulting in the death of a victim; (b) resulting in the serious bodily harm, HIV/AIDS infection or other grave consequences; (c) committed intentionally against a victim under the age of 14; (d) taking advantage of conditions of public disaster or in the cause of mass disorder shall be punished by imprisonment from 8 to 15 years" (Violence against Women, Kazakhstan: 229).

According to Article 122, "Sexual intercourse, homosexual, lesbianism or other acts of a sexual nature had intentionally with a person under 16 years of age shall be punished with deprivation of liberty for upto 3 years, or detention for up to 6 months, or limited liberty for upto 5 years." Even after such a rigorous provision in the legal system the number of reported incidents of rape in 1997 proved an increase of 1 per cent compared with 1989. At the same time the number of convictions and sentences for rape decreased by 23 per cent in 1997 compared to 1989. Additionally, there are no separate legal provisions considering trafficking in women and Kazakhstan has not still ratified the Anti-slavery Convention.

The Law "On Marriage and Family" does not consider reproductive rights separately. Article 29 (3) says that issues of motherhood, fatherhood, bringing up and education of children are to be decided jointly by both spouses. It is the only Article that can be connected to reproductive rights, but it contradicts Article 54 of the Law "On Protection of Health of the Citizens in the Republic of Kazakhstan" that authorised women with the right to make decision on motherhood by her own will. The new Criminal Code does not include criminal responsibility for forcing a woman in abortion compared to the old Criminal Code. The cost of abortion is rather high i.e. from $ 50 to $ 300 depending on a clinic. The state subsidizes abortions just for medical and social reasons *that* are performed in medical and preventive institutions of the state healthcare system (Alternative Report, 2006: 33).

Most women compared to men effectively are not able to enjoy the right of priority to get land for farming because the Land Code of the Republic of Kazakhstan grants this right to those citizens who have special agricultural knowledge and qualification as well as practical experience in agricultural business in Article 101(1). The Law of Republic of Kazakhstan of March 31, 1998 "On Farming" also requires from those who want to get a piece of land for farming to attach to the application for land a transcript from a labour record book to certify that the head of the farm has experience in agricultural business or a document on corresponding education or special training. That means that for pure formal reasons many rural women can be legally refused land for farming.

The qualification required for getting farming land which *de jure* seems fair on the surface can be assessed *de-facto* as a hidden discrimination of women. The UN Conventions on Elimination of all Forms of Discrimination against Women definitely protects rights of the rural women for equal polity in the process of land and agricultural reform. The state participants are bound to carry out corresponding measures to eliminate discrimination against women in rural regions to ensure on the basis of equality of men and women their involvement in development of rural regions and receiving benefits from such development (Alternative Report, 2006: 37-38).

Uzbek Women in Constitutional Framework

From the very first day of independence of the Republic of Uzbekistan, its President and government have focussed on the problem of the legal, economic, and social protection of motherhood and childhood, the creation of conditions for the multi-faceted development of women, and enhancing of their role in society. The Republic of Uzbekistan in the condition of a difficult transitional period and despite limited financial means has elevated concern for a healthy and happy motherhood and childhood to the level of state policy. The constitution of the Republic of Uzbekistan and more than 80 laws and other laws and regulations constitute the legal framework to ensure and protect the rights, freedom and lawful interests of women in the present conditions.

The basic law of the Republic of Uzbekistan, the Constitution, contains provision calling for protection of the rights of women. Chapter 5, Article 18, depicts, "All citizens of the Republic of Uzbekistan shall have equal rights and freedoms, and shall be equal before the law, without distinction by sex, race, nationality, language, religion, social origin, individual and social status. Any privileges may be granted solely by the law and shall conform to the principles of social justice." Chapter 10, Article 46, recommends, "Women and men shall have equal rights" and Article 117 of the Constitution guarantees the right to elect and to be elected to representative bodies (Uzbekistan – Gender Quality Indicators 2007: 2).

In Uzbekistan, at the legislative and executive levels, policy is aimed at achieving full equality between men and women, improving the legal and economic status of women, providing equal opportunity in their life and work, reproductive health, as well as changes in traditional roles in society and the family, equally for both women and men. The laws of the Republic of Uzbekistan certify to the identical conditions for work same as men as right to women, to the undeniable right of all people to equal employment opportunities, to free choice of profession, education, the right to social security in the event of retirement, unemployment, illness, disability, to healthy and safe working conditions. In addition, the laws of the Republic of Uzbekistan guarantee that women have equal status with men to access public service, participation in governance and public affairs at all levels of government (Uzbekistan, Beijing Platform for Action, 1995: 1).

Uzbek women are provided with equal opportunities as men in terms of exercise of civil legal capacity. Women enjoy equal rights in decisive contracts and agreements, managing property and during court hearings. The national legislation ensures equal rights to men and women in the freedom of movement and in choosing the place of residence. In the framework of the state strategy for ensuring the equality of women, a long-term project is being implemented, aiming to improve the national mechanism for provision of equal services on the issues of family institution consolidation, identification and consideration of children's interests (CEDAW, *www.iwraw-ap.org/resources/pdf/Uzbekistan_SR.pdf*).

Article 2 of 'The Family Code' of the Republic of Uzbekistan that was adopted in 1998, provides the equality of personal and property rights of men and women in marital relations. Women are allowed on an equivalent basis with men to implement their rights in court and to appeal against unlawful acts committed against them in administrative proceedings. The law on "Citizens' appeals" guarantees impartial consideration of an appeal.

In Article 41 of the Constitution of Uzbekistan, all citizens of the Republic have the right to education. The right to receive free education is guaranteed by the government and Article 42 of the Constitution of Uzbekistan guarantees the freedom of scientific research and engineering work and equal rights to enjoy cultural benefits. The state provides free general education for all its citizens. The equal rights of men and women to receive education are set out in the Education Act of the Republic of Uzbekistan. In Article 2 of the Physical Culture and Sport Act, the equal rights with men to physical education and sporting activity are established for women (UN CEDAW Initial Reports of States Parties, Uzbekistan, 2000: 19).

The turning point in the life of the women of the Republic of Uzbekistan was the Decree of the President of the Republic of Uzbekistan, dated 2 March 1995, "On Measures for Strengthening the Role of Women in State and Social Building of the Republic of Uzbekistan." In accordance with this, a new position was created in the Republic, Deputy Prime Minister with responsibility for the social protection of the family, motherhood and childhood (Uzbekistan: Review and Appraisal of the Implementation, 1995: (1). The National Human Rights Centre of the Republic of Uzbekistan jointly with state organisations, public organisations and NGOs, developed the Draft Law "On State protection measures of equal rights and opportunities for men and women" that is at par with international norms. In March 2006, it was introduced for consideration of the Legislative Chamber of the *Oliy Majlis* (Parliament) of the Republic of Uzbekistan (CEDAW, *www.iwraw-ap.org/resources/pdf/Uzbekistan_SR.pdf*).

In 2004, the country's Parliament introduced the amendments into the Article 22 of the Law of the Republic of Uzbekistan "On Elections to *Oliy Majlis* (Parliament) of the Republic of Uzbekistan" for 30 per cent quota for women during the selection of candidates to the country's parliament from the political parties. Since January 2005, a group of women-parliamentarians have been actively involved in the activities of public associations, non-governmental and non-commercial organisations, and undertook practical work on improving the deputies' gender awareness, lobbied the adoption of the Draft Laws "On the State protection measures of equal rights and equal opportunities for men and women in the Republic of Uzbekistan" (CEDAW, *www.iwraw-ap.org/resources/pdf/Uzbekistan_SR.pdf*).

It should be emphasised that from 1995 to the present women have occupied the position of the Human Rights Commissioner (*Ombudsman*); a woman in 2007 for the first time in the history of the State stood as candidate for the post of President of the Republic of Uzbekistan. She was the chairman of the Social Democratic Party *Adolat*, and in 2008 the first woman was elected Speaker of Legislative Chamber of *Oliy Majlis* of the Republic of Uzbekistan. This is a sign of changing attitude towards women and strengthening of their position and status in society.

The legislation of Uzbekistan prohibits any discrimination on the basis of sex and visualizes a comprehensive system of measures on protection of women's rights in the labour market. The Labour Code of the Republic of Uzbekistan secures legal mechanisms for social protection of women in the field of employment. As such, in accordance with the Article 68 of the Labour Code, the state provides additional protection measures to individuals in need of social protections, those facing difficulties in search of job and unable to compete on the labour market on equal conditions (including single parents and parents having many children under the age of 14, or disabled children), young people that just graduated from the educational institutions, disabled persons and individuals in pre-retirement age, by creating specialised enterprises, including enterprises for disabled persons.

In line with the Article 224 of the Labour Code it is prohibited to refuse women employment and decrease their salary for any reasons related to pregnancy or availability of children. There are individual article in the Labour Code of the Republic of Uzbekistan that provides additional benefit and safety measures to women with children. In accordance with the national legislation of Uzbekistan women get equal pay with men for equal work. The Ministry of Labour and Social Protection of Population jointly with the Council of Ministers of the Republic of Karakalpakstan, regional Hokim's (Head of Administration) Offices and Tashkent City Hokim's Office are responsible for ensuring equality in the field of employment and the elimination of discrimination.

The individual articles of the Labour Code emphasise additional protection measures for women and individuals busy with family duties:

- **Article 224.** Protection measures for employment of pregnant women and women with children.
- **Article 225.** Occupations where the application of women's labour is prohibited.
- **Article 226.** Transfer of pregnant women to less difficult work and work that does not allow for unfavourable production factors.
- **Article 227.** Transfer of women with children under two years of age to less difficult work and work that does not allow for unfavourable production factors.
- **Article 228.** Restriction of women's labour at overnight and overtime work, weekends and duty trips.
- **Article 228(1).** Right of women that have children less than three years of age and are employed at organisations and institutions financed from the budget to a contracted duration of working hours.
- **Article 229.** Establishment of half-time work for women and individuals busy with family duties.
- **Article 230.** Additional day off.
- **Article 231.** Benefits provided to women for annual leaves.
- **Article 232.** Additional leaves for women with children under twelve or disabled children under sixteen.
- **Article 233.** Maternity and childbirth leave.
- **Article 234.** Child rearing leave in case of children under two and under three years of age.
- **Article 235.** Leaves for individuals that adopted newborns or became guardians of those.
- **Article 236.** Breaks for breastfeeding.
- **Article 237.** Protection measures for pregnant women and women with children while implementing the labour contract.
- **Article 238.** Protection measures and benefits for people rearing children without mother.

However, despite the significant changes that have occurred in the economy of independent Uzbekistan, the employment structure in terms of gender relations has not undergone any significant changes. The share of women employed in the economy is less than 44 per cent and the share of women employed by the informal sector is increasing. In general, economic activity rate of women is slightly lower than that of men – 63.2 per cent and 78.5 per cent respectively. The tendency of women employment is increasing in low-paid sectors such as health (77.5 per cent) and education (72.7 per cent) in total. In 2006, women's wages were lower than men's by 37 per cent (Welfare Improvement Strategy of Uzbekistan, 2007: 55).

The legislation of the Republic of Uzbekistan provides for integrated measures aimed at preventing violence being committed against women. The Criminal Code of Uzbekistan stipulates various forms of punishment for violent acts committed against women. Under Article 136 of the Criminal Code, coercing a woman to enter into marriage or to continue living together in marriage or abducting a woman to enter into marriage against her will, as well as preventing a woman from entering into marriage, are punishable by a fine of upto twenty-five times the minimum wage or by corrective labour for upto three years, or by detention for upto six months or deprivation of liberty for upto three years (UN CEDAW Initial Reports of States Parties, Uzbekistan, 2000: 26).

In accordance with Article 103 of the Criminal Code, causing a person who was not materially or otherwise dependent on the accused, through cruel treatment or systematic degradation of their personal honour and dignity, to commit suicide or to attempt suicide is punishable by corrective labour for upto three years or deprivation of liberty upto five years. The same acts committed against persons who are materially or otherwise dependent on the accused are punishable by deprivation of liberty from five to eight years. The Article 115 of the Criminal Code provides for punishment by a fine of upto fifty times the minimum wage or by corrective labour for upto two years or detention for upto six months for forcing women to perform an abortion (UN CEDAW Initial Reports of States Parties, Uzbekistan, 2000: 27-28).

According to Article 118 of the Criminal Code, rape, that is sexual intercourse accompanied by the use of violence or the threat thereof, or the exploitation of the helpless status of the victim, is punishable by deprivation of liberty from three to seven years. Rape of a person known to the accused not to have attained fourteen years of age is punishable by deprivation of liberty from fifteen to twenty years or by the death penalty. Under Article 131 of the Criminal Code, the establishment or operation of brothels, as well as procurement for profitable or other base motives is punishable by a fine from twenty five to fifty times the minimum wage or by corrective labour for upto three years or by deprivation of liberty for upto three years with confiscation of property. In accordance with Article 135 of the Criminal Code, the solicitation accompanied by subterfuge for the purposes of sexual or any other exploitation is punishable by a fine from fifty to one hundred times the minimum wage or by corrective labour for upto three years or by detention for upto six months with or without confiscation of property (UN CEDAW Initial Reports of States Parties, Uzbekistan, 2000: 27-28).

Women and men in Uzbekistan and Kazakhstan generally have equal rights under the law. However, there are limited mechanisms to actively enforce those rights if they are violated. The constitutions of Kazakhstan and Uzbekistan guarantee equal rights to women and men, and other law (e.g. Family, Labour and Criminal Code) also contain non-discriminatory clauses. So far as the Labour Code is concerned the Uzbek system support women extensively as compared to the available arrangement in Kazakhstan. Both the constitutions and the 1992 Law on Citizenship prohibit discrimination on the basis of sex as well as religion, language and social status.

Although gender prejudice is illegal, the mechanism for enforcement are inadequate, women are insufficiently aware of their rights and insufficiently organised to advocate for them effectively. This lack of awareness coupled with the growing influence of more conservative strands of Islam is making all this more critical. The issues related to women's right are becoming a priority on the nation's development agenda in Uzbekistan. On the other hand, the Kazakh women are more conscious about their constitutional rights, the reason for that, first of all, there is a lack of religious rigidness and traditional attitude in the Kazakh system. Secondly, their hold in higher education is quite high and at the same time the financial dependence is less on men, as a result they are in better position to realise civil liberties and exercise their constitutional rights endowed by the Kazakh system.

Kazakh Women in International Framework

The gender equality and advancement of the status of women is essential to expedite development, peace and security. The final document of the Fourth World Conference on Women held in Beijing in 1995 and the special session of General Assembly "Women 2008: Gender Equality, Development and Peace" in the twenty-first century have a far reaching significance. They triggered the establishment of national policies and strategy for gender equality, observance to relevant international and regional instruments and increased attention to gender problem all over the world.

However, the problems related to the status of women remain an ongoing concern. Women continue to have unequal access to resources and opportunity and continue to be victim of abuse, violence, poverty and discrimination. The world is not yet free from discrimination and violence against women especially girl-child and adolescents. Throughout the transition period, the Government of Kazakhstan has demonstrated its commitment to the principles and norms of gender equality. The fundamental thrust on the advancement of women has been taking concrete measures to ensure gender equality in both legislation and practice in the country.

There is no special normative act in the legislation securing the principle of equality between men and women. But Article 4 of the Constitution gives the force of Law to international treaties ratified by Kazakhstan. As a result of the Republic of Kazakhstan joining the most important Conventions and Declarations of the UN and other international organisations protecting women's rights must promote improvement of the situation concerning the political rights of women, further the overcoming any core and evident discrimination in this field. The Vienna Declaration and the Action Programme adopted on June 25, 1993 at the World Conference on Human Rights assumed girls' and women's rights as an integral component and inseparable part of general human rights. The European Convention "On Motherhood Protection" that came into force on September 7, 1995 uses the term 'woman' to denote any female person regardless of age, nationality, race and religion, marital status (Gulsara Tlenchieva: 1).

According to "Perspectives of Gender Research Development in Kazakhstan" by Alma Abikenova, Professor at Karaganda State University, the activity of the UN office in Kazakhstan has become an intensifying factor for introduction of gender discourse in the sphere of intellectual activity and public consciousness of the state. The annual reports of the UNDP on Human Development and the UN Conventions on women's rights promotion, the documents of the international women's movements, and other materials dealing with the ideas of a social-sexual regularity have become the property of the intellectual establishment and the public associations of the republic.

The issues of the National Human Development Reports have further stimulated a turn to the gender theory implemented under the support of the UNDP (since 1995 includes the gender factor). The scholars from the leading research institutions have used gender analysis for evaluating and studying a wide range of social problems and policy. The establishment of the Gender in Development Bureau in 1996 became a major force for combining gender into social theory and practice (Galiya Khassanova, 2000: 388).

Other International Conventions on Human Rights, Conventions against Torture and other Cruel, Inhuman and Degrading Treatment or Punishment, Conventions on Child's Rights etc. have been given priority over the laws of the Republic of Kazakhstan. In 1999, the government ratified six International Labour Organisation (ILO) Conventions: the Discrimination (Employment and Occupation) Convention (Convention 111) providing protection to employees against "any distinction, exclusion or preference made on the basis of sex".

The Equal Remuneration Convention (Convention 100) calls for the implementation of principle of equal remuneration for men and women workers for the work of equal value. "On Minimal Age of Employment", "On Organisation of Employment Service", "On Cancellation of Forced Labour and others. In 2002, Kazakhstan ratified UN Convention "On Political Rights of Women" and "On Citizenship of a Married Woman". At present Kazakhstan has joined 30 international Conventions on Human Rights (Kazakhstan, Country Gender Assessment, 2006: 32).

From the point of view of realisation of political rights of Kazakhstan women the most important thing is the country's joining to the UN Conventions such as 'Convention on Elimination of All Forms of Discrimination Against Women' (CEDAW) adopted on December 18, 1979 (the Republic of Kazakhstan's law adopted on June 29, 1998), 'About Women's Political Rights' adopted on December 20, 1952 (Kazakhstan's law of December 30, 1999). The ratification of the Faculty Protocol of CEDAW made by Kazakhstan on July 4, 2001 implies that in case the Committee gets any reliable information about serious or systematic violations by the state, then it is possible to conduct an inquiry and immediately present a report to the Committee (Gulsara Tlenchieva: 1).

CEDAW Article 7, the UN Convention about Women's Political Rights require the participating countries to take all corresponding political measures, including legislative ones, in order to provide all-round development and progress of women. These international agreements strengthen women's rights on equal terms with men i.e. to vote in every election and public referendums and to be elected to all publicly elected bodies of power, participation in defining and realising the state policy and hold state positions, and also fulfil all state functions at all levels of state management. Further, to take part in the activity of NGOs and other associations dealing with the problems of the country's social and political life (Gulsara Tlenchieva: 1).

In December 1998, implementation the CEDAW conventions to strengthen the participation for women, the Council on Family, Women, and Demographic Policy was reformed into the National Commission on Family and Women Affairs under the President. Nursultan Nazarbaev, The President defined four main priorities for the National Commission: (i) promotion of the health of women and families, (ii) active participation by women in the public and political life of the country and their advancement to the decision-making level, (iii) economic empowerment of women, and (iv) eradication of violence against women (Galiya Khassanova, 2000: 390-91).

Due to the efforts of the UNDP Regional Gender Programme, women's NGOs, and the Gender in Development Bureau, the Centre of Gender Studies was established in 1998. Although the Centre is still incapable and small, it is gradually becoming the core of the school of gender research that is being organised in Kazakhstan. Much research has noted the positive role of the Gender in Development Bureau in

Kazakhstan. This UNDP project was developed on the basis of the 1990 Copenhagen Declaration and put into practice through the recommendations of the Beijing women's conference. Its purpose is to attract public attention and mobilise the political will and resources to change both the status and the living standard of women and their families. The UNDP's activities are guided by the following principles:

1. Gender equality should be included in the framework of joint activity with governments and of strategic and political documents.
2. The equal participation of men and women should be made a priority during the development, implementation, and monitoring of the programmes.
3. Benefits of programme implementation should be equally distributed.
4. There should be gender equality at all decision-making levels.

This policy is implemented by the UN system through its employees, coordinators on gender issues (Gender Focal Points), and the network of the Gender in Development Bureau. Using a method developed at UN headquarters, Kazakhstan and other CIS countries have developed their own effective programmes to respond to the challenges each country faces. The Gender in Development Bureau in Kazakhstan has established a good partnership with the women's organisations of Sweden (Swedish International Development Agency) and has successfully implemented a number of joint projects. In the framework of joint projects with the Swedish Agency on international cooperation "100 per cent of Women in Politics" and "Women's Leadership and Network Program" two conferences and 11 seminars and workshops were held for the most active women who showed their interest in politics (Galiya Khassanova, 2000: 391).

The Fourth World Conference on Women in Beijing acknowledged that human development should be pursued with due regard to the gender aspect. Women's empowerment should become an integral part of human capacity building which incorporates such areas as performance, equality, sustainability and empowerment. The Beijing Platform for Action endorsed at the conference, identified twelve critical areas of concern which are major obstacles to women's progress and require specific actions from the international community, governments and civil society: women and poverty, education and training of women, women and health, violence against women, women in and armed conflict, women and the economy, women in power and decision-making, institutional mechanisms for the advancement of women, human rights of women, women and the media, women and the environment, the girl child. To ensure the effective implementation of strategic objectives of the Beijing Platform for Action the Economic and Social Council suggested, "All UN system to actively and visibly promote policy of mainstreaming a gender perspective" (UNDP Kazakhstan: Gender Mainstreaming Strategy, 9).

After the Fourth International Conference on the Status of Women (Beijing 1995), the concept of the state policy on improving of women's status in the Republic of Kazakhstan was approved by the Decree of the President of the Republic of Kazakhstan, no. 3395 of March 5, 1997. To solve the problems of family, women and children, the Leader of the state set up a Council on Family and Women's Issues and Demographic Policy under the President of the Republic of Kazakhstan. In 1998, the Council was restructured into a National Commission on Family and Women's Affairs under the President of the Republic of Kazakhstan which was given expanded authorities (Answers to the Questionnaire on the Implementation of the Beijing Platform for Action, *www.unescap.org/.../Beijing...Questionnaire/Uzbekistan-unofficial-English.pdf*).

The strategy of gender equality and expansion of opportunities for women is stated to the fullest extent in the National Plan of Action on improving women's status in the Republic of Kazakhstan which includes twelve directions of the Beijing Platform of Action approved by the Resolution of the Government of the Republic of Kazakhstan, no. 999 of July 19, 1999. Kazakhstan acceded to the UN Convention for the Suppression of Trafficking in Persons and the Exploitation of the prostitution of others; and to the UN Conventions against Transnational Organised Crime with its two Optional Protocols – first, the Protocol to Prevent, Suppress and Punish Trafficking in Persons, especially women and children, and the second, Protocol against the Smuggling of Migrants by Land, Sea and Air. (Statement by Madina Jarbussynova, Ambassador at the Ministry of Foreign Affairs of the Republic of Kazakhstan, 2007: 4)

In 2001-2002, the project of IOM "Informational Campaign on Prevention of Trafficking in Women" was realised. The National Commission acted as a national coordinator in that project. Nineteen NGOs took part in that project by arranging hotlines in all Oblasts (provinces) of the Republic. The second joint project with IOM "Fight against Trafficking in People out of, in, via and within Kazakhstan" has been realised. The project contributed to further improvement of national legislation and promoted rendering aid to the victims of trafficking and training of the officers from the law-enforcement bodies in combating trafficking with the help of international experience (Answers to the Questionnaire on the Implementation of the Beijing Platform for Action, *www.unescap.org/.../Beijing...Questionnaire/ Uzbekistan-unofficial-English.pdf*).

UNDP in Kazakhstan has endorsed the United Nations Development Assistance Framework (UNDAF). UNDAF focuses on three interrelated areas of cooperation: (a) Developing pro-poor policies; (b) Ensuring quality of life for all; (c) Governance and participatory development. The document further suggests that the basis for coordinated and collaborative efforts should be sound policy aimed at assuring that all people across all regions benefit from the increasing prosperity of the country. "To ensure a rights-based approach that leads towards achievement of the Millennium Development Goals (MDGs), the United Nations system will focus on the most vulnerable groups of society, with explicit provisions on ensuring their free, active and meaningful participation in decision making" (UNDP Kazakhstan: Gender Mainstreaming Strategy, 10).

This framework programme was the basis for designing and elaborating UNDP programmes for 2005-2009 in Kazakhstan. UNDP in Kazakhstan endorsed the Country Programme Action Plan (2005-2009). According to the Action Plan, UNDP would provide assistance to Kazakhstan in strengthening the ability of national partners to develop pro-poor policies. The assistance would also be provided in such areas as micro-finance, globalisation, private sector development, HIV/AIDS and gender equity. The support in gender equality area will be conducive to wider integration of gender issues into national policies and legislation. The UNDP plans to place special emphasis on promotion of UN system coordination with a view to ensure a common approach to gender issues (UNDP Kazakhstan: Gender Mainstreaming Strategy, 11).

It is true that globalisation has reinforced interaction between countries and accelerated their involvement in international affairs. Being a part of the world community, Kazakhstan also joined almost all the international treaties devoted to women's interests and rights aimed at solution of gender issues, to implement these treaties and Beijing Platform for Action. A concept for state policy for the improvement of the status of women in the republic of Kazakhstan setting out basic areas of state gender policies was developed and approved.

Uzbek Women in International Framework

Since independence, Uzbekistan has been focussed on creating and improving the legislative foundation for the protection of human rights and freedoms in the country in accordance with international norms. After entering the global community as an independent country, the Republic of Uzbekistan, in accordance with the Constitution, has reiterated its recognition of the priority of generally recognised norms and international laws. As a full member of the UN, Uzbekistan is a party to international agreements regarding human rights and interests, thereby obligating it to observe and apply them in its governmental and legal practice.

During the years since independence, the Republic of Uzbekistan has recognised around 70 international agreements on human rights, including the Convention on the Elimination of all forms of Discrimination Against Women, the Convention on the Political Rights of Women, the Convention on the Rights of the Child, the Convention concerning Discrimination in respect of Employment and Occupation, the Declaration on the Elimination of all forms of Intolerance and Discrimination on the basis of Religion or Belief, the World Declaration on the Survival, Protection, and Development of Children, the Convention concerning Maternity Protection, the Hague Convention on Civil Aspects of International Child Abduction, etc. (Uzbekistan: Review and Appraisal, 1995: 3).

Since 1991 the representatives of Uzbekistan participated in a number of international forums, for instance, the Fourth World

Women's Conference (Beijing, 1995), Sessions 43-50 of the Women's Commission of the United Nations Organisation (New York, 1996-2006); Special Session on Women's Issues of the United Nations' General Assembly ("Beijing+5", New York, 2000). The country's government took a number of measures aimed to ensure a wider involvement of women's NGOs in international activities.

In particular, in the framework of preparation to a special session "Beijing+5", the Women's Committee of Uzbekistan established a partner network with NGOs, organised trainings and events to assist effective participation of NGOs in the activities of the UN and other international organisations. Women-parliamentarians and women's NGO leaders of Uzbekistan participate in meetings, conferences and trainings organised by the OSCE (Organisation for Security and Cooperation in Europe), World Bank, Asian Development Bank etc. (CEDAW, *www.iwraw-ap.org/resources/pdf/Uzbekistan_SR.pdf*).

The ILO Conventions (100) "On Equal Remuneration for Men and Women Workers for Work of Equal values"; (103) "On the Protection of Motherhood"; (111) "On the discrimination in employment and occupation"; (122) "On Employment Policy"; (138) On the Minimum Age for Admission to Employment"; (182) "On the Prohibition and Immediate Action for the Elimination of the Worst Forms of Child Labour" served as the necessary international legal base for the development at the national level of specific measures for the implementation of international standards to protect women's rights in law and practice of public bodies (Uzbekistan, Beijing Platform for Action, 1995: 1).

Uzbekistan ratified the Convention on the Elimination of all Forms of Discrimination against Women (CEDAW) on 31 August 1995. The specific efforts are being carried out to implement the recommendation of the UN Committee in Uzbekistan. A National Action Plan for implementing the suggestion of CEDAW has been developed and actively put into practice. The government of the Republic of Uzbekistan presented before the Committee one national and two periodical reports on the country's implementation of the Convention on the Elimination of all Forms of Discrimination against Women, the latest of which was presented in August 2004. The periodical reports highlighted specific programmes, activities, and major initiatives undertaken by the government from January 2001 to August 2004 aiming to enhance the status of women, as well as they outlined the planned future priorities in the activities of government in this field. This report discusses the major changes in the legislation, policies and programmes that occurred during the reporting period (CEDAW, *www.iwraw-ap.org/resources/pdf/Uzbekistan_SR.pdf*).

Since the approval of CEDAW, the Republic of Uzbekistan developed a series of national mechanisms with a view to assist the observance of women's rights outlined in the Convention. Following the recommendations of the UN Committee on CEDAW on implementation of the Convention's provisions in the national legislation, a series of measures are taken in the Republic aimed to overcome the return of direct and indirect discrimination against women. As for the country in general, the National scheme for the improvement of status of women is practised at the level of legislative and executive powers. It has also developed and actively implemented a procedure for monitoring and reporting on the implementation of CEDAW provisions that outline the country's policy priorities complying with the provisions of the Convention (CEDAW, *www.iwraw-ap.org/resources/pdf/Uzbekistan_SR.pdf*).

On 9 December 2009, UNDP's project "Legislative and Institutional Capacity Development for Women's Empowerment in Uzbekistan" in collaboration with Uzbekistan Women's Committee held a roundtable dedicated to the 30th anniversary of the Convention on the Elimination of All Forms of Discrimination against Women (CEDAW) in the Poytaxt Business Centre, Tashkent. The roundtable was aimed to promote CEDAW among state agencies and non-governmental organisations as well as the general public. It was also designed to increase the activity of governmental and non-governmental organisations in implementing and monitoring CEDAW (UNDP and Gender in Uzbekistan, The Roundtable Dedicated to CEDAW`s 30th anniversary, 2009).

A joint project of the Women's Committee of Uzbekistan and the UNDP project "Legislative and Institutional Capacity Development for Women's Empowerment in Uzbekistan" organised training on "The legal guarantees of women's right protection" in Nukus, Karakalpakstan, for students of legal clinic in 2008. The training is a part of the campaign devoted to the 30th anniversary of the Convention on the Elimination of All Forms of Discrimination against Women (CEDAW) started in October in legal clinics of Tashkent. The participants received information on CEDAW as well as the Uzbek legislation and ongoing reforms in Uzbekistan (UNDP and Gender in Uzbekistan, Legal guarantees of Women's rights, 2009).

Uzbekistan acceded to the UN Convention against Corruption and in 2008 the Parliament adopted a law on child rights. The United Nations approach in supporting Uzbekistan is articulated in the UN Development Assistance Framework (UNDAF) (2010-2015). The main emphasis will be in the three broad areas of economic well being, social services (education, health, nutrition, STI/HIV drug use prevention, social protection of children and early childhood development); environment (integrating sustainable development principles into country's policies and plans) and governance (to enhance effectiveness, accountability and inclusivity). It is important to mention that the UN has a long-standing partnership and track-record working in Uzbekistan. The UN has played a key role in the formulation of the Welfare Improvement Strategy (WIS), which was sanctioned by the government as a medium term development plan for the country in 2007 and is currently supporting its implementation (UN in Uzbekistan, 2009: 2).

In the area of education, regulations on Basic Education were revised and the UN provided assistance in developing the National Programme for the Quality and Efficiency of Education for 2008-2012. A number of partnerships were undertaken with civil society partners who have been involved in various activities dealing with protecting the rights of people with disabilities, women and children, labour migrants and people living with HIV. The UN Country Team has contributed to building the capacities of sub-national government in developing regional integrated plans for the implementation of the WIS and the National Programme of Action for Children (UN in Uzbekistan, 2009: 3).

Kazakhstan and Uzbekistan both have assent to all human right treaties including CEDAW. Both governments have sought to be associated with desired accomplishment of gender equality with the goal of integration into the world community as full and equal partners.

However, the governments themselves recognise that there are key gaps in legislation and practice. At the same time it is also a harsh fact that both these governments are far from achieving the goals considered necessary by CEDAW and other international treaties.

The implementation of policies related to gender equality is poor and there are three major reasons observable behind this inconsistency. First, legislative base is imperfect due to meagre democracy and it is not much favoured by the masses; second, the gender issues are new in these societies and people do not treat all such practices as a serious subject and third, the major obstruction that is confronted to implement all these plans and policies the lack of finance. However, both states are trying to overcome the barriers in applying women related conventions and global gender interaction in their respective states even in this difficult state of affairs.

These problems are worse in Uzbekistan than its counterpart Kazakhstan. The Uzbek society is more traditional and largely influenced by religion and centralised government system. The lack of money makes such changes more challenging because Uzbekistan does not have as much natural resources (i.e. gas and oil) like Kazakhstan. Though, the Kazakh society is also patriarchal but it is relatively more liberal in nature. The gender issues seem to be peculiar in the social format of the Kazakhs but people are principally aware about such issues. Kazakhstan is in better position as compared to Uzbekistan because the outlook of government is liberal and open. The financial resources are again a major instrument in implementing gender policies in a state and in this reference Kazakhstan has more advantages.

Kazakh Women in Institutional Framework

The Concept of Gender Policy in the Republic of Kazakhstan (2003) responded to some concerns regarding the development of a more comprehensive policy framework and institutional approach to promoting gender equality. The Concept determines major principles, priorities, and goals of gender policy in Kazakhstan in the short-term upto 2010 and long-term upto 2030. This identifies issues of ensuring women's equal access to economic opportunities and gender-based violence. The Concept also commits the government to the introduction of gender education; revision of legislation in a gender-sensitive manner; gender analysis of the budget, national plans, and programmes;

and the development and adoption of the draft law "On Equal Rights and Equal Opportunities" to advance the achievement of these policy goals (Kazakhstan, Country Gender Assessment, 2006: 24).

The Council for Family and Women's Affairs and Demographic Policy under the President of Kazakhstan was established in 1995 to address challenges faced by families, women, and children after independence. The council was reorganised to become the National Committee on Family and Women's Affairs (NCFWA) in 1998, under the President of Kazakhstan's office, as a mechanism to develop specific strategic approaches and programmes in addressing gender equality concerns. The 28-members NCFWA serves as a consultative board to work on the protection of family interests to enhance women's participation in the political, social, economic, and cultural life of the country.

The NCFWA, Chairperson has ministerial status, to facilitate participation in senior levels of decision making. A group of the parliament, composed of 33 elected deputies, guides implementation of policies and programmes to promote the status of women, families, and gender equality. The key ministries are represented on the NCFWA, including, e.g. the Ministry of Labour and Social Protection, ensuring gender concerns are incorporated into policy reviews and implementation. The NCFWA Secretariat implements programmes on its behalf (Kazakhstan Country Gender Assessment, 2006: 25).

NCFWA is represented in each oblast by the Vice-Governor and is supported by one staff member. Coordination for implementation of key programmes is facilitated through the Vice-Governor's office giving additional force. An electronic network has also been established between all NCFWA levels and with NGOs to facilitate the exchange of information. The main areas of NCFWA's activities have been implementing the National Action Plan; implementing programmes to promote women's economic advancement; combating domestic violence and trafficking, including the establishment of crisis centres and telephone hot-lines; and providing activities coordinating women's advancement with international partners and NGOs. The effectiveness of NCFWA's work remains limited due to staff capacity, especially in the areas such as reviewing legislation and policies or monitoring programme implementation. All ministries report on activities to NCFWA in every six months, based on which it submits a report to the government with its suggestions for improving the operations of certain organisations (Kazakhstan Country Gender Assessment, 2006: 25-26).

On 19 July 1999, the Government of the Republic of Kazakhstan adopted by a decree (No. 999) the National Action Plan on Improving the Status of Women in the Republic of Kazakhstan and forwarded it to the UN Commission on the Status of Women. The plan underlines its goals of improving the status of women in Kazakhstan and implementing the Platform for Action of the Fourth World Conference on the Status of Women (Beijing, 1995). The National Action Plan is developed by the National Commission on Family and Women's Affairs under the President of the Republic of Kazakhstan in cooperation with the relevant state bodies, with participation of NGOs and international organisations in accordance with a recommended UN model (Yuri Shokamanov, 2000: 1).

The strategic goal of the National Action Plan is to establish conditions and development of effective mechanisms for strengthening women's role in public and political life, improving women's status in accordance with the long-term development strategy (Kazakhstan – 2030). The National Action Plan consists of 12 priorities, identified by the Fourth World Conference on the Status of Women (Yuri Shokamanov, 2000: 1).

- **Women and Poverty:** The main goal in the policy is increasing the general level of payment for labour, including gradual increasing the minimum salary level to the subsistence level, legalisation of all incomes and increasing the salary level of employees of civil service agencies, where women predominate, and where salary level is lower than an average salary level in the republic.
- **Education and Training of Women:** In accordance with the Constitution of the Republic of Kazakhstan, all citizens are guaranteed access to secondary education in state academic institutions and women are more educated. The main targets in the area of education are: rational distribution of financial resources, especially among rural schools, improving the teaching methodology, securing access to education for children from low-income families, integration of handicapped children into regular schools.

- **Women and Health:** Programmes on increasing maternal and prenatal mortality are implemented in the republic, as well as national programmes on reproductive health protection and others. The strategy to protect women's health anticipates development of standards for reproductive health for marginalised population groups, introduction of methods of safe motherhood, provision of modern contraceptives to the population, scientific and sociological research in the area of family planning.
- **Violence against Women:** The wide spread form of violence against women is domestic violence (physical, psychological and sexual). In accordance to some experts, estimate over 60 per cent of all women in Kazakhstan have been subjected to physical or sexual violence at least once in a lifetime. It is foreseen that new laws shall be adopted and existing legislation shall be amended in accordance with international standards; effective assistance in social rehabilitation to victims of violence shall be secured; special training and education of specialists dealing with women subjected to violence shall be organised, and other activities shall be secured.
- **Women and Armed Conflicts:** Due to armed conflicts in some neighbouring states, the problem of refugees exists in Kazakhstan. There are refugees as a consequence of political, national, religious and other kind of oppression. Among refugees from Afghanistan there are many illiterate people, a significant part of them do not have any professional training or means for existence. Women constitute an especially vulnerable group. A special body for migration processes management "Agency for Migration and Demography" with responsibilities to address problems of refugees-repatriates and other migrants in Kazakhstan.
- **Women and Economy:** Among women applying to employment agencies only every sixth woman receives employment. When enterprise personnel are decreased, women constitute the majority of laid off workers. A micro-crediting programme for lowest income population is implemented in order to provide self-employment to population and development of individual entrepreneurship. A majority of

credit beneficiaries are 63 per cent women. In June 2000, the Government of Kazakhstan has adopted a programme to combat poverty and unemployment.

- **Institutional Mechanisms for Advancement of Women:** The National Commission on Family and Women's Affairs under the President of the Republic of Kazakhstan is established to protect family interests and provision of the necessary conditions for women's participation in political, social, economic and cultural life in Kazakhstan. The priority area for intervention of the National Commission is participation of women in politics, institutions of power, economy, their employment and promotion, issues of women and protection from violence.
- **Women's Human Rights:** Women in Kazakhstan have equal rights to access to education and professional training, in public, political and cultural life, to labour, to equal pay, rest and social provision. Conditions to allow women to combine employment with motherhood are being established; legal guarantee as well as material and moral support for family and fatherhood, motherhood and childhood are being provided. Kazakhstan has joined the Convention on Elimination of All Forms of Discrimination against Women. Kazakhstan envisages addressing the issue of joining the Convention on Political Rights of Women, on Protection of Motherhood, Nationality of Married Women, on Agreement to Marriage, Marriage Age and Registration of Marriage as well as other conventions relevant to family, women and children.
- **Women and Mass Media:** Mass media has a goal to facilitate formation of a non-stereotypical image of a woman, to present her as a creative personality, and an active participant of public processes of country's development. There is not enough attention given to gender issues. Towards this goal, it is envisaged to widen women's access to means of defending their interests through mass media, as well as to ensure objective and non-stereotypical presentation of women in mass media.
- **Women and Environment:** Environment is an important condition for human life and human health. There are two

large zones of environmental disaster in the country: the Aral Sea Basin (caused by drying out of the Aral Sea) and Semipalatinsk (around the Semipalatinsk nuclear test site). The National Environmental Action Plan has been adopted; a Republican Centre for Environmental Protection and Sustainable Development has been established. Twenty-six special programmes to improve the environmental situation, including those relevant to women's health.

- **Girls:** After joining the UN Convention on Child's Rights, some disciplines are included in the educational curricula in Kazakhstan: sexual education, personal hygiene, and healthy lifestyle promotion. As a rule, girls have better educational attainments than boys have. Yet, in the academic year of 1997/1998 girls constituted only 33 per cent of the total number of students in universities. The legislation ensures criminal punishment for exercising of violence against women. However, around two thousand cases of rape or attempts to rape of girls are registered annually.

The Concept of Gender Policy and the Millennium Development Goals in Kazakhstan (NCFWA, 2004) restructured the National Action Plan around the framework of the MDGs. It sets outs priority concerns and strategies to achieve gender aspects of the MDGs in areas of economy and labour, health, and the elimination of violence against women and children.

To protect family, women and children's at the legislative level a special parliamentary group on the family and a special subcommittee of the lower chamber of the Parliament on the issues of women, family, youth, tourism and sport had been created since the submission of the initial report. A section entitled "Women in Development" had been included in the indicative plan for social and economic development of the country for 2000-2005. From 2000, national legislation had been subject to gender analysis and amendments on violence against women had been introduced into the Criminal Code. The government had also started to collect statistical data disaggregated by sex and had published a statistical handbook entitled "Women and Men in Kazakhstan" (24th Session Kazakhstan, 2001: 1).

In Kazakhstan, women represented two-thirds of the unemployed at the turn of this century, and the government had recently adopted a new programme on combating poverty and unemployment for 2000-2002. The government planned to decrease the level of unemployment by 4.5 per cent to approximately 9 per cent by 2002, and it was predicted that over 400,000 new jobs would be created as a result of that programme. The government was also promoting industries in which women were traditionally highly represented. The National Commission for Family and Women had initiated a special credit line to support women entrepreneurs working in the production sector. A State programme of microcredit targeting the rural population, including women, had been successfully implemented during the period 1998-2000, and would be strengthened over the period 2000-2003 (24th Session Kazakhstan, 2001: 1).

The Non-Governmental Organisations (NGOs) are calculated as more organised and known for their socially important work. There are both positive and negative trends in the development of the NGO sector. By 2004, there were more than 6000 registered NGOs in Kazakhstan, however only about 1000 of them are actually working, and only 150-200 could be called sustainable with committed staff and strong organisational structure. A number of factors affect their work such as the Soviet legacy, lack of knowledge and skills, preferential donor support, narrow specialisation of the NGOs. However, overall, the state and citizens increasingly recognise the NGO sector for its potential in promoting and safeguarding the interests of different stakeholders in Kazakh society. The Concept of State support to Non-Governmental Organisations was developed by the government with NGO participation and approved on 23 January, 2002. The aim of the programmes was to strengthen the Government-NGO cooperation at all levels (UNDP, Government of Kazakhstan, 2004: 2).

In the beginning, women's NGOs lacked coordination, with leaders who had begun their activity by drawing attention to women's issues (women's rights, women's status in the transition period, involvement of women in enterprises). But in 1995-1996, the situation as a whole in the republic called for change in the activity of women's organisations, toward social programmes. Joining the women's organisations were groups with a social aim, working in the areas of the family, disabled children, the lonely elderly, and other vulnerable groups. There are not enough of them yet and not spread across larger territories and their financial resources are limited. Today all these organisations play a rather modest role, their emergence, however, is an important factor in women's participation in the social and economic life of the country (Galiya Khassanova, 2000: 389).

Kazakhstan Community Loan Fund (KCLF) is an economic non-governmental organisation in Kazakhstan. KCLF became the first registered non-banking lending institution in Kazakhstan. Its goal is to combat women's unemployment by injecting capital into small women-led businesses. According to Zhussupov of KCLF, "There are currently women's NGOs in Kazakhstan providing counselling in fields of healthcare, legal services, and social issues, but our loan fund is the first to offer financial assistance specifically to women. Government programmes exist but rarely reach recipients, and none focus on women entrepreneurs." The microfinance organisation not only empowers women financially, it advances them professionally. Women hold six of seven elected positions on the KCLF board of directors (Anita Wright, 2000: 17).

Women are taking an active role in the management and integrity of the fund. They lead the accounting department, the nonfinancial services unit, the information systems department and make up over 50 per cent of the loan officers. Not only does KCLF provide microcredit, it also supplies information to the community about how public organisations are governed, how financial records are kept, and what non-banking methods of credit are available. As Kazakhstan continued with its economic and social transition, the women managing KCLF were introducing democratic, participatory processes into the local business environment (Anita Wright, 2000: 18).

For spreading political awareness among women, there are 150 women's NGOs in Kazakhstan offering considerable support in protecting women's political rights. Their leaders and participants are more and more active in the sphere of politics, realising citizens' rights to elect and be elected to the bodies of power and local government. For instance, in 1998, the women's NGOs formed the women's electoral block aimed at increasing the number of women representatives in all bodies of power, supporting electoral campaigns of women candidates, propagating law concerning election in country (Gulsara Tlenchieva: 1).

A project named 'Awareness of Women's Rights' made a considerable contribution to disseminate political knowledge among the country's population. For now not all Kazakhstan women are ready enough for realising their political rights, such as freedom of unions, meetings, rallies and demonstrations, processions and resentment, and access to public service. The continuation of women NGOs work toward information improvement in this field. In this respect it is desirable that women's NGOs cooperate with political parties and the state network functions as independent administrators (Gulsara Tlenchieva: 2).

The NGOs consider equal rights and opportunities recorded in the Constitution of the Republic of Kazakhstan and other legislative documents, and advocate equal right for women and men to realise their political, civil, economical, social, cultural and other rights. For example, Women's Electoral Block NGO thinks that all political strategies and programmes must pass gender examination before their adoption. It is obvious that equal rights imply equal responsibility i.e. a human capability, regardless of sex, of having corresponding duties directed by law (Gulsara Tlenchieva: 2).

Women's NGO's have established employment and professional orientation centres, centres for promotion of small businesses and legal and juridical aid. In several Oblasts a number of seminars on establishing coordination between local executive bodies and non-governmental organisations were held together in association of NGOs. Such councils have already been functioning in some of the local areas e.g. Almatinskaya, Pavlodarskaya, Kostanaiskaya and Yuzhno-Kazakhstanskaya Oblasts (Kazakhstan: Answers to the Questions on Implementation of Beijing Platform of Actions, *www.un.org/womenwatch/daw/.../KAZAKHSTAN-English.pdf*).

Thirty-seven the most active leaders of the National and Oblast non-governmental organisations were rewarded by the National Commission with "Jubilee Medal in Honour of the 10th Anniversary of Independence of Kazakhstan." The first time in the history of Kazakhstan there was high recognition of the activities of NGO's on behalf of the State. Today in Kazakhstan political and institutional foundations for the activities of non-governmental organisations have been created and they are being actively developed in alliance with the government (Kazakhstan: Answers to the Questions on Implementation of Beijing Platform of Actions, *www.un.org/womenwatch/daw/.../KAZAKHSTAN-English.pdf*).

Besides, the NGOs are facing some fundamental problems in Kazakhstan. They have very limited financial resources and in this regard they are mostly dependant on international organisation and Western countries' assistance. Secondly, the public image of NGOs in Kazakhstan has not changed noticeably over the past years. The NGOs slowly expanded their public relation activities, such as outreach to media, but have so far failed to create a positive perception of NGOs among government officials and business sector representatives. The observations tend to be negative among government officials towards NGOs involved in political advocacy campaign.

The relations between NGOs and journalists have improved slightly though the work of NGOs does not appear in the national media as much as many would like. The degree to which an NGO is covered in the media is a function not only of the political climate or the media's attitude towards the NGO sector, but also of the NGO's efforts to actively interface and cultivate good relations with media outlets. Some NGOs seem to have reduced their outreach efforts after initial attempts to make inroads with the media failed. The public generally remains relatively doubtful or ignorant of the NGOs. Many view these NGOs as medium for advancing the interests of narrowly defined economic and political elites. This is especially true of NGOs with ties to political figures (Kazakhstan: 2000 NGO Sustainability Index, 90).

Uzbek Women in Institutional Framework

Uzbekistan has a certain framework of institutional provisions, strategies and programmes at the national level to improve the status of women as well as to protect their rights. Since the submission of initial report of Uzbekistan, the institutional mechanism on improvement of status of women continued to act and develop in the interests of protection of women's right. The Women's Committee of Uzbekistan is the largest women's organisation in the Republic established on 23 February 1991, financially supported by state and it has branches in all regions of the Republic. It has the legal status and is registered with the Ministry of Justice of the Republic of Uzbekistan.

It initiates, manages and implements governmental policy, programmes and projects aimed to improve women's conditions. In an effort to maintain the motion of improvement in status of women, the Women's Committee of Uzbekistan places high emphasis on five priority areas: women's employment and economic welfare; women's reproductive health and reproductive rights protection; women and their participation in social life, stressing women's involvement in executive positions and decision-making; as well as women and law, where special emphasis is made on the elimination of discrimination against women; women and education, stressing over the improvement of professionalism and competency through education (CEDAW, *www.iwraw-ap.org/resources/pdf/Uzbekistan_SR.pdf*).

The Committee also bears the principal responsibility for participation of the Republic of Uzbekistan in international events on women's issues. The committee is carrying out the work to strengthen links with women's organisation in Uzbekistan within the framework of international cooperation. Together with representative of the Charity Corps (USA), the women's committee has set up women's information centre and has opened five branches of it in the cities of Tashkent, Samarkand, Bukhara, Urgench and Namangan. The key role of the Women's Committee of Uzbekistan and its branches is to perform the following tasks:

- cooperate with a view to provide the government with well-considered and representative advisory services in connection with identification, development and implementation of policy reflecting the variety of opinions and conditions pertaining to women;
- reflect the entire diversity of opinions expressed by women, based on consultations with women's non-governmental non-commercial organisations, as well as other groups and organisations working on women's issues;
- act as an intermediary in the process of information exchange between the government and women's sector;
- analyse policy implemented with respect to particular fields representing a special interest for particular organisations;
- Create and support the effective administration to ensure the execution of functions and duties of regional branches of the

Women's Committee of Uzbekistan (CEDAW, *www.iwraw-ap.org/resources/pdf/Uzbekistan_SR.pdf*).

The Women's Committee of Uzbekistan, together with the Ombudsman, has created an advisory-analytic council to put into place monitoring activities regarding the implementation of the Conventions, other international documents, laws, and the normative- legal acts of the Republic with respect to interests of women and children. In accordance with the results of the monitoring activities, discussions were carried out regarding the current situation in the local areas, a National Platform for Action to improve the situation of women in Uzbekistan and to enhance their role in society was determined on 3 March 1999.

It was drawn up following consideration of all the elements and requirements of the Beijing Platform for Action with description being taken of special national features and conditions. It defines the general strategy and priority aiming state policy toward women in harmony with the Constitution of the Republic of Uzbekistan, the state's international obligations and the recommendations of the Fourth World Conference on Women with regard to Action for Equality, Development and Peace, and it takes into account the socio-economic situation in Uzbekistan. The National Platform for Action anticipates the combining efforts of the government, of parliamentarians, of state and public organisations and of the civilian sector in order to enhance the involvement of women in the formation and development of democratic society (UN CEDAW Initial Reports of States Parties, Uzbekistan, 2000: 25-26).

For Uzbekistan, the following outlines of action were highlighted:

- improving women's health, including reproductive health, and developing services for the family;
- educating women and raising their occupational and functional literacy;
- improving the economic situation of women;
- reducing the impact of ecological degradation;
- strengthening the involvement of women in political structures;
- establishing special programmes to support girls;

- shaping models of the new woman in Uzbekistan in the media, culture and art and overcoming existing stereotypes;
- carrying out gender research, including gender objectives in the social policy of the project programme;
- developing and strengthening the role of women's non-governmental organisations;
- upgrading the national mechanism to improve the situation with regard to women's status in Uzbekistan.

The National Action Plan was developed and approved by the Ministry of Justice of the Republic of Uzbekistan to implement the recommendations of the UN Committee on the Elimination of Discrimination against Women. On the basis of the second and third periodic report of the Republic of Uzbekistan, the Plan was developed with the involvement of all the Ministries and Departments, as well as non-profit organisation. Many of these plans are in the process of implementation (Answers to the Questionnaire on the Implementation of the Beijing Platform for Action, (*www.unescap.org/.../Beijing... Questionnaire/Uzbekistan-unofficial-English.pdf*).

The National Action Plan undertook to achieve the following:

- Drafting of the Concept of National Strategy on Gender Equality in the sphere of law, economy, social protection and employment.
- A comparative analysis of national and international legislation on gender equality.
- Inclusion in the curricula of law schools, professional training of judges, lawyers, law enforcement officials, as well as government officials at all levels of compulsory discipline "Gender Equality."
- Publication of a regular compendium on gender statistics.
- Develop proposals for improving the financing of the activities of NGOs, including women ones.
- Development and implementation of departmental statistical reporting of data by the law enforcement authorities about victims of crimes, including women and girls.
- Organisation of the centres providing legal advice to women in difficult family situations.

- Preparation of information on legislation to combat all forms of trafficking, including women and girls, to deal with those responsible for the act and to help the victims.
- Carrying out a sociological study on the status of women in the informal labour market.
- Preparation of information on criminal law in prohibiting polygamy in the form of cohabitation. Preparation of proposals to make appropriate changes in the provisions of the Criminal Code prohibition on polygamy.
- Development of effective measures to support gender-related progress, using the human development index, as recommended by the UN Development Programme.

In 2001, major commitments were proposed in National Action Plan for improving the status of women in Uzbekistan. The following suggestions were projected from this platform: improvement of women's health; education and raising of professional and functional level of women; women's health and the environment; women's economic status and employment; women's rights and opportunities to participate in decision-making; girl's rights; discrimination and violence against women; women in the mass media; development of women's NGOs; women for peace and security and their role against armed conflicts.

In the decree of the President of the Republic of Uzbekistan, dated 2 March 1995, "On measures for strengthening the role of women in the state and social building of the Republic of Uzbekistan", a new position of Deputy Prime Minister of the Republic of Uzbekistan was formed, with authority over questions of social protection of the family, motherhood, and childhood. Similar positions have been introduced in all the regional structures of power attached to the Cabinet of Ministers, and a Secretariat for the social protection of the family, motherhood, and childhood has been created. Thus, in all structures of power from top to bottom the policy has been set to strengthen the number of women in decision-making positions (Uzbekistan: Review and Appraisal of the Implementation, 1995: 12).

An official duly authorised by the *Oliy Majlis* for human rights (approved in 1995) carries out his activity in accordance with the law of the Republic of Uzbekistan regarding human rights

(Ombudsman, 1997). The institution of an authorised official for human rights (Ombudsman) is a parliamentary structure, which is supported with resources by the *Oliy Majlis*. The Ombudsman in accordance with the law has the power of legislative initiative. It cooperates with all national institutions, and also with non-governmental and international organisations as well as foundations in the areas of assuring women's rights, advancing their interests, and promoting gender equality (Uzbekistan: Review and Appraisal of the Implementation, 1995: 12).

The Institute for Monitoring Current Legislation of the *Oliy Majlis* of the Republic of Uzbekistan (approved in 1996) is a systematic research establishment. It cooperates actively with all democratic institutions of the Republic of Uzbekistan. The Institute participates in decision-making through taking part in developing bills and conducting scientific and legal expert assessments of bills. The State Committee on Statistics has created a system of gender-based indicators, which are derived through state statistical observation in the areas of demography and society, and through individual selective specialised research and sociological surveys. In all, 176 indicators are included in this system, reflecting the various aspects of gender development and gender balance (Uzbekistan: Review and Appraisal of the Implementation, 1995: 13).

The State Committee on Statistics functions with the vision of the users' demand of various types, in cooperation with social organisations and departments. It has published a series of statistical collections devoted to the status of women and men in Uzbekistan in agreement with a wide range of indicators employed in statistical practice. The National Centre for Human Rights has celebrated public functions on rights of the child since the date it was founded in 1998, in which they are provided legal counselling services free of charge. More than 500 people, about 65 per cent of whom are women and children, apply to the centres each year. (UN CEDAW Initial Reports of States Parties, Uzbekistan, 2000: 18) The non-governmental non-commercial organisations and women's organisations make significant contribution in the progress of civic initiatives, including those related to increasing the role of women in various fields. Their number increases year by year from two NGOs in 1991 to 84 NGOs in 2006, working in all regions of Uzbekistan.

Women's NGOs have proved to be most active non-profit organisations and the effectiveness of their activities is largely determined by the pressure of the problems during the transition period and challenges to overcome them. The rural women are more focused on economic projects – the creation of small businesses, microcredit, credit unions, marketing efforts for the development of handicrafts, etc. Urban women are focused on educational programmes (also include rural women), publications (newsletters, brochures, training manuals on civic education, campaign posters), research projects, establishment of emergency centres, etc. These projects are designed to involve women in economic and social spheres. An important thing is that women themselves develop and manage these programmes (Answers to the Questionnaire on the Implementation of the Beijing Platform for Action, *www.unescap.org/.../Beijing...Questionnaire/Uzbekistan-unofficial-English.pdf*).

The NGOs have two objectives: current and long-term. The former is directed towards the provision of assistance to orphans, support to the families who have lost their bread-winner, support to the disabled and their families. The latter objective lies in the protection of civil and political rights, civil and legal education, training of women-leaders, women's socialisation. Included among such women's NGOs are the Association of Businesswomen, the '*Olima*' Association, and the Centre for Women Leaders, the '*Khimoya*' Legal Centre and the Women's Resource Centre.

The '*Olima*' women's association was registered on 7 July 1994, currently has sections in all the regions of the country and 650 women members. The Association of Businesswomen of Uzbekistan was registered on 21 June 1991 and includes more than 3,000 women. (UN CEDAW Initial Reports of States Parties, Uzbekistan, 2000: 34) One more organisation that works with women is the National Association of NGOs of Uzbekistan, which has developed a strategy for action in all the areas of women welfare activities. But the key area is to integrate the female youth force into the national mainstream.

Women-related governmental and non-governmental institutional framework is reasonably good in Kazakhstan and Uzbekistan to compensate for gross social differences, but they are very limited in scope and quality, especially in Uzbekistan. Women and members of ethnic or religious groups have limited access to education, public office, etc. The Welfare Improvement Strategy Paper for 2005-2010, which was sanctioned by the Government of Uzbekistan, has yet to be put into practice.

There are no mechanisms that would ensure equal opportunities of employment in state institutions or guarantee equal access to public services. The absolute absence of financial or social capital (i.e. social networks) among women, the disabled, socially vulnerable groups and some ethnic minorities, constitutes the main barrier to expanding their access to public services. The government is not willing to introduce appropriate measures and system that would support these groups in society.

The violence against women is a subject of major concern in Kazakhstan and Uzbekistan. At the same time the institutional and constitutional framework of both these states has failed to overcome this problem. An increase has been recorded in number of suicide cases resulting out of violence against women in Uzbekistan in recent past. Despite, the country's great accomplishment and the effort to ensure equal rights and opportunity for men and women, Kazakh government is still facing some of serious challenges over this issue. For instance, discrimination of women in labour market, lack of awareness on gender issues among males, negative aspects of culture including sex stereotyping etc. remain a major hindrance in the advancement of women. To overcome these challenges, the government of Kazakhstan has expressed its intention to continue its effort in this direction in close cooperation with the UN agenda and NGOs.

Kazakh Women in State Policy Framework

In recent years, special attention has been paid to the development of human capital and implementing a modern social policy protecting the weak and supporting the development of a national economy. Social investment in children and families is projected in following areas. The first is social insurance and social assistance. To increase the birth rate and support the children in Kazakhstan, a system of social support for motherhood and childhood was formed. It includes:

- providing maternity leave during pregnancy and the delivery at the expense of the employer;

- a lump sum welfare payment upon the birth of a child at a rate of 15 times the monthly minimum index that in 2007 came to KZT 16380;
- an allowance for all families irrespective of level of income, to care for children until they reach the age of one;
- an allowance for children aged under 18 in needy families;
- a special welfare payment for mothers who have many children;
- targeted social help;
- an allowance for women who have given birth to more than five children who have reached the age of eight;
- the preferential right for those women to retire at the age of 53 if their professional experience comprises at least 20 years.

The allowances for children, introduced three years ago, have already positively affected the growth of the birth rate, which is also shown by analysis of basic demographic indicators. The population of the country has increased by 2.4 per cent since 2001.

The second area is in the public health services. In agreement with the State Programme on Reform and Development of Public Health Services for 2005-2010, a number of measures for the protection of motherhood and childhood have been put into practice in the republic. Since 2007, funds from the republican budget in the form of special-purpose routine transfers were provided for this purpose. These funds are allocated to supply medicines to children and teenagers who are registered at out-patient dispensaries with chronic diseases. The expenses for this in 2007 came to KZT (Kazakhstan Tenge) 1.037 billion. Supplying children under five years old with medicines added up to a total of KZT 596 million.

The supply of iron and iodine supplements to pregnant women cost KZT 665 million. The cost for preventive medical examinations of women of reproductive age (from 15 to 49 years old) including further supervision and treatment was KZT 3.888 billion. In order to improve and increase access for women and children to highly qualified medical aid, construction of the National Centre of Science of Motherhood and Childhood in the city of Astana was being completed.

In 2007, KZT 4 billion and KZT 9.1 billion was to be paid for the construction of facilities related to the protection of motherhood and childhood, namely, a maternity home, children's hospitals, and regional hospitals were allocated from National budget for the above mentioned projects (UNICEF, 2007: 97-98).

By the Decree of the President of the Republic of Kazakhstan of December 4, 1992 "On Measures of Social Support to Families Having Many Children", starting from January 1, 1993 for the families having four and more children under 18, the following benefits and privileges were determined:

- free making and repair of false tooth for mothers having many children;
- free distribution of medicine in compliance with the physician's prescriptions for children under 14;
- free city transportation and transportation on suburban and rural routes for mothers and secondary school students;
- priority placement of the children in children's pre-school medical and health institutions irrespective of their departmental membership.

Those mothers, who had four and more children under seven and did not work, were given a monthly benefit equal to a minimum wage irrespective of the family income. The Law "On Adjusted Republican Budget for 1994" of July 14, 1994 replaced that benefit by monthly money compensation for mothers having many children to the amount from 1.3 to 2.0 of minimum wages depending on the number of children. The Law "On Republican Budget for 1997" of December 1996 fixed a benefit for not working mothers who had four and more children under 7, equal to one monthly calculation index.

According to the Law "On Republican Budget for 1999" of December 16, 1998 benefits to families having children were given in the form of social assistance. That Law did not determine the size of benefit for mothers having many children, and therefore in 1999 those benefits were not paid almost anywhere. The Resolution of the Government of July 22, 1999 authorised Oblast Akims and Akims of Astana and Almaty to fix the size of social assistance. The size of that benefit was equal to one monthly calculation index. On June 30, 1992 the Law "On Social Protection of Citizens, Victims of Ecological

Disaster in Aral Area" was adopted. According to the Law women residing in the area of ecological disaster (Article 14) had the right particularly:

- to spend pre-birth vacations in specialised institutions outside the area of ecological disaster;
- to get 50 per cent compensation for food products for children that are on dispensary registration;
- to send children every year to specialised children's health institutions;
- to have free trip together with a sick child for medical treatment (that extends to another accompanying person if a mother for some reasons cannot go herself).

On March 20, 1994 distribution of those benefits was suspended, and on April 7, 1999 they were finally cancelled. During the last several years many other pays and benefits for the neediest people have been stopped which were given earlier:

- benefits to single mothers (fathers) were cancelled on January 1, 1997;
- benefits to minor children during the search period for their parents who evade paying alimony – were cancelled on January 1, 1997;
- benefits for utilities payments for poor families after birth of twins were cancelled on January 1, 1999;
- benefits for the children infected with immune deficiency virus and for children sick with AIDS were considerably reduced from January 1, 1997; they were reduced by almost a half from January 1, 1999 and were completely abolished in November 1999 (Alternative Report, 2006: 24-25).

Today education is rightly considered as a principal factor of political, social and economic progress. The qualitative and higher education is an important feature to measure women's position in a social order and Kazakh women are undoubtedly in better footing in education. In this connection, efforts in the sphere of education are aimed at creating a system of quality education and production. The Kazakh government is taking special pains in improving the education sector, especially in the area of Computer, Technology and Language.

By 2010, it was planned to provide 6238 organisations with linguaphones and multimedia rooms that will promote improvement in language studies for children. Currently, the sector programme, "Children of Kazakhstan" for 2007-2011, has been developed. For this programme KZT 203 billion in allocations from the state budget is planned. On the other hand, expenditures on education that in 1991 came to 6.5 per cent of GDP, and was 3.4 per cent of GDP in 2006, which is a decrease of two times. Expenditures on public health services were 3.6 per cent of GDP in 1991; in 2006 it was only 2.3 per cent of GDP. And expenditures on social protection were 4.3 per cent of GDP in 2006 while in 1991 they came to 4.9 per cent of GDP in 1991 (UNICEF, 2007: 110).

The indicator of maternal mortality in Kazakhstan is increasing steadily for the past several years. According to the national estimates based on clinical data, maternal mortality was 36.9 in 2004, in 2005 it grew to 40.5 and in 2006, according to preliminary data, the rate was 44.9 per 100 thousand live-births. Indicators of maternal mortality in 2006 had grown in seven regions and in the city of Almaty. The major reason for maternal mortality is the low level of the health of women. Only 20-30 per cent of women are healthy, and the others are suffering from various diseases (UNICEF, 2007: 116).

The changes currently taking place in the economy have negatively affected the situation of women in the labour market. Women represent two-thirds of the unemployed, and the government adopted a new programme on combating poverty and unemployment for 2000-2002. The government planned to decrease the level of unemployment by 4.5 per cent to approximately 9 per cent by 2002, and it visualised that over 400,000 new jobs would be created as a result of that programme. The government was also promoting industries in which women were traditionally highly represented. The National Commission for Family and Women had initiated a special credit line to support women entrepreneurs working in the production sector. A State programme of microcredit targeting the rural population, including women, had been successfully implemented during the period 1998-2000 and would be strengthened over the period 2000-2003 (UN Report of the CEDAW, Twenty-fourth session, 2001:11).

The efforts to change traditional stereotypes and attitudes regarding the role of women in society include the drafting of a law on advertising, which would prohibit the sexual exploitation of women, and, from 2001, the introduction of gender studies in higher and secondary education. The representative informed the Committee that the government was paying a serious attention to the issue of violence against women, especially domestic violence. The conclusions and recommendations of the comprehensive study conducted by the government on the issues of violence against women would constitute the framework for a draft law on domestic violence. A network of crisis centres had been established in various cities of the country. The government had also reinforced legislation and measures against trafficking in women and girls (UN Report of the CEDAW, Twenty-fourth session, 2001:12).

In the Republic of Kazakhstan certain measures have been taken against violence and trafficking in respect to women. Since 2001 the Resolution of the Government "On Coordination of State Bodies, Organisations and Public Associations, Involved in the Problems of Violence against Women" has been realised. The legislation which was in effect before 2000 has been brought to conformity with international norms of rights, especially with regard to imposing a more severe penalty to persons who committed crimes against women. In Kazakhstan, the most wide-spread form of violence against women is domestic violence. The Ministry of Internal Affairs worked out a draft law "On Prevention and Suppression of Domestic Violence". In case of violence in the family a woman can also turn for help to specialised police departments on protection of women against violence that was established by the Decree of the President of the Republic in 1999 (Kazakhstan: Answers to the Questions on Implementation of Beijing Platform of Actions, *www.un.org/womenwatch/daw/.../KAZAKHSTAN-English.pdf*).

At present a special Inter-departmental Commission on combating illegal export, import and trafficking in people has been established under the Government of the Republic of Kazakhstan with the Minister of Justice at the head. A National Plan on combating, prevention and suppression of crimes in trafficking in people for the period of 2004-2005, was adopted. According to this plan the state bodies undertake certain activities against trafficking in people on a regular basis.

The preparation work is being carried out for adopting international documents on combating trafficking in people and exploitation of prostitution by the third persons in Kazakhstan. In 2001-2002, the project of IOM "Informational Campaign on Prevention of Trafficking in Women" was also recognised (Kazakhstan: Answers to the Questions on Implementation of Beijing Platform of Actions, *www.un.org/womenwatch/daw/.../KAZAKHSTAN-English.pdf*).

The National Commission acted as a national coordinator in that project. 19 NGOs took part in that project by arranging hotlines in all Oblasts of the Republic. The second joint project with IOM "Fight against Trafficking in People out of, in, via and within Kazakhstan" has been completed. The project contributed to further improvement of national legislation and promoted rendering aid to the victims of trafficking and training of the officers from the law-enforcement bodies in combating trafficking with the help of international experience. A large regional informational campaign "Life without Violence –This is our Right" was held (2001 – 2003) together with UNIFEM with participation of 9 CIS countries and Baltic Republics (Kazakhstan: Answers to the Questions on Implementation of Beijing Platform of Actions, *www.un.org/womenwatch/daw/.../KAZAKHSTAN-English.pdf*).

Uzbek Women in the Framework of State Policy

One of priority areas in the state policy of the Republic of Uzbekistan is legal, economic, and social protection of motherhood and childhood. It is trying utmost in shaping conditions for improving women's social and financial status, promoting women's participation in the reforms in all areas of public life and in the country's modernisation. Such policies are implemented by the means of Laws of the Republic of Uzbekistan, Decrees of the President of the Republic of Uzbekistan, government decrees, and state programmes aiming to improve women's political, economic and social status. At present the social support to the population of the Republic is provided in the framework of two large programmes i.e. for families with children and for low-income families (CEDAW, *www.iwraw-ap.org/resources/pdf/Uzbekistan_SR.pdf*).

Since 1994 in case of the low income families support programme and since 1997 in case of the programme of support to families with children, the funds allocated from the budget are distributed by local self-governance bodies – *mahallas*. The significant support to socially vulnerable groups of society is provided in the form of low-income family grants, made available from the state budget funds (just as assistance to families with children under sixteen). The main criteria in making the decision on provision of such assistance is an average family income per capita as a rule, not exceeding the amount of the established minimum wage.

The additional characteristics are also taken into consideration, such as the property status of family members, their labour market status, and effectiveness of using the farmhouse land allocated for agricultural purposes, composition of family. The types of benefits and allowances provided to families with children are included in the unified system of the state assistance to families: monthly allowances to families with children under sixteen; monthly childcare allowance for mothers (before the child reaches the age of two); extraordinary grant at childbirth; maternity allowance (CEDAW, *www.iwraw-ap.org/resources/pdf/Uzbekistan_SR.pdf*).

The special features of the demographic situation peculiar to Uzbekistan have a significant impact on the standard of living of the population. The high level of fertility produces a high proportion of children in the population, as a result of which the population of working-age carries a higher economic burden. The eradication of unemployment and poverty and the enhancement of social integration and development are among the main aims of Uzbekistan's social policy which lies under the control of the President and Government of Uzbek Republic (UN CEDAW Initial Reports of States Parties, Uzbekistan, 2000: 48).

In the State Pension Provision Act, there is provision for granting preferential pensions irrespective of age, preferential pensions with a 5 to 10 years relaxation of the generally specified retirement age and pensions due to industrial injuries or occupational diseases. The preferential pensions were enjoyed by over 120,000 people, including 8249 people with pensions regardless of age on completion of service; 122,529 people with pensions below the generally specified age and 180,000 people with pensions due to industrial injury or occupational diseases in 2000. (UN CEDAW Initial Reports of States Parties, Uzbekistan, 2000: 49)

A range of legislative acts have been passed to increase allowances for workers, including women, employed in unfavourable working conditions. The decision (No.117) of the Cabinet of Ministers of the Republic of Uzbekistan dated 17 March 1999, on the preferential taxation of incomes of women employed in jobs with especially risky and tough conditions was approved. The Republic of Uzbekistan has its own state system as in many developed countries of social insurance which is designed to protect the population against potential social risks including, temporary incapacity to work (sickness), old age, disability and loss of the breadwinner. (UN CEDAW Initial Reports of States Parties, Uzbekistan, 2000: 50) The current system of social insurance includes a range of payments granted to people when the above-mentioned risks arise:

- an allowance for temporary incapacity to work is granted through the workplace and paid for days of sickness at rates of 60 per cent, 80 per cent or 100 per cent of the average monthly wage, according to the length of service in the job;
- a maternity allowance is granted through the workplace at the rate of aggregate average earnings for 126 calendar days;
- a one-off maternity grant is granted through the workplace or place of study of the parents, or, if they are not working or studying, through the social security agencies, at the rate of twice the minimum wage;
- a one-off burial grant is paid out at the rate of three times the minimum wage;
- pensions are granted and paid out by social security agencies.

The system of social insurance provides significant benefits for women, and the greater part of expenditure is targeted at them. In addition, recent years have seen a trend of relative decline in the proportion of maternity allowances and of maternity grants in total expenditure on benefits payments through the system of social insurance. The maternity allowances are curtailed every year, respectively 42.5 per cent in 1996; 33.2 per cent in 1997 and 33 per cent in 1998 and One-off Maternity grant was slashed from 8.3 per cent in 1996; to 6.8 per cent in 1997 and 5.5 per cent in 1998 (UN CEDAW Initial Reports of States Parties, Uzbekistan, 2000: 50).

Uzbekistan has made substantial progress in the restructuring of different layers of health services, such as primary care, emergency care, and secondary and tertiary care. Two major initiatives have been undertaken so far with the aim of restructuring primary healthcare in Uzbekistan. The first initiative, project "Health" (1998 – 2005; subsequently renamed "Health 1"), was the result of a collaboration between the World Bank and the Uzbek Government and piloted several new mechanisms and frameworks for the delivery, financing and management of rural primary care.

The new approaches mainly involved general practice and family medicine-based clinical practices. A per capita payment system was launched for rural primary healthcare providers. The second primary care initiative, consisting of project "Health 2" of the World Bank and the "Women and Child Health Development Project" of the Asian Development Bank (2005 – 2010) aims to expand the rural primary healthcare reforms throughout the country. There are plans to implement similar new pilot projects with regard to urban primary healthcare reforms as well as to introduce new shift to maternal and child health, public health, and monitoring and evaluation, in order to make stronger the primary healthcare sector (HiT Profile in Brief: Uzbekistan, 2008: 5).

In Uzbekistan, emergency care services have undergone extensive reforms, particularly in regard to hospital-based emergency care. Throughout the country, a vertical network of emergency departments has been organised. In 2004, the emergency care framework consisted of one Centre of Emergency Care in the capital, Tashkent, 12 branches and 204 ambulance stations. However, at the same time, the specialised care has become less accessible especially in rural areas. Between 1997 and 2003, overall bed capacity was reduced by 50 per cent, with a reduction of the number of hospitals in rural areas by 50 per cent and in urban areas by 20 per cent. Although funding reforms resulted in the establishment of a state-financed basic benefits package, the development of pooling schemes and third-party payers might be useful for improving access to health services, and for strengthening the value of the country's health system (Azimov and Ahmedov, 2007: 12).

The violence against women is again one additional leading problem related to women in Uzbekistan. Despite of a number of existing laws and regulations women are incapable to conquer this problem. The institute of family and community are main violators so far as violence against women is concerned. The family creates conditions chiefly for domestic violence and community for rape and trafficking against women and all these issues need a serious concern. The authorities do not notice domestic violence unless it does not turn into suicide cases. The problems of female suicide cases also have not escaped the attention of state official in Uzbekistan. The government report submitted to the CEDAW in January 2001 showed that the number of female suicides increased between 1995 and 1998 especially; 1327 cases in 1995, 1460 cases in 1996, 1573 cases in 1997 and 1560 cases in 1998 were registered in reference to female suicides in Uzbekistan (Carin Benninger Budel and Joanna Bourke Matignoni, 2003: 306).

There are no civil remedies such as protective order in Uzbekistan. No laws exist to remove abusive men from their homes for a period or on occasion. Divorce presently appears the only way for women to escape a violent marriage and further divorce is again a very tough decision for women to take. On the other hand, the victims of domestic violence face many difficulties in filing divorce, but when men would like to file divorce, the *mahalla* seems to be very supportive to them. The state bodies together with social non-governmental and international organisations are conducting a series of seminars, round table discussions, conferences, and meetings, the topic of which is increasing the legal literacy of women and raising gender sensitivity in civil society regarding violence against women (Carin Benninger Budel and Joanna Bourke Matignoni, 2003: 306).

The government, internal affairs offices, and the general prosecutor's office of the Republic, yearly study the situation about the observance of laws regulating the rights of women, and in this regard materials of general applicability are considered at coordinating meetings of law enforcement bodies. The purpose of the study of these resources is to make suspected discrimination come to light. The prosecutors' offices in all regions, together with social and non-governmental organisations as well as organisations of self-government in the localities put into practice a series of measures intended to restore women's rights.

Uzbekistan has joined the Conventions on the Suppression of Traffic in Persons and the Exploitation of the Prostitution of Others to bar the illegal migration of women (by resolution of the *Oliy Majlis* of the Republic of Uzbekistan, dated 12/12/2003). At the level of the government, the work of state, social, and non-governmental organisations and the media is being coordinated with connection to preventive measures to be taken against the unlawful transportation of people (Uzbekistan, Beijing Platform for Action, 1995: 36).

In recent years, transformation in education sector in Uzbekistan has shown some favourable results. Most notably, this has been achieved by adding the secondary special educational level and later increasing investment in the facilities for primary and secondary education. The transition to a new form of schooling at this level, along with extending the period of compulsory education from 10 to 12 years in 2007, has resulted in lower but still strong secondary school attendance rates, with 93 per cent of children aged 12-17 attending secondary school or higher. In 2005-2006, 670 schools serving 249,000 pupils were rehabilitated, and 968 schools serving 505,000 pupils underwent major renovation (Uzbekistan Country Analysis United Nations Country Team, 2008: 37).

The government has sought to maintain very high levels of expenditure on education, at more than 10 per cent of GDP and representing 38 per cent of the total budget. However, much of this investment has been spent on physical building of new secondary special schools. In the Post-Soviet era one important feature is observed i.e. a great down turn in women's involvement in higher education in Uzbekistan. To deal with these circumstances, the Republic of Uzbekistan is applying a number of measures to put it in order.

The special National Programme for Personnel Training was developed and has been implemented in the country. The environment was created for women to obtain education and increase their qualification in Uzbekistan. The non-stop system of education was introduced in the Republic. The Law on Education was developed and adopted (1997), envisaging the equal rights for women and men in terms of choosing their vocation and obtaining education in any educational institution (CEDAW, *www.iwraw-ap.org/resources/pdf/Uzbekistan_SR.pdf*).

The network of schools is mounting; new types of educational institutions, academic *lyceums*[2] and vocational colleges were established and put into operation. By the beginning of the academic year 2004-2005 as many as 65 academic lyceums and 827 vocational colleges were operating in the educational system of the Republic. 30,500 students were learning in the academic lyceums, out of which 35.9 per cent were girls. The vocational colleges provided education to 757,600 students, including 47.3 per cent of girls. As many as 2,600 teachers were employed in the academic lyceums of the Republic, of which 76.2 per cent were women. The vocational colleges had 40,000 teachers in the staff (59.5 per cent of which were women) (CEDAW, *www.iwraw-ap.org/resources/pdf/Uzbekistan_SR.pdf*).

The Uzbek government has adopted a number of state policies to improve the position of women but due to the lack of finance and centralised government system it could not achieve the desired success. The ongoing market reforms have aided economic recovery and increased expenditure on social welfare, health and education followed the rise. The state budget allocation for all social sectors increased to 55 per cent in 2008. About 12 per cent of GDP is devoted to education, 3 per cent to health and 2 per cent to social assistance for poor families. Despite this expenditure human capital has dropped, unemployment has risen and access to health and education is falling. The continued environmental degradation also helped poverty stood at 26 per cent in 2005. The government has committed to reducing this level to 14 per cent by 2015.

However, over the years since independence the rate of infant mortality has declined from 38.1 to 18.3 for 1000 lives births; maternal mortality has declined from 42.8 to 33.5 in 100,000 live births; and the number of abortions over the last 12 years has been reduced in Uzbekistan. The government policies enhanced the level of women's political participation. The number of women in the lower house of parliament has increased from 17 per cent in 2004 to 22 per cent in 2009; in this reference the condition of Uzbek women is far better than their counterpart in immediate neighbour Kazakhstan. But in the sector of Higher Education the position of Uzbek women is not satisfactory.

In 2002, the ratio of girls to boys was 47.8 per cent in preschool institutions, 49 per cent in general education schools, 35.3 per cent in academic lyceums, 40.9 per cent in professional colleges, and 38.9 per cent in institutions of higher learning. A decline in the percentage of female students in institutions of higher learning is associated with specific conditions connected to early marriage and the birth of children, essentially at the ages from 18 to 22. It means that even after the implementation of the state policies for women, the desired results are a distant dream; and it seems that such policies failed in improving women's place in society. After independence, the patriarchal and traditional forms are reviving in Uzbekistan. As a result, women are confining themselves again to the boundary of four walls, they are no more interested in jobs and outside works. Such signs are not at all favourable for a healthy society.

On the other hand, the Kazakh government is dragging its feet on social welfare policies. But the participation of women is increasing in higher education, market economy. In this way, Kazakh women are trying their best to overcome unemployment. Though the Kazakh women are not enjoying much service provisions as used to be in the Soviet times but the openness of Kazakh society and opportunities of market economy allowed smooth progress of women even without the help of government.

At the same time it is true that women in Kazakh society are far from having equality with men. Their percentage in decision-making is very low in comparisons to the Soviet period and even Uzbekistan. But their stronger footing in the economy of Kazakhstan is a condition that can slowly and steadily improve their presence in political affairs too. Though the Kazakh women are struggling a lot in relation to earlier times but undoubtedly they are moving on fast in a very positive manner without looking back to the past.

Changing Policies for Women from Soviet to Post-Soviet Period

Before 1991, Kazakhstan and Uzbekistan both were parts of the Soviet Union. In this way, a number of the policies they inherited as the Soviet legacy and the policies for women was also a part of all this. After attaining independence, some of the gender policies were pursued, some were left-out and others modified accordingly by the contemporary system of these states, which were basically started by the Soviet system. For example, the 1972 Labour Code of Kazakh SSR (Soviet Socialist Republic) contained several restrictions on women employment in various activities; heavy work under harmful condition, as well as underground work prohibited; pregnant women or women with children upto three years could not be employed in night shifts, overtime or weekend work or sent on business trips.

The new Labour Code of Kazakhstan holds no restriction for women's employment. Simultaneously, some more progressive norms were abolished; e.g. the legal norms that existed earlier and allowed additional leave for both parents to care for a child both men and women were replaced with a new regulations allowing only women to take such leave. In comparison, Uzbek's new Labour Code is carrying out most of the earlier set of laws implemented in the Soviet times.

In the Soviet Union women had such privileges as paid maternity leave for upto one year, or upto three years unpaid. During that time it was illegal to dismiss a woman from her job (the time of leave also counted as working time for the calculation of her pension). Women took for granted the state's healthcare system of obstetric and gynaecological clinics, health resorts, and delivery centres that cared for women free of charge. There were also a low-cost childcare system (free for disabled or sick children); free public education; government allowances for families with children; and state support for families with many children, including additional allowances, inexpensive children's clothing, housing privileges, and so on, which helped women maintain their home and family (Galiya Khassanova, 2000: 385).

Today, all such services are less available and more expensive, and working women have to juggle responsibilities at both the work place and at home. The double burden is a barrier to the advancement of women at work and at the same time is areas on for marital discord at home. The gender roles have become rigidly differentiated and both men and women repeatedly stated that regardless of women's level of employment or income, the "man is the leader," especially at home. Allocation of a certain number of seats for women in the Supreme Soviets of the USSR and Union Republics created an outward show of equal participation of men and women in the state government. The activity of women leaders in district committees and city committees of the Communist Party, as well as in executive committees, was quite evident (Susan Somach and Deborah Rubin, 2010: 18).

In the Law of the Kazakh SSR, women are given the right to make a decision on maternity alone. With an idea of protecting women's health, there are provisions on the use of modern methods to prevent unwanted pregnancies; sterilisation may only be performed with the woman's consent and based on medical indications. However, local women's organisations fear that anti-abortion legislation may be introduced to try and reverse the population decline in Kazakhstan. The abortions later than four months into a pregnancy are to be performed in public medical institutions and only upon medical advice. While earlier forcing a woman to have an abortion used to be a crime punished by correctional labour for upto one year, or two years if it resulted in serious consequences, the new Criminal Code no longer considers this a crime. The number of illegal abortions and abortions performed outside medical institutions are very high and common because the cost of legal abortion is very high (Violence against Women, Kazakhstan, *www.onlinewomeninpolitics.org/kz/kazakhstan.pdf*: 225).

Few women hold powerful policy-making positions in the executive branch, and those that do have tended to serve in Ministries dealing with social issues, such as health and education. According to Herman, it would not essentially be true to conclude that Central Asian Women today have a weaker voice in politics than they did in Soviet times, despite the drop in formal representation. The birth of civil society has provided new opportunities for women to enter the country's political life, though the NGOs remain reasonably weak. However, they have an effective system, which may be slow but it leads to the crucial process of group interests of women and giving them forceful representation (Robert Herman, 1996: 23-24).

Uzbekistan still largely maintains the gender equality in education and health access that used to exist during the Soviet times. Historically, the labour market situation for women differed somewhat in Uzbekistan due to the high birth rates, especially in rural areas, and labour surpluses. Despite the Soviet constitutional guarantee of the right to employment, fewer Uzbek women were working outside the home than in other parts of the USSR. Although urban women were inclined to have full-time employment, rural women were more likely to be engaged in low-paid seasonal work. Moreover, even working women were responsible for maintaining the family and home. Nevertheless, the majority of women in Uzbekistan were active in political and economic life.

Since independence, the economic challenges of the transition period have resulted in less access to health and social services. With recent efforts to reassert a national identity, more restrictions on women and girls are being imposed by families. For example, families are reluctant to permit their daughters to study away from home (where they would need to live in a dormitory), resulting in a drop in women in higher education. There is also an increase in early marriage, increased pressure on young wives, denying women the right to divorce, and restricting women's role in public life. According to unofficial reports, violence against women, including domestic violence, rape, and trafficking are on the rise. The economic challenges have led to migration abroad for employment; consequently, sometimes these women become the victims of trafficking.

Under the Soviet system, women had high sort of participation in the local and national government, if not at the topmost positions in the party. The quota systems ensured 33 per cent representation by women in the Supreme Soviet. At present, the involvement of women in the formal political sphere and in political party activity is not high, although there are no formal barriers to women's involvement and there are a number of prominent women in highly noticeable positions. Kazakhstan holds a rank of 74 among over 140 countries in terms of women's participation in national parliament. The lack of the financial resources needed to engage in pre-election campaigning, negative stereotypes against women in leadership positions, and the logistical burdens of employment and domestic chores have all been cited by respondents and in research studies as reasons restricting women's political engagement at the national level. The President has resisted the calls of women's NGOs and international groups for a quota for women's participation in decision-making positions.

In the most recent parliamentary elections (2007), women comprised approximately 15 per cent of the total number of candidates, but the final seating is determined by the parties rather than by the exact number of votes they receive. After the 2007 election, women held 18 of 107 seats in the *Majhilis* (just under 17 per cent of the total), up from 8 women members (10 per cent of the total of 77) in 2003. The Senate has only two women members (4.3 per cent) at present. (Susan Somach and Deborah Rubin, 2010: 16) On the other hand, according to the Women's Committee, an Uzbek quasi-governmental organisation whose Chair is the Deputy Prime Minister, 67 per cent of Uzbekistan's small business are owned by women, 12 per cent of *Mahallahs* are headed by women, and the number of women in the lower house of parliament has increased from 17 per cent in 2004 to 22 per cent in 2009.

Under the Uzbek law, women must constitute at least 30 per cent of those nominated for deputy candidate posts by each political party. For the December 2009 parliamentary elections, 33 per cent of candidates were women. Before the number of deputies was expanded to 150 in December 2008, there were 21 women in the 120-member lower chamber of the parliament and 15 women in the 100-member senate. There is however only one woman in the 28 member cabinet. Uzbek women thus are not lacking much behind the Soviet times while the Kazakh women are left behind in the political participation and decision-making (Susan Somach and Deborah Rubin, 2010: 59).

Divorce in the former USSR times was not difficult, especially if the application was made with the mutual consent of both spouses. However, at the same time, there were some legal provisions which aimed to protect women in these situations. For instance, a husband could not divorce his wife if she was pregnant or if they had a child less than one year of age. This provision has not changed. The rate of divorce in Uzbekistan is half that in the Russian Federation because of the strong influence of traditional social norms regarding women which force them to remain obedient and not to create the situation which could lead to divorce.

As a result, many women who may have valid grounds for divorce, do not exercise their legal right to divorce out of fear that their parents and relatives would hold them responsible for the breakdown of the marriage. Instead, they tolerate domestic violence, polygamy and humiliation for preserving the family unit and for the sake of their children. Women are aware that the threat of divorce puts them at a serious economic disadvantage (UN Promoting Women's Rights as Human Rights, 1999: 129).

In economic terms the gap in wages has increased between men and women since independence. It was reported that even educated women do not actively seek employment outside the home, but are expected to take care of their families especially in Southern Kazakhstan and Uzbekistan. There are many restrictive attitudes that hamper women's increased participation in business, such as a fear that the women will grow "too independent" and not fulfil their household responsibility and also raised concerns about women's interactions with other men outside the home. Basically, it can be said that the revival of religion and patriarchal form of society is creating a barrier to the advancement of women in the rural areas of these states especially. As a result, the average wage gap between men is increasing from 30 per cent in 1990 to 38 per cent in 2002 (Susan Somach and Deborah Rubin, 2010: 19).

Notes

1. Social reasons for abortion include:
    1. death of a husband during pregnancy period;
    2. confinement of a woman or her husband;
    3. cases when a woman and her husband are officially recognised as unemployed;
    4. if a woman is not married;
    5. availability of the Court decision on deprivation or limitation of parental rights;
    6. pregnancy as a result of a rape;
    7. if a woman has a status of a refugee or forced migrant;
    8. an invalid-child in a family;
    9. divorce during pregnancy period;
    10. many children in a family (4 and more children).
2. ***Lyceum*** is a category of educational institution defined within the education system of many countries, mainly in Europe. The definition varies between countries; usually it is a type of secondary school. In reference of Uzbekistan, Lyceums also emerged in the former Soviet Union countries after they became independent. One typical example is Uzbekistan, where all high schools were replaced with lyceums ("litsey" is the Russian term, derived from French "lycée"), offering three-year educational programme with a certain major in certain direction. Unlike Turkey, Uzbek lyceums do not hold University entrance examination, which gives students the right to enter a University, but they hold a kind of "mock examination" which is designed to test their eligibility for a certain University. (Source: *http:// en.wikipedia. org/wiki/Lyceum*)

Chapter - 6

Conclusion

Whenever the question of women's equality, women's right and women's liberty is raised, then new aspects of feminism came to the forefront. The term Feminism was firstly used in Western world basically from 1970 to 1980. Three types of feminism was identified as – Liberal, Radical and Socialist feminism. Liberal feminism focuses on eliminating gender inequality. According to liberal feminism, society consists of individual who are equal, and therefore all people must have equal rights. There is a clear division between the role of state and individual freedom. Radical feminism seeks to redress the power balance between men and women. Radical feminism considers the social structure against women and radical feminism aims to challenge and to overthrow patriarchy by opposing standard gender roles and what they see as male oppression of women. Socialist feminism theory is the gist of Marx and Engels' view about feminine ferment. Marx believed that in a society two classes always exist – the exploiter and the exploited. Women come under the exploited class because they do not any resource of production. The capitalist societies are fundamentally male-dominated society and in such a setting women are always treated as unpaid labour.

Actually socialist feminism connects the oppression of women to Marxist idea about exploitation, oppression and labour. Besides, in the end of twentieth and in the beginning of twenty-first century, some of other types of feminism were also being observed, i.e. Cultural Feminism, Black Feminism, Colonial Feminism and Islamic Feminism. So far as Central Asian women are concerned, they were influenced by socialist and Islamic feminism mainly. Islamic feminism is a new concept that favours women's rights, their progress and to free them from exploitation, but they never talk about the change in social structure, dominance of males and women equality. The role of various feminist movements (socialist, Islamic and liberal) was also influencing the position of Central Asian Women in different times in different situations.

The status of Central Asian Women transformed according to a variety of times, ruling regimes and governments. Kazakhstan and Uzbekistan are two important states in this region and these special effects also governed the position of women in these states. During the Russian Empire, the condition of women was certainly worse in social, political and economic terms. Both these societies are different from each other in several ways and by nature. However, women in both these societies were also facing the common evil of *Kalym*, *Paranja*, polygamy and bride kidnapping etc. The Kazakh women being a nomad society was a little in liberal condition than the Uzbek counterpart. But decisively women in both societies were living the life of beasts where they have not any rights regarding property and divorce; additionally, the condition of widows was also pathetic. In pre-USSR period Central Asian Women didn't have any share in economy; they were completely engaged in domestic labour for which they were even not paid a single penny. The political participation was an entirely a distant dream for them.

The Soviet era proved to be the golden period for Central Asian Women. The government completely banned all the ill-practices which were against women. Their education level was enhanced from 2 per cent to 99 per cent during this time. The economic participation of women was extensively encouraged and to increase women's involvement in external affairs (outside home) they were given some additional facilities (to ease them from domestic and family responsibilities) like crèche, kindergartens, childcare centre, community kitchen etc. Various kinds of leave provisions were launched to facilitate the working environment for women. These efforts of the Soviet government made possible for the Kazakh and Uzbek women to record their presence in all spheres of life. She was able to defeat some of the social evils and a positive change could be observed in her approach towards life.

Women and men were treated equally in constitutional laws. Women were also given the right to divorce, the right to equal inheritance of property, the right to education without discrimination, the right to vote, the right to be witness in court on equal basis as men and right to hold public offices. According to Article 122, in the USSR, women enjoyed equal rights with men in all spheres of economic, state, culture, social and political life. This is ensured by granting women equal rights with men to work, remuneration of labour, leisure and rest, social insurance and education. The Soviet government acknowledged that Central Asian Women were in an exploitative situation. The patriarchal form of society and the tradition of Islamic practices were holding back women's progress in these societies. Women were given equal rights to men in all affairs by the Soviet administration and in this way somehow it reduced the ill-effects of patriarchy. Religion was forcibly banned from public spheres with all its conventional practices and this was the beginning of a new era in some manner.

In this period women was associated with social, political and economic life, feeling freed from her confinement. The Zhenotdel (Women's Department of Communist party) was set up to draw women into public life. During the meetings organised by the Zhenotdel in villages and cities women were imported skills with sewing, trade, reading and writing. This was a mode that gave women a public awakening and provided a platform where women shared their social problems. Further, women's and children's health was given a special preference during this period.

All expected mothers were placed under medical supervision from the very first months of pregnancy. As a rule all women gave birth in maternity homes where professional staff was easily available. A large number of research institutes of mother and child care were established. Actually, it was the first attempt when women's health was given any consideration and first experience for women when some special attention was offered to them as citizens at government level.

The changing status of Central Asian Women from Pre-USSR period to USSR period was extremely constructive. At the same time it is also a fact that even after these phenomenal changes women have not achieved parity with men. The 'double burden', wage gap and their number among top positions (which was very nominal) were some of the challenges women still faced in the Soviet period. Despite of these, this was certainly a new dawn for women in these societies. During the USSR period, Kazakh and Uzbek women had positively benefitted in social, political and economic fields.

Since 1991, after the disintegration of Soviet Union again a great change has been noticed in the position of Kazakh and Uzbek women which is again very complicated to analyse and conclude whether it is negative or positive. Now both these states are under different government systems and independence has provided an occasion to evoke traditions and religion for the masses. If both these states are comparatively analysed then Uzbekistan has been much affected by traditional and religious resurgences. Some of the ill practice like early marriage, polygamy and *Paranja* was again visible. Besides, it seems that the Uzbek women herself approved such changes in her life. Such changes reduced women's involvement in skilled working force and higher education in Uzbekistan. On the other hand, the Kazakh society was much influenced by European culture and it could save itself from the negativity of religion and tradition to some extent except some complaints of polygamy and bride-kidnapping in Kazakhstan.

It is true that today, the involvement of women in political sphere and in political party activity as well as in decision-making authority is not high in Kazakhstan. For example, 12 per cent of the members of the parliament are women and only one woman is minister. In local governmental bodies, the percentage of women's participation is a little bit higher but nowhere does it exceed 20 per cent. Kazakhstan holds the rank of 74 among over 140 countries in the level of women's participation in national parliament. The Kazakh constitutional laws and governmental policies do not allow any quota for women concerning their political participation.

On the other hand, there is a 30 per cent quota for women in political parties to encourage their participation in decision-making in Uzbekistan. As a result, women's strength was recorded 22 per cent in the lower house in 2009. Under the Uzbek law, women must constitute at least 30 per cent of those nominated by parties as candidates for parliamentary elections. In December 2009 parliamentary election 33 per cent candidates were women. It is only the government support and policies that improved women's political participation in decision-making in Uzbekistan and they have a far better position in this regard than in Kazakhstan. Undoubtedly, political participation is an important milestone in women empowerment.

So far as the women rights and gender equality is concerned, Kazakh government however supported a range of legislative efforts ensuring that gender equality was formally written in Kazakh constitution, government policies and legal structures. A council that is known as National Commission for Women Affairs and Family Demographic Policy was formed to ensure gender equality. The government of Kazakhstan has also associated the accomplishment of gender equality with its goal of entering into the world community as an equal partner. It has signed about 60-70 International agreements, including the key declarations related to gender.

The Kazakh legislation base in reference to women equality is still not much stronger. The Soviet Labour Code provided women social assurance (maternity leave, government daycare institutions and child-care leave etc.) and gave a special security to women. There is a considerable gap between the provision of equality for men and women declared by the constitution and its implementation in practice and the government itself is aware of these key gaps in legislation and practice. The implementation of gender equality policy approach is inadequate and the governmental stand seems faulty. In some areas, there still exists a lack in protecting rights, promoting them to executive positions and proper equality between men and women. Although Article 1 of the national constitution particularly prohibits discrimination, it does not contain any definition of discrimination.

So far as the legal rights are concerned, it seems that Uzbek women are in a better and stronger position than Kazakh women, especially in the matter of labour law. The Uzbek Labour Law expansively provides facility of social security and social insurance to women in the country. The Kazakh women are at par with Uzbek in Constitutional and Criminal Code. Uzbekistan has also agreed to all human rights treaties including CEDAW. Though, there is the active role of Human Right Commission, Ombudsman, National Action Plans and other institutional frameworks for improving women position in Uzbekistan even then they do not have enough budget.

But within the families the situation is really severe; the revival of traditional standards and religious rigidness, and more restrictions on women and girls are being imposed. Because of these problems, the existing institutions and machinery are unable to accomplish their desired objectives and work. On the other hand in Kazakhstan, whatever the available set up, they are more successful and doing well in empowering women's position, though the measures established for women's equality in the Soviet times are now to some extent getting blurred in both these states. In Kazakhstan, Gender Based Violence (GBV) is a serious problem and reflects the lack of equality between men and women. The definition of GBV is wider than only violence against women or violence that occurs only within the home i.e. domestic violence. It can entail rape, date-rape, sexual harassment, and such violence that even leads to homicide. The occurrence of GBV in Kazakhstan is difficult to measure as it has been neither well defined nor well recorded by either the police or hospitals.

Since 1999, a division on women's protection from violence has operated within the Ministry of Internal Affairs. They have branches throughout the country which are supposed to offer legal assistance and to analyse data on the issues. The recent signing of the new "Prevention of Domestic Violence" law calls for more accurate record keeping of the incidence of domestic violence. Despite of all these arrangements, in 2004–2005 among young women aged 17 to 29, 29 per cent reported having experienced violence at work or at school and women accounted for 91 per cent of the victims of a violent crime, and 65 per cent of those were sexual assaults.

In 2008, crisis centres around the country counted a total of 21,679 calls made to hotlines, of which 28 per cent reported acts of physical violence against women. ADB (2006) and UNDP (2005) reported that in some aspects gender inequality have exacerbated since independence. The practice of gender inequalities is rising among the young generation in the southern region of Kazakhstan because it is close to Uzbek border and, especially in the rural regions masses are influenced with traditional and patriarchal norms.

Although domestic violence is still largely a forbidden subject in Uzbekistan, the government however has also committed to pass a Domestic Violence Law. Therefore, there should be political willpower to enhance support for promoting domestic violence prevention and protection activities that currently exist, e.g., the shelter in Bukhara. The health programmes may provide an entry point by establishing protocols for domestic violence screening for patients. The forms of women trafficking and violence against women are very serious problems and needs a concern on the part of the government. In this matter the existing laws are not enough to curb these threats. A number of suicide stories are reported, which occurred out of domestic violence in Uzbekistan. Such situations are even more alarming in both these states as compared to the Soviet times.

In economic terms, Uzbekistan is a state centralised economy and it has not much resource to implement all the women favoured policies. On the other hand, Kazakhstan economic condition is comparatively very sound because of its natural resources (oil, gas and uranium etc.). After independence, Kazakhstan introduced open and market economy which has been discussed in fourth chapter. The market economy provided an infinite prospect to Kazakh women to grow. They are an important part of Kazakhstan economic life, but their contribution differs from those of men. They are noticeable everywhere in offices and marketplaces, reflecting a relatively high rate, though it is deteriorating in terms of labour force participation now. The 80 per cent participation of women in the early 1990s is at present only 66.7 per cent share as compared to 76.1 per cent for men. The high degree of horizontal sex-segmentation in the work force ensures that their contribution to GDP is lower than men's.

Despite the presence of a few women in key positions as leaders of business, women in general are estimated to hold only 3 per cent of management positions. In Kazakhstan, women are most visible in education and healthcare, where they hold 74 per cent and 80 per cent of jobs; yet women's salaries are 86 per cent and 82 per cent of men's earnings, respectively. In 2003, women's average wages were estimated to be 67.6 per cent of men's. In 2008, the gap between men and women was approximately 32.4 per cent in average wage. Women are minimally represented in the higher paying jobs in the mining and petroleum industries which account for 35 per cent of the national GDP. Not only are there legal prohibitions for women against operating heavy machinery, but few women study the subjects in university that would qualify them for these positions in engineering and industrial management.

Women's proportion is also rising in the much lower paying agricultural sector in Kazakhstan. They are legally entitled to land on equal terms as men according to the Land Code of 2003, but in practice social attitudes limit their ability to manage their own farms. The legislation also restricts the allocation of land only to individuals with special agricultural knowledge or qualifications, or practical agricultural experience. Additionally, a small number of rural women who are farmers have had adequate training in agriculture or agri-business that would entitle them to accessing their rights to participate in farm management. Thus, despite being a sizeable alternative of agricultural workers, women face significant barriers in moving from farm worker to be farm manager or owner.

Women comprise a slight majority of all self-employed workers i.e. 51 per cent at the national level. In rural areas, 64 per cent of women are reported as self-employed, primarily in agriculture. This work offers no pension or benefits, and typically returns only a low level of compensation. The predominance of women in the agricultural sector and in self-employment or informal employment explains much of the overall high levels of poverty among women; in 2006, women were estimated to account for 60 per cent of the poor. All the above statistics show that Kazakh women are facing dire consequences in conventional employment and now she has to deal with the present market economy system to improve her position. Though gender disparity and lack of government support are enhancing women's difficulties, at the same time, the unlimited opportunities in the new context confer them at least a platform to strive for better life in Kazakhstan. As a result, a positive shift can be noticed in women's position after 2000 and all credit for this change goes to the market economy system and efforts made by Kazakh women. But such shift is again giving rise to new problems like migration.

Further, to enhance women's position in Kazakhstan, the government has to implement gender equality policies in a proper manner. The channels of communication have to strengthen so that the women can know and get benefited from the programmes and schemes run for women. Women should be facilitated with family care and social assistance to increase their efficiency at workplace. The promotion of linkages to other local microcredit programmes would boost women's ability to start and maintain their enterprises. On the other hand, Uzbek women are fully supported by the government system. She is accessing social security (daycare schools, maternity leaves etc.) which was launched by the previous Soviet system.

Uzbekistan is experiencing the negative effects of migration to Russia and Kazakhstan, both for those who leave and those who stay at home. While it is generally considered an acceptable option for men to seek employment abroad, it is less so for women. Even when jobs are available at home, the daily rate for labour in Kazakhstan can be as high as ten times of what it is in Uzbekistan. However, legally migration is permitted but the number is limited. Both men and women eager to migrate for work are often suspiciously exposed to being trafficked. Meanwhile, those family members who remain at home face other challenges such as being in a separated family, dependent on payment, and vulnerable to risk of the migrating spouse starting a new life abroad. When migrants do return home they may bring health problems that compromise their future earning potential and worsen family relations, such as when the migrants have suffered dangerous working or living conditions, experienced abuse related to being trafficked, or become infected with Sexually Transmitted Infections (STIs).

Women are left behind when husbands migrate and take on new roles, including earning money. Moreover, the lack of agricultural and non-agricultural employment opportunities in rural areas is driving a growing number of women to seek temporary, informal, and often exploitative employment in the cities. Thus, there is a need of both an opportunity to work and to develop their entrepreneurship capacity and to assist them in starting income-generation projects. Financing is still an essential barrier to small and medium-sized enterprise (SME) development, especially for potential and existing women entrepreneurs. The government has to expand agri-business programmes to strengthen Uzbek women from the economic point of view. The quality and quantity of agri-business training centre and technical assistance need to be improved. The funding of small scale business, banking reform activities and development of consumer products should be ensured.

Gender equality implies a society in which women and men enjoy the same opportunities, outcomes, rights and obligations in all spheres of life. The equality between women and men exists when both sexes are able to share equal distribution of power and influence; have equal opportunities for financial independence through work or through setting up businesses; enjoy equal access to education and the opportunity to develop personal ambitions. Yet despite many international agreements related to women's rights, progress on gender equality is uneven. Women in Central Asia, especially the two countries studied are still much more likely than men to be poor and illiterate. They have less access to medical care, property, credit, training and jobs. They are also far less likely than men to be politically active and far more likely to become victims of domestic violence.

Appendices

Appendix 1

Key Aspects of the National Action Plan for the Improvement of Women's Status in Uzbekistan

The implementation of the National Action Platform for the Improvement of Women's Status in Uzbekistan is designed to provide the support needed by women in Uzbekistan to ensure their advancement. The nine key priority areas targeted by the National Action Plan were briefly outlined in Chapter 1. The following explanations provide more detail on these priority areas.

Women's Health

(i) Give particular consideration to the health of women of all age groups;

(ii) Design special programmes to fight widely spread diseases, such as breast cancer, HIV/AIDS, heart disease and infectious diseases (including hepatitis);

(iii) Raise the quality of basic medical knowledge among the population and students at institutions of higher learning with the cooperation of the government, Ministry of Health and Ministry of Higher and Specialised Education;

(iv) Continue the implementation of measures aimed at reducing maternity and infant mortality undertaken by the Ministry of Health jointly with other agencies concerned;

(v) Provide pregnant women and nursing mothers with free medical services guaranteed by the State;

(vi) Organise the production of various foodstuffs for children by relevant ministries and agencies with the purpose of improving the health and nutrition of women and children; and

(vii) Design awareness-raising programmes to educate women and girls on the negative consequences of alcohol, drug and tobacco addiction.

Women's Education

(i) The Ministries of Education and of Higher and Specialised Education will collect data on women and girls' educational level in cities and rural areas; and

(ii) Relevant government agencies and NGOs will monitor gender equity in access to education; for example, survey the number of overseas training provided to highly qualified women professionals, assess women's access to information technologies, etc.

Women and Ecology

The government should pursue a preventive approach to ecological disaster. Steps also need to be taken to ease related social tensions. It will be necessary to Uzbekistan Resident Mission.

(i) Elaborate and implement a series of measures aimed at further upgrading government guarantees and indemnity of the Aral Sea residents. A special programme designed for women from the Aral Sea is also required;

(ii) Set up specialised environmental focal points in affected zones and coordinate their performance;

(iii) Formulate basic regulations to achieve reasonable nutrition for specific professional and age categories of the population, in particular for women. Such measures need to take into account adverse environmental impacts that cause poor nutrition and growing disease rates;

(iv) Continue organising ecological conferences, meetings and training programmes dedicated to women and environmental issues.

Women's Economic Status and Employment

The government must continue its commitment to improving women's working conditions, job creation opportunities, and strict observance of Labour Code provisions. With a view to expanding women's employment, it is necessary to

(i) Upgrade mechanisms for continued professional advancement of women to support their competitiveness in the labour market; and

(ii) Improve social and legal basis for the promotion of gender awareness initiatives and approaches directed at women.

In addition, the government has to stipulate the following measures:

(i) Expand support to the needy groups of population;

(ii) Set up retraining centres for women; and

(iii) Create more workplaces for women in state-run enterprises.

Women's Rights and Opportunity to Participate in Decision Making

The international gender standard is that women should comprise not less than 30 per cent of the staff in any entity. For this reason, surveys are required to measure and monitor women's level of participation in elected bodies, political parties, the Parliament, the Cabinet of Ministers, ministries and agencies, law enforcement bodies, local authorities, diplomatic institutions and international organisations. In order to create conditions for promoting women to leadership positions and preparing women to perform as government officials it is necessary to

(i) Amend the Government Service Act and regulations within ministries and agencies so that they encourage greater gender equity;

(ii) Amend legislative acts to protect women's rights and interests in line with international conventions and agreements;

(iii) Compile and implement a programme on women's preparation for assuming responsibilities within government management structures and ensure equal access to decision-making positions at all levels of administration;

(iv) With the help of government institutions, NGOs and the mass media, enhance legal awareness among women; and

(v) Legislate equal opportunities and introduce a quota system to enable women to be elected to the Parliament of Uzbekistan and other government bodies.

Girls' Rights

The government should implement a state programme aimed at supporting the education and upbringing of girls to imbue them with national and cultural values.

Discrimination and Violence against Women

In order to prevent violence against women, which is regarded as a flagrant violation of the provisions of the Declaration on Human Rights, the UN Convention on the Elimination of all Forms of Discrimination against Women, etc., steps should be taken to

(i) Upgrade administrative and criminal codes with the aim of strengthening punishment for violence against women, whether in the home or workplace, including prostitution and compelling women through drug addiction; and

(ii) Strengthen women's rights in marriage and divorce, including the division of property, and moral and material indemnity in case of divorce on the husband's initiative, in the Marriage and Family Code to raise women's status within the family and in decisions regarding the education of children.

Women in the Mass Media

The creation of a new "Uzbek woman" in the mass media, culture and arts should overcome existing stereotypes. For this purpose it will be necessary to

(i) Increase the number of specialised newspapers for women as well as TV and radio programmes dedicated to women's issues;

(ii) Design a comprehensive programme aimed at expanding social debate on gender issues in all forms of media;

(iii) Explain through mass media women's rights and obligations to disseminate legal knowledge in the area of equal rights and opportunities and other issues of gender concern in the society;

(iv) Raise awareness in society and create conditions for widespread discussions on the role of women in society, including the historical development of roles assigned to men and women, as well as acute social problems arising from gender inequality; and

(v) Publish scientific and other types of publications that contribute to the creation of a new image of Uzbek womanhood.

Women's NGOs

To promote and strengthen the role of women's NGOs it will be necessary to

(i) Collect data and distribute information on women's status in Uzbekistan;

(ii) In cooperation with the Ministry of Macroeconomics and Statistics, undertake gender statistical surveys and disaggregated analyses based upon new methodological approaches;

(iii) Promote the activities of the NGO "Women and Society" Institute to ascertain women's status in the economic, political, cultural, social, educational and scientific spheres of the country, to give practical recommendations and design mechanisms to enhance the role of women in the ongoing democratic transformation of Uzbekistan;

(iv) Publish an annual report highlighting women's status in Uzbekistan, as well as brochures and leaflets on gender analysis; and

(v) Encourage the establishment of NGOs and their integration into the international women's movement.

Appendix 2

National Millennium Development Goals: A framework for action in Central Asia: Kazakhstan, Kyrgyzstan, Tajikistan, Turkmenistan, Uzbekistan.

Goal 1: Eradicating Extreme Poverty and Hunger in Central Asia

- By the end of the 1990s, an estimated 23 million people (over 40 per cent of Central Asia's population) lived on less than

Real GDP growth in Central Asian countries *(in per cent)*

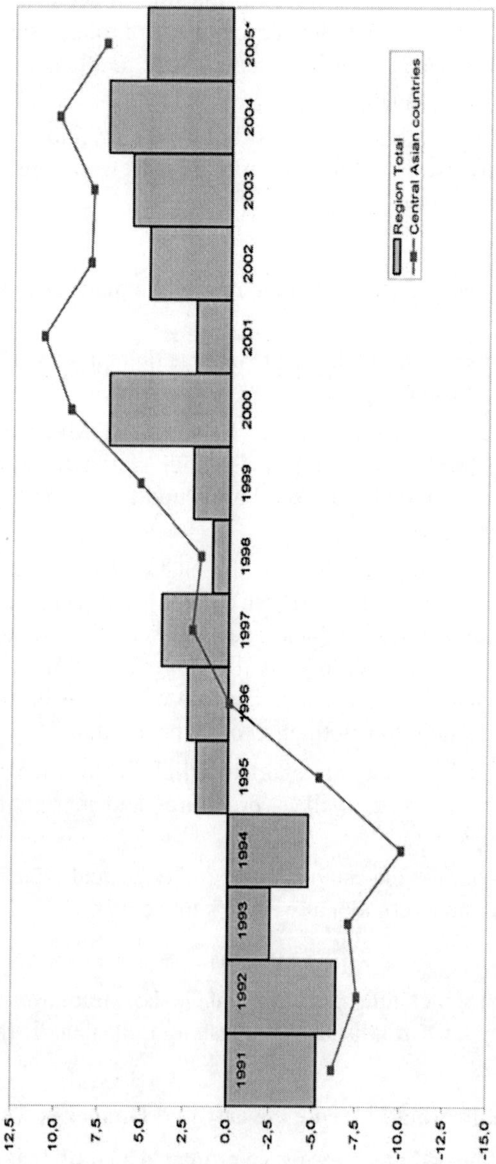

Source: Author's estimations based on IMF, World Economic Outlook 2005 data

PPP $4.30 a day; 10 million experienced extreme deprivation (living on less than PPP $2.15 a day).

- Tajikistan reduced the share of those living on less than PPP $2.15 per day from 91 per cent to 74 per cent during 1999 – 2003.
- The percentage of the population classified as living below the subsistence minimum in Kazakhstan dropped from 39 to 24 per cent during 1999 – 2002, and declined further since (to 16.1 per cent in 2004).
- Per-capita GDPs reported by Tajikistan, Kyrgyzstan, and Uzbekistan are on par with some African countries' per-capita income levels.

Goal 2: Achieving Universal Primary education in Central Asia

- All Central Asian countries institutionalised universal primary school education enrollment during the Soviet period. While this standard has been maintained in many Central Asian countries, in some it has not.
- In Tajikistan, primary school attendance dropped to 88 per cent in 2003, with larger declines occurring in rural areas–affecting girls more than boys.
- Kyrgyzstan also reported declines in primary school enrollment (albeit not as steep); increasing enrollment trends have been noted in recent years.
- Sharp reductions in funding for public education, combined with growing numbers of young people, have also put unprecedented pressures on access to quality post-secondary education institutions in Central Asia.
- Turkmenistan experienced a sharp contraction in university attendance during the 1990s (down to 4 per cent of the population in 2000) and introduced changes (e.g., reducing the length of compulsory primary education) that drew sharp criticism from international observers.

Goal 3: Promoting Gender Equality and Empowering Women in Central Asia

- Gender inequality is a major concern in Central Asia, one that manifests itself in education, labour markets, and elsewhere.

Even in countries where women have strong educational backgrounds (e.g., Kazakhstan, Kyrgyzstan), this does not necessarily translate into equal incomes or opportunities in the workplace.

- Women in Central Asia are concentrated in rural and public service employment, where wages are one-fourth to one-eighth the levels paid for industrial work.
- Women's relative wages have declined during the last 10 years: whereas women in Kazakhstan and Tajikistan earned upto three quarters of men's wages during 1996–1998, by 2001 they had fallen to 58 and 65 per cent respectively.
- Combined with large declines in the real value of state-funded social benefits (on which women rely particularly heavily), falling wages have accelerated the feminisation of poverty in a number of Central Asian countries. Single-mother families (which, on an average, contain four children in Tajikistan) remain particularly vulnerable to poverty.

Goal 4: Reducing Child Mortality in Central Asia

- The Central Asian countries have the dubious distinction of being the only states in the Commonwealth of Independent States (along with Azerbaijan) to record infant mortality rates above 50 deaths per every 1,000 births.
- All the Central Asian countries (with the partial exception of Tajikistan) are more or less on track to reach the infant and child mortality goals set out in their national MDG reports.

Goal 5: Improving Maternal Health

- In contrast to Central Asia's infant and child mortality, most Central Asian countries reported significant improvements in maternal mortality trends after 1990; by three quarters in Turkmenistan, half in Tajikistan, and one-third in Kyrgyzstan.
- Only Kazakhstan reported reversals in maternal mortality during this period. On the other hand, these levels remain among the highest in the Commonwealth of Independent States.

- Indicators in Central Asia are more favourable than in other CIS countries: around three times as many women in Kazakhstan, Kyrgyzstan, Turkmenistan and Uzbekistan use modern contraceptive methods as do women in the Caucasus.
- Survey data indicate that more than one-third of Central Asians do not use modern contraceptives, the availability of which in poorer, rural areas is significantly lower.
- The numbers of abortions in Central Asia (under 1.5 times in a lifetime) are significantly lower than in the rest of the Commonwealth of Independent States, which can be perhaps explained by the greater influence of tradition and religion.
- The more secular Central Asian States with larger Russian minorities (Kazakhstan and Kyrgyzstan) report abortion rates that are nearly twice those of their more homogeneous and traditional neighbours, Turkmenistan and Uzbekistan.
- In Uzbekistan, the abortion rate has reported a steady decline ever since independence to 99.4 induced abortions per 1,000 live births in 2003.

Goal 6: Combating HIV/ AIDS, TB and Other Diseases in Central Asia

- HIV/ AIDS and TB are recognised as a prime health threat, as are such diseases as malaria, typhoid, and brucellosis.
- The numbers of people living with HIV/AIDS seem to be relatively low in Central Asia at or under 0.1 per cent of the general population. UNAIDS estimates place this figure at less than 30,000; national reporting indicates less than 6,000, with most of the reported cases in Kazakhstan and Uzbekistan.
- The spread of HIV in Central Asia seems to be closely linked to intravenous drug use, much of which is associated with the burgeoning heroin trade coming out of Afghanistan.
- Malaria has become particularly problematic along Tajikistan's border with Afghanistan: 30,000 new cases were recorded in Tajikistan in 1997 alone. Although the incidence subsequently declined (to around 6,000 in 2002), the total number of people living with malaria in Tajikistan is estimated at 300,000 to 400,000.

Goal 7: Ensuring Environmental Sustainability in Central Asia

- Domestic sources of running water are not available to at least 10 per cent of households in Kazakhstan, Kyrgyzstan and Uzbekistan, and to over a quarter of the residents of Tajikistan and Turkmenistan.
- The situation is critical in rural areas in Tajikistan, where nearly three-quarters of the population do not have access to running water in their dwellings. At least a quarter of the population in all five countries lacks access to proper sanitation facilities.
- The Central Asian countries' are the global leaders in carbon dioxide emissions per unit of GDP: Turkmenistan, Uzbekistan, and Kazakhstan are among the seven dirtiest countries in the world in this respect (along with Ukraine, Azerbaijan, North Korea and Mongolia).

Appendix 3

Mahbuba Ergasheva, UZBEKISTAN

Expert Group Meeting on Regional Implementation and Monitoring of the Beijing Platform of Action and the Outcome of the third Special Session of the General Assembly relating to Women 2002 (2-4 December 2002 Bangkok)

Gaining of the Independence have created an opportunities for women to participate in all transformations in Uzbekistan. At the same time the problems of development and creation of conditions for the realisation of women's potential and their interest is becoming key issue in Uzbekistan. In this connection the government of Uzbekistan have made an important step for the improvement of the women's status in the country. For example, adoption of the presidential decree in March 1995 titled: Enhancing Women's Role in the State and Social Development of Uzbekistan. This political structure designed to encourage women's participation in public life. Another decree "Strengthening government support of the families with children", Resolution of the Cabinet of Ministers titled, "State program for 1998 on ensuring the family interests" and announcement of the 1999 as a "Year of Women", announcement of the year 2000 as a "Year of Maternity and child." This move was designed to draw attention to gender issues that adversely affect women's ability to participate in society.

In 1997, the Women's Committee developed and adopted the National Platform for Action. The twin objectives of the national Action Plan are improving women's status in Uzbekistan and enhance their role in society. In is hoped that the objectives and targets of the National Action Plan are achieved by the year 2005. Of the 12 areas of concern detailed in the Beijing Action Platform (1995), the nine key priority areas were selected as the focus of the Uzbekistan National Action Plan.

Uzbekistan represented its initial report on the implementation of the *"Convention on the Elimination of all forms of Discrimination against Women"* on January 25-30, 2001. It was accepted as a satisfactory with 47 recommendations and more than 40 concerns.

Problems in the Field of Gender Equality

Despite of the government efforts in raising women's status women's participation in political structure of Uzbekistan has fallen during transition period. Notably, a presidential decree: Enhancing Women's Role in the State and Social Development of Uzbekistan established the position of Deputy Prime Minister of Women's Affairs, responsible for monitoring and enhancing women's participation in society. This decree set in place a formal political structure designed to encourage women's participation in public life. Similar positions at the deputy governor level were concurrently established for women at three administrative levels of government, that is, at the provincial, regional and city level (365 Deputy Governors within the country in executive bodies of the government). Despite of these efforts of government the women's participation in high political decision-making remained low. Out of 250 seats women occupy 23; it constitutes 9.2 per cent in Parliament.

Since Uzbekistan is currently in transition to a market economy, it is experiencing a rapid development of our private sector and denationalisation of many factories and plants. Although the privatisation process has opened new opportunities for men who occupied previously high administrative positions, it has presented challenges for the women. Women have to choose between work and home. They are either forced to participate in informal sector of economy. Women 45-50 years of age often find it impossible to re-enter the labour market. If they succeed they have been channelled into marginal, low-paying, low status sectors. Moreover, some efforts to solve women's problems from the top and encourage women to resume their maternal roles have become common for mass media and government officers of Uzbekistan. Radio and TV also encourage this by giving historical explanations for women's naturalistic positions, which basically translates as a women's place in the home.

Both before and since independence, women have received generous benefits and maternity leave, but now this is problematic for their professional careers. Women have three years maternity leave with the assurance that they keep their jobs. Women receive 70 per cent of their salaries for 18 months. However, this creates a challenge for them during their three years stay at home, as women lose their professional skills. We are becoming more competitive where professionalism is very important. Women are currently finding that when they return, after three years maternity leave, they have lost their professional skills which means they lose also their job positions. In the transition to the market economy, many women are finding that their rights are no longer enforced, and that companies discriminate against women and especially mothers. In most cases, employers in the private sector try not to hire women of child-bearing age, because of frequent maternity leave with the ensured salary for a year and a half as well their job position. Privatized factories and plants are often unable to pay their assurance therefore giving more job positions to men. In addition, discrimination in salaries within private sector, a woman earns 20-30 per cent less than a man with similar experience and qualifications. These and many other factors came women to be involved in the informal sector of the economy and increase unemployment among them. Women in Uzbekistan are also very dependent economically on the family because they are mostly involved in the health care or educational systems. Both systems pay poorly. This situation has placed women in awkward positions and subsequently they have become passive and have accepted subordinate positions in their families voluntarily. They cannot see solutions of their economically dependent situations.

The current labour legislation grants working women a number of benefits that make employers reluctant to employ them except for certain female type jobs. It is not surprising then that although women comprise 42 per cent of the labour force, they account for 63 per cent of the registered unemployed. Also, current legislation prohibits discrimination against women in recruitment and employment for the managerial position but in reality often the preference will be given to the male candidate.

The third and an important issue is the violence against women in family. First of all it is psychological violence, which a young woman practices in the husbands' family, from his side as well as his relatives. Conducted interview with young families showed that, in most cases decisions for young bride in low about the work place, quantity of children, family expenditures will be accepted by mother in low or by husband. Due to the high conflict situations in young families there are suicide cases among women at the age 17 – 28 years old. In order to prevent such cases it is necessary to have accessible network of crisis centres throughout of the country. The numbers of non-government crisis centres are working mainly in large cities in the country which is not enough of course.

Measures taken for Gender Equality

Uzbekistan has introduced a number of legislative changes and legal reforms designed to guarantee the interests and status of women. In general, women in Uzbekistan are accorded equal rights with men and enjoy a number of special provisions that acknowledge and protect the position of women. According to the Constitution of Uzbekistan, all citizens enjoy equal rights and freedoms irrespective of sex, race, ethnic origin, language, religion, social background, convictions, personal or social status (article 18). Article 46 guarantees equality of rights for men and women. However, in practice many women are not served well by these laws because of poor implementation and lack of compliance. In order to ensure the equal opportunities for women and men in decision making it is planned to make some changing's into the ministries and authorities, creation of the state program for the support and training women leaders.

As I mentioned earlier that Uzbekistan has adopted the National Platform of Action. Unfortunately, the National Platform of Action does not pay enough attention to the problem of violence. There is not statistical data on violence against women and monitoring such crimes in Uzbekistan, except Ministry of Internal affairs which are closed for public. As well as out of 67 ratified International legal Acts only 10 have been translated into Uzbek language in particular Beijing Declaration and Platform of Action.

Family and labour codes are often the systems of law most directly bearing on women's status. The Family Code adopted in 1998 regulates marital and family relations, property rights and disputes. According to the Family Code, spouses enjoy equal rights. Polygamy is illegal and only civil marriage is recognised as legal. But according to the Criminal Code can be considered as a fact, when a man will have two or more women in one household. But if wives live separately it is not accepted as polygamy. Two issues not directly addressed in the Family Code are discrimination against women on the basis of their family status and prohibition of violence against women. The Family Code however does contradict with the provisions outlined in the CEDAW where the marriage is set at 18. Another area of concern is how the Family Code allows young women to marry at 17 and even at 16 in some exceptions.

Social changes in the life of Uzbek people also create initiative for women intellectuals to promote women's rights. The growth of women's NGO's is one of the most positive achievements in terms of women's political participation in Uzbekistan. Currently, there are more than 200 registered NGO's in Uzbekistan. Many non-governmental organisations raise issues on human rights, combating violence against women in their activities. Also, almost all women's NGO's in Uzbekistan are in the initial state of formation. Most of them are having the lack of funding and achievements of some women's NGO are explained by the support of international foundations. The present legislation on NGO adopted in 1998 does not provide a favourable environment for the fruitful activity of women's NGO. Therefore, women's NGO's are not protected by the government legally as well as materially. Despite of obstacles women's groups are able to render services to their clients and take an active part in economic, social and political transformations in the country.

The Main Obstacles of Women's NGO's in Uzbekistan

- Shortage of knowledge on NGO development within NGO itself and government structures;
- Shortage of information about NGO activity and their role in formation of the civil society;
- Weak management of NGO's and in confidence of their own power;
- Absence of solidarity among NGO's;
- Weak legal literacy of Women's NGOs as well as government structures;
- Absence of favourable environment for NGO development and unequal access to the opportunities;
- Presence of an extra guardianship on NGO's.

Bibliography

Abazov, Rafis (1998), "Political Islam in Central Asia: Leaving Political Scene or Gathering Momentum", *International Journal of Central Asian Studies,* Vol. 3.

Abajov, Rafis (2004), *Historical Dictionary of Kyrgyzstan*, Scarecrow Press, Oxford.

Abazov, Rafis (2007), *Culture and Customs of the Central Asian Republics,* Greenwood, London.

Abdullaeva, Marifat (2006), "Review of Central Asian Countries", UNESCO, web source: *http://unesdoc.UNESCO.org/images/0014/001459/14593e.pdf* accessed on 14 July 2008.

Abramson, David (2006), "The Political Culture of Islam, Gender and Development in Uzbekistan", *The National Council for Eurasian and East European Research*, Washington DC.

Agadjanian, Victor (1999), "Post-Soviet Demographic Paradoxes: Ethnic Differences in Marriage and Fertility in Kazakhstan", *Sociological Forum,* Vol. 14, No. 3.

Ahmed, Leila (1992), *Women and Gender in Islam: Historical Roots of Modern Oebats,* Princeton, NJ: Yale University Press.

Ahmedov M, Azimov R et al. (2007), *Health Systems in Transition: Uzbekistan*, Copenhagen, WHO Regional Office for Europe on behalf of the European Observatory on Health Systems and Policies.

Al-Hatimy, Said Abdullah (1983), Women in Islam: A Comparative Study, Islamic Books, Lahore, Pakistan.

Ali, Farhana (November 2006), "Rocking the Cradle to Rocking the World: The Role of Muslim Female Fighters", *Journal of International Women's Studies*, Vol. 8, No. 1.

Alimdjanova, Dinara (2009), Gender Aspects of Agricultural and Rural Employment: Application for Uzbekistan, Gender Study Centre, Uzbekistan.

Alimova, Dilarom A. (1998), "A Historian's Vision of Khudjum", *Central Asian Survey,* Vol. 17, No. 1.

Aminova, Alena (2005), "Only Few are Aware: That Bride Kidnapping is a Criminal Offence", *CaucAsia,* Fifth Issue.

Aminova, R.Kh. (1985), *The October Revolution and Women's Liberation in Uzbekistan*, Nauka Publishers, Moscow.

Among Uzbekistani Women, Little Difference Exists between Actual and Desired Level of Fertility (March 1998), DIGESTS, Vol. 24, No. 1.

Anderson, John (1993), "Out of the Kitchen, Out of the Temple, Religion, Atheism and Women in the Soviet Union" in S. Ramet (ed.), *Religious Policy in the Soviet Union,* Cambridge University Press, Cambridge.

Anderson, Kathryn H. and Becker, Charles (2008), "Religious Affiliation and Family Formation in Post-Soviet Central Asia" a project report from *The National Council for Eurasian and East European Research*, 25 April.

Answers to the Questionnaire on the Implementation of the Beijing Platform for Action (1995) and the decisions taken at the twenty-third special session of the General Assembly (2000), web source: *www.unescap.org/.../Beijing...Questionnaire/Uzbekistan-unofficial-English. pdf* accessed on 23 December 2010.

Arabsheibani, G. Reza, Altay Mussurov (2006), *Returns to Schooling in Kazakhstan: OLS and Instrumental Variables Approach,* Discussion Paper, No. 2462, Institute for the Study of Labor, Bonn.

Asad Alam and Arup Banerji (November 2000), Uzbekistan and Kazakhstan: A Tale of Two Transition Paths?, *World Bank Research Series*, Working Paper No. 2472.

Asian Development Bank (2005), *Uzbekistan, Country Gender Assessment Report*, Philippines.

Asian Development Bank (2006), *Kazakhstan, Country Gender Assessment Report*, Philippines.

Atkin, Muriel (1992), "Religious, National and Other Identities in Central Asia" in Jo-Ann Gross, Muslim in Central Asia, Duke University Press, London.

Atkinson, Gerald L., "Radical Feminism and Political Correctness", web source: *www.lifesitenews.com/ldn/2005_docs/PC5.pdf* accessed on 12 July 2008.

Badawi, Jamal (1980), "Women in Islam" in Islam: Its Meaning and Message by Kurshid Ahmed, Islamic Foundation, Leicester.

Badran, Margot (1985), Islam, Patriarchy, and Feminism in Middle East, *Trends in History*, Vol. 4, No. 1.

Badran, M. and Cooke, M. (eds) (1990), *Opening The Gates: A Century of Arab Feminist Writing,* Indiana University Press, Bloomington & Indianapolic.

Barrett, Michele (1980), Women Oppression Today: Problems in Marxist Feminist Analysis, Verso, London.

Bart, Jody, "Feminist Theories of Knowledge: The Good, The Bad, and The Ugly", web source: *www.dean.sbc.edu/bart.html-46k-* accessed on 4 August 2008.

Becker, Charles M. et al. (2003), "Short Term Migration Responses of Women and Men during Economic Turmoil: Lessons from Kazakhstan", *Eurasian Geography and Economic,* Vol. 44, No. 3.

Becker, Charles M and Seitenova, Ai-Gul S. (March 2005), "Fertility and Marriage in Kazakhstan's Transition Period: Implications for Social Security Policy", PIE Discussion Paper Series, *Institute of Economic Research workshop on Pension Reform in Transition Economies*, Hitotsubashi University.

Bell, Susan Groag and Offen, Karan M. (eds.) (1981), Women, the Family and Freedom: The Debate in Documents II, 1880-1950, Stanford University Press, Stanford.

Bridger, Susan (1970), *Women in the Soviet Countryside: Women's Role in Rural Development in the Soviet Union,* Cambridge University Press, Cambridge.

Bryson, V. (1999), *Feminist Debates*, Macmillan, Basingstoke.

Buckley, Cynthia and Barrett, Jennifer (2004), "Reproductive and Sexual Health among Young Adults in Uzbekistan", *Studies in Family Planning,* Vol. 35, No. 1.

Budel, Carin Benninger and Matignoni, Joanna Bourke (2003), "Violence Against Women: 10 Reports/Year 2002 for the Protection and Promotion of the Human Rights of Women", *World Organisation Against Torture (OMCT),* Geneva, Switzerland.

Bureau of Gender and Development and the State Department of Statistics (1999), *Women of Uzbekistan: Statistical Collection*, Tashkent.

Burgess, Amanda (January 2006), "Intersection of Race, Class, Gender and Crime", *Feminist Criminology,* Sage Publications, Vol. 1, No. 1.

Burnaby, Frederick (2002), A *Ride to Khiva: Travels and Adventures in Central Asia*, Oxford University Press, Oxford.

Buvinic, Mayra (1999), "Promoting Gender Equality" *UNESCO 1999,* Blackwell, Oxford.

CEDAW (2006), Monitoring of Implementation of Recommendations of the Committee on the Elimination of Discrimination against Women to the Primary National Report of the Republic of Kazakhstan (Alternative Report), Almaty, Kazakhstan.

CEDAW (2001), 24th Session Kazakhstan, the Initial Report of Kazakhstan, *490, 491 & 497 Meetings*, 18 & 23 January 2001.

CEDAW, Monitoring of the Implementation of Provisions of the Convention on the Elimination of All Forms of Discrimination against Women in the Republic of Uzbekistan, web source: *www.iwraw-ap.org/resources/pdf/Uzbekistan_SR.pdf* accessed on 18 Jan.2011.

CEDAW (November 2006), Monitoring of Implementation of Recommendations of the Committee of the Elimination of Discrimination against Women to Primary National report of the Republic of Kazakhstan, Almaty, Kazakhstan.

Central Asia: Islam and the State (2003), 10 July, *ICG Asia Report,* no. 59, Cosid /Brussels.

Central Asia and Caucasus, web source: *http://www.law.emory.edulife/region/centralasia.html_TIK* accessed on 8 June 2008.

Chenoy, Anuradha M. (1996), "Islam, Women and Identity in Contemporary Central Asia", *Economic and Political Weekly,* 2 March.

Chenoy, Anuradha M. (2005), "A Plea of Engendering Human Security", *International Studies,* Vol. 42, No. 2.

Chow, Esther Ngan-Ling (2003), "Gender Matters: Studying Globalisation and Social Change in the 21st Century", *International Sociology,* Vol. 18, No. 3.

Chua, Amy L. (1998), "Markets, Democracy and Ethnicity: Towards a New Paradigm for Law and Development", *The Yale Law Journal,* Vol. 108, No. 1.

Combating Gender Based Violence: A Key achieving the MDGs (March 2005), United Nations Population Fund (UNFPA) in collaboration with the United Nations Development Fund for Women (UNIFEM).

Compass 2020 Report (2007), *Central Asia: The Struggle for Power, Energy and Human Rights,* Berlin.

Constitution of the Republic of Kazakhstan (1992).

Constitution of the Republic of Uzbekistan (1992).

Conze, Susanne (2001), "Women's Work and Emancipation in the Soviet Union, 1941-59" in Melanie Ilic (ed.), *Women in Stalin Era*, Palgrave, New York.

Coomaraswamy, Radhika (2003), "Integration of the Human Rights of Women and the Gender Perspective: Violence against Women" *United Nations Economic and Social Council,* 27 February.

Cooper, Belinda and Traugott, Isabel, "Women's Right and Security in Central Asia", web source: *www.worldpolicy.org/journal/articles/wpi03-1/cooper.pdf* accessed on 14 July 2008.

Cornhiel, Susanna Lastarria and Garcia-Frias, Zoraida, "Gender and Land Rights: Findings and Lessons from Country Studies", web source: *www.fao.org/docrep/008/a0297e/a0297e08.htm* accessed on 2 October 2009.

Culture of Uzbekistan, web source: *www.everyculture.com/To-z/Uzbekistan.html* accessed on 11 June 2008.

Culture of Kazakhstan, web source: *www.everyculture.com/ja-ma/kazakhstan.html* accessed on 11 June 2008.

Custer, Peter (1997), Capital Accumulation and Women's labour in Asian Economies, Saye/ Zed Books, New Delhi/ London.

Daly, John C.K. (March 2008), "Kazakhstan Emerging Middle Class" The Silk Road Paper Series, *Central Asia-Caucasus Institute & Silk Road Studies Program*, School of Advanced International Studies, Johns Hopkins University, Washington.

Darsky, Leonid and Scherbov, Sergei (1995), "Marital Status Behavior of Women in former Soviet Republic", *European Journal of Population,* Vol. 11.

Dave, Bhavna (October 2004), "Minority Rights: Cultural Diversity and Development in Central Asia", *United Nations Office of the High Commissioner for Human Rights*, Bishkek.

Disparities between Men and Women in Transition Countries of Europe and Central Asia, Washington, September 18, 2002, Web source: *http://lnweb18.worldbank.org/ECA/eca.nsf/General/ F55E7337BA 69423985256BFA0053F091?OpenDocument* accessed on 28 July 2009.

Domagalskaya, Natalya (May 2005), Polygamist, Traditions and Gender, *CaucAsia, International Coalition of Gender Journalists*, Issue 5.

Dodge, Norton (1966), *Women in the Soviet Economy,* The John Hopkins Press, Baltimore.

Dubrovina, Lyudmila (1957), "Women's Right to Education in the Soviet Union" in L. Petrova and S. Gilevskaya (compiled by), *Equality of Women in the USSR,* Foreign Languages Publishing House, Moscow.

Economy in Uzbekistan, web source: *http://www.world66.com/../ economy* accessed on 28 September 2010.

ECPAT International (End Child Prostitution, Child Pornography and the Trafficking of Children for Sexual Purposes) (2002), web source: *http://www.ecpat.net/EI/Publications/WhoWeAre/EI_2nd_ Aseembly.pdf* accessed on 9 October 2010.

Edgar, Adrienne (Summer 2006), "Bolshevism, Patriarchy and the Nation: The Soviet Emancipation of Muslim Women in Pan-Islamic Perspective", *Slavic Review,* Vol. 65, No. 2.

Education Statistics: Uzbekistan, web source: *http://www.childinfo.org/ files/CEECIS_Uzbe...* accessed on 28 August 2009.

Ehrenreich, Barbara (1976), "What a Socialist Feminism?", *Working Papers on Socialism & Feminism* published by the New American Movement (NAM), web source: *http://www.marxists.org/subject/women/authors/ehrenreich-barbara/socialist-feminism.htm* accessed on 8 July 2008.

Eisenstein, Hester (1983), *Contemporary Feminist Thought,* G. K. Hall, Boston.

Engels, F. (1884), The Origins of Family, Private Property and the State, Introduction by Pat Brewer, web source: *readingfrom theleft.com/PDF/EngelsOrigin.pdf* accessed on 19 June 2008.

Falkingham, Jane (April 2000), "Women and Gender Relations in Tajikistan", web source: *http://www.adb.org/../prelims.pdf* accessed on 13 April 2010.

Family Law Code of Uzbekistan (1998).

Fathi, Habiba (1997), "Otines: the Unknown Women Clerics of Central Asian Islam", *Central Asia Survey,* Vol. 16, No. 1.

Fazylov, Djamoliddin and Smirnova, Galina (2008), "The Development of Education: National Report of Uzbekistan", 26 September, web source: *www.ibe.unesco.org/National_Reports.* accessed on 25 August 2010.

Fernea, Elizabeth (1998), In Search of Islamic Feminism: One Woman's Global Journey, Anchor Books, New York.

Foster, Charles (2007), "Law: Modern Family Law, 1800 – Present", *Central Asia and the Caucasus,* 7/11/.

Gender Briefing Kit in Uzbekistan (2004), web source: *http://www.un.org/womenwatch/daw/news/gender.htm* accessed on 12 August 2009.

Gender Equality: Legal and Institutional Framework on Women's Rights and Equal Opportunities; De Jure and De Facto Discrimination", Kazakhstan, web source: *www.onlinewomenin-politics.org/kz/kazakhstan.pdf* accessed on 7 November 2010.

Gidadhubli, R.G. (1994), "Economic Transition in Uzbekistan", *Economic and Political Weekly*, 5 February, Vol. 29, No. 6.

Gidadhubli, R.G. (1996), "Reshaping the Uzbek Economy", *Economic and Political Weekly*, January 27, Vol. 31, No. 4.

Gills, Dong-Sook S. (2002), "Globalisation of Production and Women in Asia", *The Annals of the American Academy of Political and Social Science*, 581; 106.

Glichman, Rose (1990), "Soviet Scientist Talking: An Official Debate about Women by Marry Buckley", *Russian Review,* Vol. 49, No. 1.

"Global Justice Now: Investing in Women Leaders as Key Players in Transitional Democracies", Global Justice Center: Human Rights through the Rule of Law, web source: *http://globaljusticecenter.net* accessed on 7 July 2009.

Gorsghenin, K. (1958), "Soviet Women Enjoy Equal Civil Rights with Men", *Equality of Women in the USSR*, Foreign Language Publishing House, Moscow.

Gros, D. and Steinherr, A. (2004), *Economic Transition in Central and Eastern Europe: Planting the Seeds*, Cambridge University Press, Cambridge.

Gumppenberg, Marie-Carin von (September 2007), "Kazakhstan – Challenges to the Booming Petro-Economy: FAST Country Risk Profile Kazakhstan" Working Paper 2/2007, *Swiss Peace*, Bern.

Haffmann, David L. (1994), *Peasant Metropolis: Social Identities in Moscow, 1929-1941*, Cornell University Press, New York.

Halle, Fannina W. (1938), *Women in Soviet East*, Martin Secker & Warburg Ltd., London.

Hashimov, Umida (2009), "Financial Crisis Hits Uzbekistan" *Analyst CACS* 1/28/2009.

Hausmann, Ricardo et al. (2008), The Global Gender Gap Report, *World Economic Forum*, Geneva, Switzerland.

Heer, D.M. and Youssef, Nadia (1977), "Female Status among Soviet Central Asian Nationalities: the Melding of Islam and Marxism and its Implications for Population Increase", *Population Studies,* Vol. 31, No. 1.

Herman, Robert et al. (1996), *Gender Considerations in Central Asian Republics: A Preliminary Assessment*, Prepared by USAID/ CAR.

Highlights on Health in Kazakhstan (1999), web source: *www.euro.who.int/document/E72497pdf* accessed on 15 June 2008.

HiT profile in Brief: Uzbekistan (2008), Health Systems in Transition: Uzbekistan, European Observatory on Health Systems and Policies, web source: *www.euro.who.int/__data/assets/pdf_file/0012/98895/E90673sum.pdf* accessed on 14 June 2010.

Horgan, Goretti, (Autumn 2001), "How does Globalisation affect Women?", *International Socialism Journal,* Issue 92.

Horowitz, Jonah (2005), A Critique of Marxist Feminism, Feminist Theory, Short Paper, 8 February, web source: *www.explodingcow.com/~jonah/foo/MarxistFeminism.pdf* accessed on 4 June 2008.

Human Right Watch (September 2006), "Reconciled to Violence", web source: *http://hrw.org/reports2006/kyrgyzstan0906/.* accessed on 15 June 2009.

ICG (International Crisis Group), Interview with Rural Youth, Kyrgyzstan, May 2003 web source: *http://www.csudh.edu/dearhabermas/centralasiayouth.pdf* accessed on 18 August 2009.

ICG (International Crisis Group), Interview with Medical Specialist, Bukhara, Uzbekistan, March 2002, web source: *http://www.csudh.edu/dearhabermas/centralasiayouth.pdf.* accessed on 18 August 2009.

ICG Report (International Crisis Group) (July 2003), *"Central Asia: Islam and the State"*, no. 59, 10.

Ihlamur, Suna Gulfer, (2003), "Gendering Central Asia: Historically Reconstructed Role of Woman as Identity Bearers and Markers" in *Turkish Review of Eurasian Studies,* OBIV, Cilt 3.

Ilic, Melanie (ed.) (2001), "Introduction" in *Women in the Stalin Era,* Palgrave, New York.

Ilkhamov, Alisher (Winter 2001), "Uzbek Islamism: Imported Ideology or Grassroots Movement?", *Middle East Report*, no. 222.

ILO (2008), *Global Wage Report 2008/09: Minimum Wages Collective Bargaining: Towards Policy Coherence*, Geneva.

IMF (1999), *Economic Reforms in Kazakhstan, Kyrgyz Republic, Tajikistan, Turkmenistan, and Uzbekistan,* Occasional Paper 183, Washington DC.

ILO Report (International Labour Office) (November 2003), *The Impact of "Transition" and Afghanistan Crisis on Employment and Decent Work Concerns in Kyrgyzstan, Tajikistan and Uzbekistan,* Geneva.

IOM Report (International Organisation for Migration) (April 2005), *Fertile Fields: Trafficking in Persons in Central Asia,* Vienna.

International Women Rights Action Watch report, Uzbekistan, web source: *http://iwraw.igc.org/publications/country reports.htm* accessed on 28 July 2010.

Jackson, Nicole J. (2006), "International Organisations, Security Dichotomies and the Trafficking of Persons and Narcotics in Post Soviet Central Asia", *Security Dialogue,* Vol. 37, No. 3.

Jawad, Haifaa A (1998), The Rights of Women in Islam: An Authentic Approach, Macmillan, New York, web source: *http://msacalgary.com/books/ethics/The%20Rights%20of%20Women%20in%20Islam.pdf* accessed on 11 April 2008.

Kamilov, R.T. (1964), "Growth of the Working Class of Uzbekistan (1953-58) Part 1", *Soviet Sociology,* Vol. 3, No. 1.

Kamp, Marianne (2002), "Pilgrimage and Performance: Uzbek Women and the Imagining of Uzbekistan in the 1920s", *International Journal of Middle East Studies,* Vol. 34, No. 2.

Kanddiyoti, D. (2003), "The Cry for Land: Agrarian Reforms", *Journal of Agrarian Change*, Vol. 3, No. 1-2.

Kandiyoti, Deniz and Azimova, Nadira (2004), "The Communal and the Sacred: Women's Worlds of Ritual in Uzbekistan", *The Journal of the Royal Anthropological Institute,* Vol. 10, No. 2.

Kasymova, Sofia, "Gender Socialisation: Central Asia" web source: *http://www.genderedu.freenet.tj/izabel.pdf* accessed on 12 July 2009.

Kazakhstan (2002), Country Report on Human Rights Practices, web source: *http://www.state.gov/g/drl/rls/hrrpt/2002/18373.htm* accessed on 25 May 2009.

Kazakhstan: 2000 NGO Sustainability Index, web source: *http://www.usaid.gov/locations/europe_eurasia/dem_gov/ngoindex/2000/kazakhstan.pdf* accessed on 25 August 2010

Kazakhstan: Answers to the Questions on Implementation of Beijing Platform of Actions (1995) and Resolutions of the 23rd Special Session of the UN General Assembly (2000), web source:

www.un.org/womenwatch/daw/.../KAZAKHSTAN-English.pdf accessed on 13 May 2010.

Kazakhstan Profile, web source: *http://www.ifrc.org/../05AA075 profiles.pdf* accessed on 12 September 2010.

Kazakhstan Today (2003), About 5000 cases of Human Trafficking from Kazakhstan Registered Annually, *BBC Worldwide Monitoring*, 19 January.

Kelly, Liz (April 2005), "Fertile Fields: Trafficking in Person in Central Asia", *IOM (International Organisation for Migration)*.

Kelly, Liz and Regan, Linda, "Violence against Women: A Briefing Document on International Issues and Responses", web source: *http://www.britishcouncil.org/waw.pdf* accessed on 6 April 2009.

Kennedy-Pipe, Caroline (2004), "Whose Security? State Building and 'Emancipation' of Women in Central Asia" *International Relations*, Vol. 18, No. 1.

Khalid, Adeep (1998), *The Political Politics of Muslim Cultural Reform: Jadidism in Central Asia,* Berkeley.

Khalmurzaev, Nurollo (2000), "Small and Medium-Sized Enterprises in the Transition Economy of Uzbekistan", *Central Asian Survey*, Vol. 19, No. 2.

Khassnova, Galiya (Summer 2000), "On the Way to Democracy: Women's Activism in Kazakhstan" *DEMOKRATIZATSIYA, The Journal of Post-Soviet Democratisation*, Vol. 8, No. 3.

Khassnova, Galiya (2001/2002), "Women in Democratic Institutions in Kazakhstan", *Central European University, Centre for Policy Studies,* web source: *www.policy.hu/document/200808/ Khassanova.pdf&letoltes=1* accessed on 12 July 2009.

King, Jennifer S. (2003), "Islamic Feminism vs. Western Feminism: Analyzing a Conceptual Conflict", An Abstract of Thesis submitted Central Connecticut State University, New Britain, Connecticut.

Klaveren, Maarten van et al. (May 2010), "An overview of women's work and employment in Kazakhstan", Working Paper 10-93, *Amsterdam Institute for Advanced Labour Studies (AIAS)*, University of Amsterdam.

Kovrigina, Maria (1957), "Public Health and Mothers and Child Welfare in the USSR", *Equality of Women in the USSR,* Foreign Language Publishing House, Moscow.

Lapidus, Gali Warshopsky (1975), "Political Mobilisation, Participation and Leadership: Women in Soviet Politics", *Comparative Politics,* Vol. 8, No. 1.

Larsson, Johan Fredborn (2010), *The Transition in Kazakhstan: from Command to Market Economy*, Minor Field Study Series 199, Department of Economics, University of Lund, Sweden.

Lenin, V.I. (1965), *Collected Works,* web source: *http://www.marxists.org/archive/lenin/works/cw/index.htm.* accessed on 12 August 2009.

Levin, Theodore (1993), "The Reterritorialisation of Culture in the New Central Asian States: A Report from Uzbekistan", *Yearbook for Traditional Music,* Vol. 25, Musical Processes in Asia and Oceania.

Lubin, Nancy (1981), "Women in Soviet Central Asia: Progress and Contradiction", *Soviet Studies,* Vol. 33, No. 2.

Lubin, Nancy (1991), "Energy Wealth, Development and Stability in Turkmenistan", *NBR Analysis*, Vol. 10, No. 3.

Lubin, Nancy, et al. (2002), "Narcotics Interdiction in Afghanistan and Central Asia", A Report of the Open Society Institute, web source: *http://www.Eurasianet.org/policyforum/Lubin012902.ashml* accessed on 22 November 2008.

Luong, Pauline Jones and Weinthal Erika (1999), "The NGO Paradox: Democratic Goals and Non-Democratic Outcomes in Kazakhstan", *Asia Studies,* Vol. 51, No. 7.

Macauley, Alastair (1987), *Women's Work and Wages in Soviet Union,* Allen and Unwin, London.

Malysheva, Marina, "Revisiting the Labour Market Debate from a Gender Perspective: Transition Countries (1995-2005)", web source: *http://www.Econpolunisi.it/iserhtm/2005/Malysheva%20firstdraft.pdf.* accessed on 7 November 2008.

Marx, Karl and Engels, Friedrich (1848), The Communist Manifesto, web source: *www.marxists.org/archive/marx/works/1848/communist-manifesto/* accessed on 10 June 2008.

Massal, Greagory J. (1974), *The Surrogate Proletariat,* Princeton University Press, Princeton.

Maternal Mortality in Central Asia (2008), *Central Asia Health Review*, 2 June, web source: *http://www.cahr.info_files/page0023.htm* accessed on 21 April 2010.

Mattar, Mohamed Y., "State Responsibilities in Combating Trafficking in Persons in Central Asia" *Loy. L.A.Int'l & Comp. L.Rev*, Vol. 27, No. 145.

Mawdudi, S.A.A. (1976), Purdah and the Status of Women in Islam, Islamic Publications Ltd., Lahore, Pakistan.

Mc Dermott, Patrice (Summer 1998), "The Meaning and Uses of Feminism in Introductory Women's Studies Textbooks", *Feminist Studies,* Vol. 24, No. 2.

Medlin, William K. and Cave, William M. (1964), "Social Change and Education in Developing Areas: Uzbekistan", *Comparative Education Review,* Vol. 8, No. 2.

Mee, Wendy (February 2001), *Women in the Republic of Uzbekistan*, Country Briefing Paper, web source: *www.adb.org/.../Country_Briefing_Papers/Women...Uzbekistan/women_in...* accessed on 5 January 2009.

Michaels, Paula A. (Summer 2001), "Motherhood, Patriotism, and Ethnicity: Soviet Kazakhstan and the 1936 Abortion Ban", *Feminist Studies,* Vol. 27, No. 2.

Minnesota Advocates for Human Rights Report (December 2000), *Domestic Violence in Uzbekistan*, Minneapolis.

Mohan, R. Vasundhra (2002), "A Study of Uzbekistan", *Contemporary Central Asia,* Vol. 6, No. 1.

Mojab, Shahrzad (Winter 2001), "Theorizing the Politics of Islamic Feminism", *Feminist Review*, No. 69.

Mojab, Shahrzad and Gorman Rachel (2001), The Struggle over Lifelong Learning: A Marxist-Feminist Analysis, Paper presented at the annual Meeting of the Adult Education Research Conference (42nd, Lansing, June 1-3), web source: *www.edst.educ.ubc.ca/aerc/2001/2001mojab.htm.* accessed on 6 August 2008.

Molyneux, John (2007), "Marxism and Oppression", March 16, web source: *johnmolyneux.blogspot.com/2007/03/marxism-and-oppression.html.* accessed on 24 December 2009.

Morrow, Merrill, "Central Asia: New laws Adopted but Change a Long Way Off", *Asia and the Pacific*, web source: *http://www.wedo.org/../gmr2005_asiapac.pdf* accessed on 28 August 2009.

Moser, Robert G. (2001), "The Effects of Electoral System on Women's Representation in Post-Communist States", *Electoral Studies,* Vol. 20.

Mossell, Gregory J (1974), *The Surrogate Proletariat: Moslem Women and Revolutionary Strategies in Soviet Central Asia, 1919-1929,* Princeton University Press, Princeton.

Munro, Vanessa. E. (2006), "Stopping Traffic? A Comparative Study of Responses in Trafficking in Women for Prostitution in BRIF", *J.CRMINOL,* Vol. 46.

National Human Development Report (1995), Uzbekistan, web source: *http://undp.org/../UZBEKISTAN_1995_en.pdf* accessed on 28 December 2008.

Northrop, Douglas (2000), "Languages of Loyalty: Gender Politics, and Party Supervision in Uzbekistan, 1927-41", *Russian Review,* Vol. 59, No. 2.

Northrop, Douglas (Spring 2001), "Subaltern Dialogues: Subversion and Resistance in Soviet Uzbek Family Law", *Slavic Review,* Vol. 60, No. 1.

OSCE (2007), Uzbekistan – Gender Quality Indicators 2007, web source: *www.osce.org/gender/30847* accessed on 18 March 2009.

Ozkaya, Gunseli (1981), *From Captivity to Freedom: Woman's Fight,* Turkish Women's Association Publication.

Pankatova, Anna (1957), "Soviet Women have Equal Political Right with Men and Take an Active Part in Government" in L.Petrova and S.Gilevskaya (compiled by), *Equality of Women in the USSR,* Foreign Languages Publishing House, Moscow.

Patnaik, Ajay (1989), *Perestroika and Women Labour Force in Soviet Central Asia,* New Literature, New Delhi.

Patnaik, Ajay (1996), *Central Asia: Between Modernity and Tradition,* Konark, New Delhi.

Perevedendsev, V. (1975), "Statistics: almost All about Women", *Current Digest of the Soviet Press*, Vol. 27, No. 23.

Petrone, Karen (1999), "Gender and Heroes: The Exploits of Soviet Pilots and Arctic Explorers in the 1930s" in *Women and Political Change: Perspective from East-Central Europe,* by Sue Bridger (ed.), Macmillan, London.

Pomfret, Richard (2000), "The Uzbek Model of Economic Development 1991-1999", *Economics of Transition*, Vol. 8, No. 3.

Pomfret, Richard (2001), "Economic Development Strategies in Central Asia since 1991", *Asian Studies Review*, Vol. 25, No. 2.

Pomfret, Richard (May 2010), "Central Asia after Two Decades of Independence", *World Institute for Development Economics Research,* Working Paper No. 2010/53.

Popova, Nina (1957), "Equality of Soviet Women in the Economic Spheres" in *Equality of Women in the USSR,* Foreign Languages Publishing House, Moscow.

Price, B.R. and Sokoloff, N. (2004), *The Criminal Justice System and Women* (3rd ed.), McGraw Hill, New York.

Ramchandran, Sudha, "Central Asia: Uzbekistan's Femmes Fatales" web source: *http://www.atimes.com/../FD28Ag01.html* accessed on 11 November 2009.

Rasid, Ahmed (2000), *Taliban: Militant Islam, Oil and Fundamentalism in Central Asia,* New Haven, Yale University Press.

Rasul, Amina (2004), "Muslim Women: Hear US, See US," in *Center for the Study of Islam and Democracy,* Washington.

Republic of Uzbekistan (2007), *Welfare Improvement Strategy of Uzbekistan*, Full Strategy Paper for 2008 – 2010, Tashkent.

Rifkatovna, Ismagilova Nuria, "Women in Politics and Gender-based Corruption in Central Asia: Realities and Responses" web source: *http://www.10iacc.org/content-ns.phtml* accessed on 20 April 2010.

Schrand, Thomas G. (1999), "The Five-Year Plan for Women's Labour: Constructing Socialism and the 'Double Burden', 1930-1932", *Europe-Asia Studies,* Vol. 51, No. 8.

Sacks, Karan (1975), "Engels Revisited: Women, the Organisation of Production and Private Property" in R. Reiter (ed.), *Towards and Anthropology of Women*, New York.

Schuster, Alice (1971), "Women's Role in the Soviet Union: Ideology and Reality", *Russian Survey,* Vol. 30, No. 3.

Schwartz, Stephen (2004), "Hizb Ut-tahrir in Uzbekistan and Kazakhstan: A Comparative Analysis", *Terrorism Monitor,* Vol. 2, Issue 16.

Schwartz, Janet S. (1979), "Women under Socialism: Role, Definitions of Soviet Women", *Social Forces*, Vol. 58, No.1.

Seibert, Anita and Pintera, Ewa (2009), *Through their Eyes: Images of Economic Situation of Women from the Developing Countries of Central Europe, the Balkans and Central Asia*, Karat Coalition, Warsaw.

Sergeyeva, G. P. (1975), "Women's Education and Scientific and Technological Progress" in *Soviet Women: Some Aspects of the Status of Women in the USSR,* Progress Publishers, Moscow.

Shahidian, Hammed (1998), "Islamic Feminism" Encounters "Western Feminism": An Indigenous Alternative?, Paper Presented to the Feminism and Globalisation Seminar, 12 February, Women's Studies Program, Illinois State University, Illinois.

Sharma, R. R. (1979), A *Marxist Model of Social Change, Soviet Central Asia: 1917-1940*, Macmillan, Delhi.

Shokamanov, Yuri (2000), "Kazakhstan: The National Action Plan on improving the Status of Women in the Republic of Kazakhstan and Improving of Gender Statistics" Working Paper No. 8, Orvieto, Italy.

Siddiqui, M. (1988), The Rights of Women in Islam: An Authentic Approach, Adam Publishers, New Delhi.

Smith, Sharon (Fall 1997), "Engels and Origin of Women's Oppression", *International Socialist Review,* Issue 2.

Somach, Susan and Rubin, Deborah (March 2010), USAID Gender Assessment: Central Asian Republics, United States Agency for International Development (USAID).

Sommers, C. (1994), "The Feminist Revelation", *Social Philosophy and Policy*, Vol. 8, No. 1.

Statement by Mrs. Madina Jarbussynova (2007), Ambassador at Large of the Ministry of Foreign Affairs of the Republic of Kazakhstan at the 51st Session of the Commission on the Status of Women, 28 February, New York.

Stites, Richard (1991), *The Women's Liberation Movement in Russia: Feminism Nihilish and Bolshevism in 1860-1930,* Princeton University Press, Princeton.

Stites, Richard (1996), "Zhenodel: Bolshevism and Russian Women", *Russian Women,* Vol. 3, No. 1.

Studying Islam in the Soviet Union (2008), Inaugural Lecture Delivered on 11th December, University of Amsterdam.

Taksanov, Alisher (2003), "Modern Slavery hits Uzbekistan", *Times Central Asia*, 25 June, web source: *http://www.times.kg/news/1084110.html* accessed on 14 May 2009.

Tatibekov, Bolat L. (February 2004), "Peculiarities of Demographic Processes and Labour Market Development during the Transition period in Kazakhstan", *Fourth PIE International Workshop on Pension Reform in Transition Economies*, Hitotsubashi University, Tokyo.

Teplova, Tatna (2007), "Welfare State Transformation, Childcare and Women's Work in Russia", *The Author 2007,* Oxford University Press, Oxford.

The Concept of Gender Policy and the Millennium Development Goals in Kazakhstan, web source: *http://www.mdgender.net/uplocal/tools/kazak_MDG_English.pdf* accessed on 8 July 2008.

The Oxford Companion to Politics of the World (1993), Oxford University Press, Oxford.

The Republic of Kazakhstan: the second periodic report on the implementation of the Convention on the Elimination of All forms of Discrimination against Women, New York, 16 January 2007, web source: *www.un.org/womenwatch/daw/cedaw/cedaw37/.../CEDAW2007.pdf* accessed on 25 July 2010.

Thegenova, Gulden and Shedevova, Nazym (2000), "The Problems of Trafficking Women" Risk Factors and Prevention in Kazakhstan", *The Times of Central Asia,* Vol. 2, No. 37.

Thoenes, Sander (1996), "The 1996 Diary of Deals", *Financial Times*, 17 July.

Three Wave of Feminism: From Suffragettes to Girls, web source: *http://www.sagepub.com/upmdata/6236_Chapter_1_Krolokke_2nd_Rev_Final_Pdf.pdf* accessed on 8 July 2008.

Tinbai, Kengjali (2010), "Kazakh and Uzbek Economic Diverge", web source: *www.businessweek.com/globalbiz/cont.* accessed on 13 January 2011.

Tlenchieva, Gulsara, "Development Problems and Prospects of the Political Activeness of Kazakhstan Women" web source: *http://www.genderstudies.info/english/eng_text7.php* accessed on 29 July 2010.

Togan, Isenbike (1999), "In Search of an Approach to the History of Women in Central Asia" in Korkut A. Erturk (ed.), *Rethinking Central Asia: Non Eurocentric Studies in History, Social Structure and Identity*, Ithaca Press, Cornell.

Tong, Rosemarie (2009), Feminist Thought: A More Comprehensive Introduction, Westview Press, Boulder and San Francisco.

Transparency International Corruption Perceptions Index (2003), 7 October, web source:*http://www.transparency.org/pressreleases_archive/2003/dnld/cpi2003.pressrelease.en.pdf* accessed on 18 July 2009.

Umarov, Kairat (2007), "Kazakhstan Today" Speech by His Excellency Ambassador of Kazakhstan to India on 16 May 2007 at the Centre for South, Central, South East Asian and South West Pacific Studies, School of International Studies, JNU, New Delhi.

UN in Uzbekistan (April 2009), Published by UN Office in Uzbekistan, Tashkent, web source: *http://www.unic.un.org/aroundworld/.../tashkent_UN_Uzb_Newsletter_latest.pdf* accessed on15 February 2011.

UN Millennium Development Goals (MDG) Indicators, web source: *http://mdgs.un.org/unsd/mdg/Data.aspx* accessed on 22 September 2010.

UN (2001), Report of the Committee on the Elimination of Discrimination against Women, Twenty-fourth session (15 Janury-2 February 2001) Twenty-fifth session (2-20 July 2001), Supplement No. 38 (A/56/38), New York, web source: *www.un.org/documents/ga/docs/56/a5638.pdf* accessed on 19 September 2010.

UN (2000), Consideration of Reports submitted by States Parties under Article 18 of the CEDAW, Uzbekistan, CEDAW/C/UZB/1, 2 February 2000.

UN (2008), Kazakhstan Country Analysis, web source: *http://europeandcis.undp.org/home/show/64C...*accessed on 9 March 2010.

UN (2010), Kazakhstan Achievement, Issues and Prospects: A Perspective by the United Nations, web source: *www.hks.harvard.edu/.../UNDP%20Common%20Country%20Assessment%20for%20Kazakhstan.pdf* accessed on 17 March 2011.

UN (1999), *Promoting Women's Rights as Human Rights: Studies on Women in Development*, Economic and Social Commission for Asia and the Pacific, United Nations Publications, New York.

UNAIDS Report (January 1999), *UN- Facilitated Response,* Almaty.

UNCTAD (2009), *World Investment Report*, New York and Geneva.

UNDP (2005), *Central Asia Human Development Report*, UNDP Regional Bureau for Europe and the Commonwealth of Independent States.

UNDP (2005), *Gender equality in Uzbekistan: Facts and Figures*, 2000 – 2004, Statistical Bulletin, State Committee of the Republic of Uzbekistan on Statistics, Tashkent.

UNDP (2004), "Strengthened Capacity of Civil Society Organisations for Participation in 2004 Parliamentary Elections in Kazakhstan", Government of Kazakhstan, web source: *www.undp.kz/projects/files/135-14936.pdf* accessed on 11 July 2010.

UNDP Kazakhstan (2004), "National Human Development Report for 2004, Education for all: the Key Goal for a New Millennium", Almaty.

UNDP Kazakhstan: "Gender Mainstreaming Strategy" web source: *http://europeandcis.undp.org/gender/kazakhstan/show/08FCC922-F203-1EE9-B3360D15BA11580A* accessed on 4 November 2010.

UNDP and Gender in Uzbekistan (2009), "The Roundtable Dedicated to CEDAW`s 30th anniversary", web source: *http://www.undp.uz/en/news/story.php?id=1204* accessed on 12 December 2010.

UNDP and Gender in Uzbekistan (2009), "Legal guarantees of Women's rights considered in Karakalpak legal clinic", web source: *http://www.undp.uz/en/news/story.php?id=1201* accessed on 12 December 2010.

UNDP (2008), *UNDP Human Development Indices,* web source: *http://hdr.undp.org/en/media/HDI_2008_EN_Tables.pdf* accessed on 12 May 2010.

UNDP (2009), Human Development Report: Overcoming Barriers, Human Mobility and Development, web source: *http://hdr.undp.org/en/reports/global/hdr2009/* accessed on 25 February 2010.

UNDP Report (October 2004), *Report on the Status of Official Statistics Related to Gender Equality in Eastern Europe and The CIS Countries,* Geneva.

UNDP (March 2003), *Tajikistan: Human Development Report 2001-2002*, Dushanbe.

UNICEF (2007), Presentations from the International Conference "*Increasing Social Orientation of Budget and Efficiency of Public Expenditures at National and Local Levels in the Best Interests of Children and Families in Kazakhstan*", 9-10 April, Senate of Republic of Kazakhstan, Astana.

UNICEF report (1999), *Women in Transition: A Summary,* Florence, web source: *www.unicef-irc.org/publications/pdf/monee6sume.pdf.* accessed on 28 July 2010.

United Nations Secretariat Report (December 2006), *UNDP Programme to Improve Gender Statistics in Uzbekistan*, New York.

Usha, K.B. (2005), "Political Empowerment of Women in Soviet Union and Russia: Ideology and Implementation", *International Studies,* Vol. 42, No. 2.

Utebaev, Mussiraly (2008), "The Role of Parliament of the RK in the Process of Social Budget Appropriations in the Best Interests of Children and Families", *Increasing Social Orientation of Budgets and Efficiency of Public Expenditures at National and Local Levels in the best Interests of Children and Families in Kazakhstan*, UNICEF Kazakhstan, Astana.

Uzbekistan: Polygamy in Central Asia, web source: *http://www.wluml.org* accessed on 9 May 2009.

Uzbekistan (1995): Review and Appraisal of the Implementation by the Republic of Uzbekistan of the Beijing Platform for Action adopted at the Fourth World Conference on Women, Beijing.

Uzbekistan Country Analysis United Nations Country Team (2008), Tashkent. web source: *europeandcis.undp.org/uploads/.../UZB%20Country%20Analysis_final.pdf* accessed on 8 March 2010.

Uzbekistan Country Report (2010), BTI 2010, November 18, 2010. web source: *www.bertesmanntransfomation-index.de/* accessed on 8 February 2011.

Uzbekistan in Transition, web source: *www.adb.org/documents/books/country.briefingpapers/women_in.Uzbekistan/chap_1.pdf* accessed on 28 September 2008

Violence against Women, Kazakhstan, web source: *www.onlinewomeninpolitics.org/kz/kazakhstan.pdf* accessed on 2 November 2010.

Vodzinskaio, V. V. (1973), "Orientations Toward Occupation" in *Social Stratification and Mobility in USSR* by Murry Yanowitch and Wesley (eds.), International Arts and Science Press, White Plain.

Wallin, Dawn C. (1999), "Liberal Feminism and Educational Administration: Recruiting and Supporting Women in Educational Administration", web source: *www.eric.ed.gov/ERICWebPortal/recordDetail?accno=ED441285* accessed om 8 June 2009.

Wilding, Faith (2007), "Monstrous Domestically", web source: *www.feministezine.com/feminist/domesticity.html* accessed on 7 July 2008.

Wolff, Kristina (2007), "Gender Studies: Sociology of Sex, Gender and Sexuality" in Blackwell Encyclopedia of Sociology, ed. by George Ritzer, Blackwell.

Women in Contemporary Turkey, web source: *http://www.tawsf.org/Women.htm* accessed on 10 June 2008.

Women in Parliament in 2008, the Year in Perspective, web source: *http://www.ipu.org/../wmn08-e.pdf* accessed on 28 September 2010.

Women's Political Rights and Participation in Public Life, Kazakhstan, web source: *www.onlinewomeninpolitics.org/kz/kazakhstan.pdf* accessed on 28 October 2010.

Women's Social and Economic Rights, Kazakhstan, web source: *www.onlinewomeninpolitics.org/kz/kazakhstan.pdf* accessed on 12 August 2010.

World Bank Report (May 2008), Europe and Central Asia Region and Global HIV/AIDS Program, web source: *http://siteresources.worldbank.org/INTECAREGTOPHEANUT/Resources/cablood-bankstudy.pdf* accessed on 28 September 2010.

World Bank (2004), *Kazakhstan – Dimensions of Poverty in Kazakhstan. Volume I: Policy Briefing.* Report No. 30294-KZ. W.p.

World Bank (2005), Getting Competitive, Staying Competitive: The Challenge of Managing Kazakhstan's Oil Boom. Washington, DC. Web source: *www.indexmundi.com/kazakhstan/total_fertility_rate.html* accessed on 12 January 2011.

Wright, Anita (Summer 2000), "Microfinace NGO in Kazakhstan Funds Women Entrepreneurs", *Give & Take: A Journal on Civil Society in Eurasia*, Vol. 3, No. 2.

Yankova, Z.A. (1975), "The Women and the Family" in *Soviet Women: Some Aspects of the Status of Women in the USSR,* Progress Publishers, Moscow.

Yazykova, V.S. (1975), "The Socialist Mode of Life and Women's Free Time" in *Soviet Women: Some Aspects of the Status of Women in the USSR,* Progress Publishers, Moscow.

Youth in Central Asia: Loosing the New Generation (2003), *ICG Report (International Crisis Group)*, No. 66, 31 October 2003.

Zellerer, Evelyn and Vyortkin, Dmitriy (2004), "Women's Grassroots Struggles for Empowerment in the Republic of Kazakhstan", *Social Politics,* Vol. 11, No. 3.

"16 Days of Activism against Gender Violence Creating a Culture that says No to Violence against Women", November 25 – December10, 2002, web source: *http://www.mpa.gov.uk/downloads/committees.* accessed on 22 July 2009.

Index

D

E

F

O

P

Q

R

S